Sinkhole

SID STEPHENSON
and
AARON F DIEBELIUS

AuthorHouse™ UK
1663 Liberty Drive
Bloomington, IN 47403 USA
www.authorhouse.co.uk
Phone: UK TFN: 0800 0148641 (Toll Free inside the UK)
        UK Local: 02036 956322 (+44 20 3695 6322 from outside the UK)

Published by AuthorHouse 03/31/2021

ISBN: 978-1-6655-8763-1 (sc)
ISBN: 978-1-6655-8764-8 (hc)
ISBN: 978-1-6655-8767-9 (e)

Print information available on the last page.

This book is printed on acid-free paper.

Foreword.

All my life I loved stories. I fell into them like slipping into a warm river that took me effortlessly to South-west Texas, Kathmandu, The Simpson Desert, Timbuctoo and endless other mythical places. Beguiling characters drifted across my story landscape like wraiths, informing my value system and driving the evolution of my passions. It followed that books, comics and then movies took me into those specific genres where the stories were expressed visually and graphically, and with a crystalline pure logic.

The writers, directors, technicians and actors who facilitated this accessible and immersive storytelling became my heroes, one of which, Cormac McCarthy wrote haunting tales of mono-syllabic characters in vast surroundings clawing their way through the cusp of apocalyptic change. His characters transfixed me, one said:

> *"You might think you could run away and change your name and I don't know what all. Start over. And then one mornin' you wake up and look at the ceilin', and guess who's layin' there"*

Over time my views, interests, thoughts and opinions have changed along with my vocations. Craftsman, Teacher, Educationalist, Aid Project Manager, Academic Writer, MSc Tutor, all exploded into crystal clarity with the random collision of influences from Cinematographer Mike Fox, and Pro-Screenwriter Aaron F Diebelius, now my Co-Writer. The collision of bodies often means a catastrophe, particularly for the smaller of the two. In this case it was three, I was the third, and I was carrying with me the first draft of a story named 'Sinkhole', this follows below, and has evolved into a new storytelling genre Aaron and I have named 'SCROVEL'.

SCROVEL is a movie that plays in the reader's head, while they read.

The unique visual imagery and dialogue impact is generated from a direct relationship between the writer and the reader, unlike a movie, which is the product of a dedicated team. SCROVEL is a powerful storytelling genre which freely and unashamedly draws from its two 'parents', the Novel and the Screenplay – two entirely different beasts.

The Novel is a freely expressed fictional narrative of a story, and a Screenplay is a stark visual description of a story that is intended to be seen on-screen. The screenplay demands extreme clarity expressed in a rigidly formatted structure.

The Screenplay's readership specifically targets the film-making team who will construct and act in the movie. The Novel's readership is everyone else. SCROVEL is a new storytelling genre that combines both elements.

SCROVEL is dedicated to Screenwriters everywhere. They are the creative heart of the movie business. All movies begin from their keyboards and their ability to tell a story, but to be successful they have to be very much more than storytellers. They have to format and figure out how to get their story out to the decision-makers who will read it, then gamble and balance a business process leading to a finished movie product. A tiny percentage of screenwriters are successful in this arduous process. The greater percentage will fail, and heartbreakingly, their stories will never be told. My message to them is this; continue to do what you do, keep on keeping on, but maybe... use SCROVEL to tell your story. Your readers will become part of your process and together the writer and reader will make a 'movie'.

Aaron and I hope you enjoy your personal journey through Sinkhole. Maybe one day we will all watch it on screen, what a day that would be!
Sid.

Co-Writers: Sid Stephenson and Aaron F Diebelius

SINKHOLE
A Drama.

Co-Writers:

Sid Stephenson
+44 (0) 7555096959
E: sidstephenson@aol.com

And

Aaron F Diebelius
+44 (0) 7703768689
E: AaronFDiebelius@outlook.com

Log-line

Two unworldly but highly skilled HUNTERS blunder into an evolving crime. The encounter ejects them headlong into a deadly world of international politics and assassination

Synopsis

The Synopsis follows at Page 415.

Writing Style

This document is written in a genre that the writers euphemistically call 'SCROVEL'. This is a crossover between a NOVEL and a SCREENPLAY.

SCROVEL targets two specific user groups, (1) Readers and Movie Buffs who read 'Film Tie-Ins' and (2) Screenwriters who never get the opportunity to finally bring their project to the screen.

SINKHOLE is dedicated to SCREENWRITERS everywhere who have a story to tell. It may inspire them to seek an alternative platform to reach an audience.

VO: - Voice Over
OS: - Off Screen
INT: - Interior
EXT: - Exterior

SINKHOLE (title fills screen)

Teaser.

(Rolling white type on black
screen with Voice Over)

NEWS HEADLINES. (16 years ago).

BBC Cumbria: Major Arms find in OLD TIN MINE WORKINGS

CUMBRIA POLICE BELIEVE THAT A CRATE OF GUNS FOUND IN AN
ISOLATED SPOT NEAR ULVERSTON ARE PART OF A SHIPMENT EN-
ROUTE TO WORLD TROUBLE SPOTS.

FOLLOWING INTEGRATED INVESTIGATIONS WITH SEVERAL
POLICE FORCES, INCLUDING INTERPOL, THE GUNS WERE FOUND
SUBMERGED IN OLD TIN MINE WORKINGS, KNOWN AS SINKHOLES,
WHICH HAVE BEEN FLOODED IN LIVING MEMORY. THE GUNS WERE
ENCLOSED IN A METAL CRATE WHICH INCLUDED AMMUNITION
AND OTHER SPARE PARTS. SOME OF THE AMMUNITION WAS TIPPED
WITH TRACER MATERIALS FOR USE IN DARKNESS. THE GUNS AND
AMMUNITION WERE MILITARY GRADE, IN PERFECT CONDITION,
AND WOULD BE CAPABLE OF FIRING 500 ROUND PER MINUTE,
OVER A 1 KILOMETRE RANGE.

NO BOMB PARTS OR INCENDIARY DEVICES WERE FOUND.

A SENIOR POLICE SPOKESMAN SAID THAT THE OWNER OF THE LAND
WAS NOT BELIEVED TO HAVE KNOWN THAT THE ARMS WERE THERE,
AND THERE WAS NOTHING TO INDICATE A LOCAL CONNECTION
BETWEEN THE ARMS AND ACTIVITIES IN ANY DESIGNATED 'WAR
ZONES'.

NO-ONE HAS BEEN ARRESTED IN CONNECTION WITH THE FIND,
BUT INVESTIGATIONS ARE CONTINUING WITH LOCAL POLICE,
NORTHERN IRELAND POLICE AND INTERPOL.

TITLE AND CREDITS PLAYING OVER ACTION SEQUENCE

In the early dawn a car pulls up outside a terraced house and stands, engine running, orange streetlights reflecting on wet pavements. The front door opens and a HUNTER in country clothing carries rifle and shooting paraphernalia. He deposits it into the raised tailgate of the car, slams the tailgate, gets in, car door slams shut.

The car pulls away, camera zooming upwards to show a small town with frenetically busy main road running through it. The car threads small streets, finally joins the traffic on the main road, soon lost in the melee.

PRESENT DAY:

EXT. CUMBRIA. WOODED COUNTRYSIDE ON AN ALLUVIAL PLAIN NEAR MORECAMBE BAY COASTLINE. AUTUMN. EVENING, LAST LIGHT.

AERIAL SHOT: TWO MEN WALKING THROUGH ROUGH ROCKY BRUSH COUNTRY. CUTTING TO WIDE PANNING SHOTS.

STIV (22) and BOB (24) had been friends since school. They had shared the heady days of being young bucks together, girlfriends, their first cars, pubs, and overall, they shared their passion for rifle shooting. This passion ranged from shooting wild game for the pot, to blasting tin cans and other targets. They avidly read specialist shooting magazines and spent their spare cash on equipment with abandon.

It is evening. They have been hunting the coastal woods and rough fields along Morecambe Bay for several hours. Apart from shooting at a few prominent, but inert targets, they had little to show for their efforts.

As the light began to fail, they head the four or five miles of gently sloping coastal brush homewards to Ulverston, their hometown. They are in no rush, rifles on leather slings over their shoulders, binoculars and the paraphernalia of shooters in bags across the other shoulder.

WIDE TO MEDIUM SHOTS

The land becomes monochrome as dusk approach's, bushes and trees reduced to black clumps of shadow, but the sky over the Bay, still retaining the fading promise of the day. Streaks of deep colour gathering low on the horizon, blues deepening to purple, then grey and black towards mountains to their right and behind. A silver slither of moon emerges and disappears in black clouds.

The two young men are in good spirits, talking occasionally as they meandered through low lying brush, other times lost in thought, comfortable in each other's presence, easy with the silences.

> STIV
> You are quiet mate, you ok?

> BOB
> (Grinning)
> Enjoying the evening, I guess. I like this time of day when the light drops. I'll be glad to get home and eat though.

> STIV
> How's Iris's cooking these days, she improved?

> BOB
> (Grins)
> Hardly, it's not her strong point. Since the old man left she lost interest in all that stuff.
> (A beat)
> I manage, used to it now.

Two miles to their right on slightly higher ground, the A590, the single main arterial road, carries its usual frenetic traffic load to and from the Barrow shipyards and Motorway system 30 miles east. Lights, exhaust fuel and vehicles of all sizes highlighting a different world of relentless noise, clamour, stress and pulsing flares of white and red lights.

                    BOB (CONT'D)
          What about you? Do you actually
          cook the stuff we shoot?

                    STIV
          Yep, some of it. I'm on my own these
          days, so I give the rest away. I have
          to skin it and get it ready for the pot,
          but yes, it's OK. Stuff that you've
          hunted and shot always tastes
          better I reckon.
                    (A beat, looking around)
          Wow, the light is dropping fast now
          Bob, maybe we left it a bit late
          today.

                    BOB
          I have a torch in my pack, don't
          like using it much because my eyes
          get dependent on it. Can't see shit
          when I switch it off.

Deep in these coastal woods it is still. The distant sounds of the road muted and sometimes silent as winds changed. Both men were used to walking rough ground and the deepening darkness did not pose a major problem, albeit they were more watchful in their progress.

                    STIV
          Iris could cook for me any day, or
          not cook.
                    (A beat, grinning at Bob in
                    the semi-darkness)

I know she's your Mother, but she has
been in my fantasies for as long as I
can remember, she…

                    BOB
Oh, fuck off Stiv, come on, not that
stuff again. I tell you what, I'll tell her
what you...

                    STIV
                (Quickly)
Shit don't do that mate, I'd bloody
die. Would never come round your
place ever again.

Stiv came to a sudden halt, looking intently at something on rising
ground to his right front.

                STIV (CONT'D)
                (In a low voice)
What was that? Did you see
something over there?
                (A beat)
2.o clock high (pointing)

                    BOB
I'm looking mate,
(Long pause)
Nope. You are seeing things maybe

                    STIV
                (Thoughtful)
Hmm, maybe you're right, weird.
There's nothing up there in that spot
is there.

Stiv was looking intently at a wooded area several hundred
yards in front of them and to the right in slightly rising ground. He
stopped and focused.

STIV (CONT'D)
There was a light, I'm sure. Just for an
instant. Maybe someone 'lamping'
do you think?

BOB
(Laughing easily)
We can wander over in that
direction Stiv, but I doubt its anything
mate.
(Looking around and
upwards)
It's gonna be pitch dark before
long. Only idiots like us still out here
fucking around.

WIDE TO MEDIUM

The two young men change direction slightly to their right and
move casually forward towards the rising ground. It is now almost
dark, the pool of light over the Bay darker, but still lighter than the
rest of the sky.

BOB
(Low and urgent)
Stop mate, there is someone there in
that copse. I saw it now. Just a flash,
then gone. What the fuck?

STIV
This is weird Bob. I've walked all this
area many times for years now,
there's nothing there, a few old sink
holes maybe, nothing.
(Low voice, looking at Bob)
Let's take a quiet look shall we...?
Might be someone having a shag,
you never know...
(Smiling)
Come on, let take a look see.

Bob grins, his imagination caught by the idea. The two young men separate slightly and begin to make their way slowly and stealthily into the outer trees of the copse. It is very dark in the trees with occasional piles of boulders.

CUT TO:

EXT. INSIDE THE COPSE. NIGHT.

Once inside the trees proper, and closer, the light they had seen momentarily before, is now flickering through the partially clad autumn trees and illuminating the underside of branches. The two men, now separated, stealthily make their way forward, both increasingly carried away with curiosity, but also, as they work their way closer, with the beginnings of indefinite and inarticulate feelings of unease.

They are within a stone's throw of their homes, but here they are sneaking up on something that is slightly bizarre and out of the ordinary, with a vague feeling of illicit excitement which tickles both their imaginations.

STIV
(Whispering)
Who the hell is it? This is weird.

Stiv steps quietly up to a pile of boulders and carefully peers over. In front of him is a SINKHOLE from some OLD MINE WORKINGS. It is filled to the top with black water, maybe twenty feet across. On the other side of the sinkhole, some 30M away, is a back end of a 4*4 reversed up to the side of the water. The back of the 4*4 hatch door is open, and it is filled with equipment. On the ground nearby are air bottles and the various paraphernalia associated with scuba diving.

The area is brightly lit by a single spotlight on a tripod, pointing downwards illuminating the water with a dazzling white circle. Stiv traverses slightly to his right to improve his view, then settles with his chest against a rounded rock.

Standing by the water, lit starkly along one side stands the black silhouette of a man, immobile. He is staring intently at the circle of light dancing on the rippling water's surface.

Slightly around to his left, Stiv sees a slight movement in the shadows as Bob's pale face rises slowly above some rocks opposite, 10M away. Both watching men are experiencing increasing unease now, feeling like they should immediately withdraw as quietly as possible and head homewards. He gestures to Bob to keep low and sees his head sink below the top of the rock.

This situation is somehow out of their comfort zone in ways neither could explain, it felt dangerous. They independently arrive at the conclusion that they are both seeing something that they should not be seeing.

CUT TO:

MEDIUM CLOSE

The surface of the water breaks suddenly in circle of bright light. A DIVER's head emerges, water cascading in dazzling explosions of light, grotesque, heaving in the black water like a primitive creature, glistening in the spotlight. The tops of his dive tank and oxygen pipes showing behind his neck. The diver removes his air mask and pushed up his goggles.

                    DIVER 1
                (Excited, in Bulgarian)
        I think I've found it. I'm going back
        down. Throw me the hook.

                    DIVER'S ASSISTANT
                    (Excited)
        Fuck! OK, hang on. I'll throw it out to
        your right side. Watch out, this hook
        is heavy.

The assistant scrabbles among his equipment, uncoiling ropes, then swinging a hook twice, throws the hook with its attached rope, out across the water and past the diver. The diver catches the rope deftly, turning easily in the water, one arm upwards with his thumb extended in the universal gesture of 'OK'.

DIVER 1
Right, got it. I'm going down.

The diver disappears under the water. The black water swirling and closing over his head leaving boiling clusters of bubbles.

The DIVER's ASSISTANT paces back and forth along the edge of the sinkhole, staring at the spotlight's bright circle on the surface. Watching from the rocks, Stiv and Bob are transfixed, held in position, both now unable to back away from the unfolding scene, even though it felt somehow dangerous and out of their comfort zone. Both young men, even though they were unable to communicate at that moment, feel that these men would do them harm if they were spotted and caught.

Several minutes passes, the diver emerges again shaking his head, water cascading in bright droplets in the pool of light, breathlessly ripping away his breathing bask and goggles.

DIVER 1 (CONT'D)
(Excited)
Its hooked. Can you take up the
slack?

The diver's assistant goes to the 4*4 and starts the engine. He comes back to the rear of the car, uncoiling ropes, then presses a button on some equipment. There is the whine of an electric motor, and the rope begins to wind inwards on a winch.

DIVER 1 (CONT'D)
Slow now, I don't want to slip the
hook. Carefully, yes, good.
(Sharply)
Stop now, I'll go back down and
check it's all OK.

The diver disappears beneath the surface again. The assistant stays by the winch. The rope now taut, a quivering black line. The diver emerges again.

                    DIVER 1 (CONT'D)
          OK, it's fine.
                    (A beat)
          Carefully now, haul her up.

The winch sounds again, the note changing as it goes under load. The 4*4 begins to sink slightly on its suspension as the weight on the rope increases.

Both Stiv and Bob watch intently as the rope continues to coil inwards. The diver disappearing several times ensuring that whatever was is the end of the rope, is still OK. The winch changes as the motor takes the load, and the 4*4 suspension pulls down low, the rope now close to the side, a black glistening line straight and rigid with tension.

                    DIVER 1 (CONT'D)
                    (Excited, exultant)
          Yes, here we go. Slow down now.

The top edges of something black, rectangular, glistening in the white light, is now showing above the surface. It spins slowly on its axis, glittering. Guided by the diver in the water, the rectangular box shape gradually emerges from the water, sliding inch by inch up towards the straining winch, finally out of the water and laid flat on the ground near the edge.

The box is metallic, very heavy, possibly over a meter long by half a meter, and half a meter deep. There doesn't appear to be any other markings other than heavy locks and hinges.

                    DIVER 1 (CONT'D)
          Excellent! Good job.
                    (Extending his arm upwards)
          Here, give me a hand will you.

The assistant braces himself against the 4*4 and pulls his friend out of the water. The diver quickly pulls off his tank and other equipment, takes off his rubber head mask and flippers and throws them into the back of the 4*4, briefly towelling his face and neck. The assistant pulls the spotlight around to shine down on the box.

DIVER'S ASSISTANT
Well done my friend. Let's have a
look at this bad boy now shall we.

Both men pull the box slightly up and away from the edge of the sinkhole and bend over the locks. Metallic sounds carrying over to where the two watchers were concealed. The assistant rummages in the back of the vehicle, bringing out a handful to TOOLS. Both men hunch down to the task of opening the metal box.

Both watchers' strain to see what would be revealed as the box was opened.

CUT TO:

MEDIUM TO CLOSE SHOTS ON THE BOX

The lid of the box finally screeches open, water cascading. The assistant reaches down into the box, pulling out a heavy object, long and dripping with water, it is wrapped in some sort of waxed paper. He strips the paper in several layers. Beneath, the object is metallic, covered in heavy grease. The diver produces rags to wipe away the grease.

Both watchers experience the same quickening of heart rates as the box gives up its contents, one by one unwrapped and the protective grease wiped away, are 30 or more MILITARY ASSAULT RIFLES, with MAGAZINES and BOXES OF SHELLS.

By this time Bob is leaning high above the rock, his face white with tension, glistening in the side glow from the spotlight. Stiv realizes that if either of the men glance upwards, they will see Bob in plain

13

view. He gestures again wildly to Bob, waving him to get down. Bob glances at him and immediately drops down again behind the rock.

Starkly lit by the floodlight, the two men begin clearing up their operation. Methodically packing their extensive diving gear, loose paper wrappings and rags, and finally the assault rifles into the back of the 4*4. Finally, they extinguish the spotlight, its filament slowly dying. One of the men walks around the vehicle, switching on the headlights to complete their operation.

They tip the now empty metal box back into the sinkhole, pace the area, glancing around the whole surroundings, their eyes momentarily sweeping past where Bob and Stiv are hiding, then walk around to the front of the car, getting in the seats.

The car remains stationary, engine running quietly.

The passenger door opens again, and the dark figure of the assistant gets out. He is carrying a torch. He walks back to the side of the sinkhole, playing his torch over the water. He appears to be searching for something. He walks around the sinkhole, eventually approaching near the rocks where Stiv is concealed.

He stands by the water, his torch pointing downwards. Stiv freezes in place, not daring to breathe, willing Bob to do the same. The torch goes out, the copse turns to black darkness except for the rear lights of the 4*4 40 feet away.

Both young men are completely still. Stiv sits with his back to the rock, holding his breath, with no idea where the Assistant is. The faint glow from the rear lights of the 4*4 go out and the darkness is complete. There is no sound.

The black silence continues for a minute, then two minutes, then the torch comes on again. Stiv hears the sound of the assistant moving and cautiously peers over the top of the rock. The assistant is walking back to 4*4, his torch playing around the copse. The 4*4 starts up again, its lights flaring.

The man converses with his companion briefly, voice raised slightly. He turns suddenly, then walks back to the rocks close to where Bob is hiding.

CUT TO:

CAMERA HOLDING ON STIV

Stiv crouches down, not breathing.

> DIVER'S ASSISTANT (OFF SCREEN V/O)
> (Exclaiming)
> Fuck!
> Who the hell are you?

Stiv hears scuffling.

> DIVER'S ASSISTANT (OFF SCREEN V/O) (CONT'D)
> (Shouting to his mate)
> Hey, get over her, now.
> (To Bob)
> Come out from there, hey!
> (To his mate)
> He's got a fucking gun!

More scuffling. Stiv stays down, out of sight, petrified.

> DIVER 1 (O.S.) (V/O)
>
> So, what do we have here now, 22 cal Brno Hunting Rifle? You a rabbit shooter mate, or are you something else?

> BOB (O.S.) (V/0)
> (Very frightened)
> I was heading home, been out rabbiting all day. Saw your light.
> Sorry.

DIVER 1 (O.S.) (V/O)
(To the Assistant)
Now we have a real fucking
problem don't we.
(To Bob)
Over here, where I can see you

CUT TO:

PULLING BACK TO MEDIUM SHOT FROM BEHIND STIV

Stiv eases carefully upwards, peering. The two men are herding
Bob at gunpoint, with his own gun, over to where their 4*4 stood
idling, its lights on. Bob has his hands laced on top of his head,
stumbling, being roughly pushed.

DIVER 1
(To Bob, roughly)
Sit, over there.

Stiv watches as Bob is pushed over to the base of a large rock.
He slides down into a sitting position, eyes wide upwards to his
captors. The Assistant, after rummaging in rear of the 4*4, slides
a black plastic tie over Bob's wrists, brutally pulling it tight. Bob
yelps.

DIVER'S ASSISTANT
(To his mate)
He's a kid. He's got a gun and
shooting stuff in his bag. Looks like
he's been out rabbiting like he says.
(A beat)
Now what?
We can't just leave him, can we?

The Diver, who seems to be in charge, stands still, thinking.

DIVER 1
We need to move, fast.
We'll rig it, an accident.

Put one in his head, chuck him in
the sinkhole. When they find him,
they'll think he did it himself, either
deliberate, or whatever.

We need to go. Let's just do it and
get the fuck out of here.

                    DIVER'S ASSISTANT
          OK, yes, you are right, I guess. Was
          he on his own...?

                    (Looking around the copse)
          This is fucking crazy. We should be
          well away from here by now.

Stiv is transfixed. Bob is whimpering incoherently. The Diver jacks a
shell into Bob's BRNO RIFLE, checking the safety catch.

Stiv is breathless. They are really going to kill Bob before his eyes.
How can this be! He pulls his own 22 Cal rifle from his shoulder
pack, clicks in a TEN ROUND MAGAZINE and hardly breathing,
quietly jacks a round into the breech, leaning onto the rock.

                                                            CUT TO:

VIEW THROUGH TELESCOPIC SIGHT SHOWING CROSS HAIRS

The head of the Diver springs into sharp relief in Stiv's TELESCOPIC
SIGHT. The cross hairs illuminated in red with the night-sight's auto
function. Stiv is rigid with the mind stretching stress of the moment,
heart rate soaring. Nothing in his entire existence has prepared
him for the split-second decision he is about to make.

                                                            CUT TO:

CLOSE UP ON STIV

They are going to shoot Bob, unless he intervenes. If he shows himself, his advantage is lost. His choices are few.

> DIVER'S ASSISTANT
> Come on, we need to get going.
> Shoot this fucker.
>> (Louder)
> Do it.

CUT TO:

MEDIUM AND CLOSE SHOTS

The diver walks over to Bob, who has his head down, mewling low, like a baby. The Diver leans forward, holding Bob's rifle muzzle up to Bob's head.

Stiv doesn't hear his shot.

The effects are extra ordinary. The Diver is holding the rifle outwards towards Bob, one handed. The Assistant to one side, watching, waiting for the shot.

CUT TO:

ACTION SHOTS AND CUT-AWAYS

The Assistant hears a muted shot, but Bob doesn't change position. A spray of blood and brain matter erupts across the rock, glistening in the car lights. The Diver lowers the rifle, takes two faltering steps towards the rock, then his knees giving way, sits down awkwardly, gradually leaning against the rock in an upright position.

> DIVER'S ASSISTANT
> What are you doing? What the
> hell---

18

The Diver Assistant steps hesitantly towards his friend, a hand outstretched. A look of total amazement, turning to horror on his face. He is bending towards his friend when Stiv's SECOND SHOT hits him below his armpit, erupting through his chest cavity and exiting bloodily above his collar bone, then ricocheting off the rock with a screech.

Bob rolls away as the Assistant's weight falls onto him. The man rolls over onto his back, gasping, a look of shock and outrage on his face, feet kicking out. His hands moving frantically over his chest, feeling for the wound, looking in horror at his bloody hands.

CUT TO:

MEDIUM

Stiv comes from behind the rocks, around the sinkhole, and runs towards the tableau, lit theatrically by the car lights. The whole thing looking like a movie he once saw. He goes to Bob first, pulling out a knife and cutting the plastic tie from his wrists.

> BOB
> (Breathless, in shock)
> Bloody hell Stiv, He was gonna do
> me. That fucker was going to kill me.
> You saved me.

Stiv goes to the Diver, takes Bob's rifle away. The man is clearly dead, the exit wound gaping, grotesque. The metallic smell of blood heavy in the air.

The Assistant is still alive, feet kicking spasmodically, helplessly staring up at the under-lit branches above, taking huge, ragged gasps, each breath a fine gurgling spray of red mist. As they watch dreadfully fascinated, he stops, a long exhalation, then he is still, then an imperceptible sinking followed as the tension in his body relaxes.

CUT TO:

MEDIUM AND CLOSE

Stiv sits against the rock, Bob by his side. They look at the two men, both now still in grotesque death. The 4*4 still idling quietly nearby, its exhaust smoke curling white in the light. The pile of guns glistening in the stark light.

                    STIV
          You OK Bob? They didn't---

                    BOB
          No. I'm OK, what about you?

                    STIV
          I dunno...
                    (Head sinking down to his
                    knees, tears starting)
          Fuck Bob, I just killed two men. I
          don't even know them.
                    (a long drawn out pause)
          What do we do now?
                    (Now crying)

Both young men sit with their backs against the rock. Both white-faced, shocked to their core. Both wanting to crawl into the bosom of their Mother and disappear. Their lives from this point forever changed, no longer boys, but by no means yet, the men they will become.

                                        CUT TO:

WIDE AND AERIAL

In the distance, the A590's frenetic snake of COMMOTION, TRAFFIC NOISE and PULSATING LIGHTS continued unabated, and above, the final last streaks of pale light over the BAY faded to black.

                                        FADE TO BLACK

20

EXT. WALNEY ISLAND DIVE CENTER. A DIVING EQUIPMENT HIRE COMPANY. AFTERNOON. ESTABLISHING SHOTS

The DIVE CENTER is a fenced off enclosure on a 40-meter square industrial area near the Docks. The enclosure is crammed with equipment, compressors, cabling, ropes, air tanks. At one end is a rusted workshop area and office, the worktops covered in papers, brass air valves, spanners, dirty coffee cups, a couple of phones.

CUT TO:

MEDIUM CLOSE

DAVE GEDDINGS (53) former PARA and Nth Sea Oil diver, now owner of a diving equipment supply and hire company, frowns, consulting his watch. He looks across the clutter at his friend and partner MIKE KRAMER (41) also former PARA.

> DAVE
> I wonder if those buggers have
> done a runner? They should have
> had that gear back here an
> hour ago.
>   (a beat)
> There was something about those
> two you know...

> MIKE
> Hmm, I know what you mean. They'll
> be back mate.

> DAVE
> Where were they diving anyway?
> Most people go down on the wreck
> in the Bay, they didn't even seem to
> know about it.

> MIKE
> Give them an hour or two mate,
> then I guess we'll have to report it,

Police and Coastguard. Rules are
pretty clear in this situation.

CUT TO:

WIDE

A BLACK RANGE ROVER with darkened glass pulls up outside their
corrugated tin gate. A hard looking man, casual dress, 50s, steps
out, pushing Ray Bans upwards into his hairline. He pushes through
the gate and walks over to Dave.

CUT TO:

MEDIUM CLOSE

                    DANIEL LAIDLOW
Hello, I'm DANIEL, I'm just checking
on some friends of mine. I believe
they hired some diving gear here
yesterday.
          (A beat)
You didn't hear from them at all, by
any chance?

                    DAVE
Hi Daniel
          (Handshake)
Nothing yet here. They should have
been back an hour ago. We were
just talking about it.
          (Indicating Mike)
Mike, my partner.
          (Glancing at Mike, who was
          staring quizzically at the
          visitor)
We have some fairly stringent rules
about this sort of thing. Two hours
late and we have to alert police
and Coastguard.

At the mention of POLICE, Dave sees a momentary trace of reaction in Daniel's eyes.

> DANIEL
> Really now, is that so. I guess its
> the possibility of something going
> wrong, yeah,
>> (Smiling reassuringly, a beat)
> Ah, they'll be fine I think. Just held
> up somewhere maybe, or they
> got carried away with the dive.
> I shouldn't worry about alerting
> anyone.

The man returns Mike's stare, turns slightly back to face Dave, sizing him up, dropping his Ray-Bans back down.

> DAVE
>> (Flatly)
> No, we'll stick with our rules. Two
> hours that's in 25 mins from now, we
> will make the police call as required.

Daniel regards Dave for a beat, doesn't reply. He gives Mike a further measuring glance, seems about to say something, then turns away with a terse nod and goes back to his car.

> DAVE (CONT'D)
>> (Calling after him)
> You don't know where they were
> diving do you? It might be useful to
> know where to look if things go tits up.

CUT TO:

WIDE

The Range Rover takes off at speed. Taking the turn at the top of the road with a faint screech of tires. Mike gazes after the departing car, frowning.

                    DAVE
               (Looking curiously at his
               partner)
          What...?

                    MIKE
               (not meeting Dave's eyes)
          Nah... nothing. He reminded me of
          someone.

Dave goes back into their cluttered office, dropping into his usual
swivel chair. Mike stays where he was, standing by the road,
staring after the Range Rover.

                                                    FADE OUT

                                                    FADE IN:

**EXT. BOB'S HOUSE. A TERRACE IN A NARROW STREET IN ULVERSTON,
CUMBRIA. CARS PARKED BOTH SIDES. AFTERNOON. ESTABLISHING
AND MEDIUM**

Stiv knocks on the door and waits. Voices inside, movement in the
obscure glass, then Bob's Mother IRIS 40s, short dark hair, petite
and beautiful, opens the door.

                    IRIS
               (Dazzling smile)
          Oh hello Stiv.
               (Standing aside, indicating)
          Come in, he's in the front. He's not
          wonderfully well, but I'm sure he'll
          be OK to see you.

Iris backs against the wall and Stiv passes her in the narrow passage,
her perfume wafting over him, but his usual stab of unspoken guilty
desire for Iris is missing because of his raised stress level.

Bob is sitting by a large TV on silent. He is pale and nervous
looking. Greetes Stiv with a gesture towards a chair. Stiv sprawls.
Both look at the silent screen.

24

                    IRIS (OS)
                (From the kitchen)
        You guys want a drink? tea, coke?

They both decline in unison.

                    STIV
              (Still looking at the TV)
        You want to go out? We can't talk
        here.

                                              CUT TO:

WIDE

They walk along the street of terraces, finally emerging into a
small park area with swings and dilapidated kids' playground
equipment.

                                              CUT TO:

MEDIUM

They sit on a low wall, watching a half-hearted football kick
around with a few local kids.

                    BOB
                (Shaky)
        That fucker was going to kill me Stiv.
        Like I was nothing. With my own gun.
                (Shaking his head head
                down)
        You fucking did him though, Both of
        them. I never slept you know, kept
        replaying it in my head.
                (Eventually looking up at Stiv)

        You OK mate?

STIV
No, not OK.
(With feeling)
Not I'm not fucking OK at all. Hardly
surprising is it...
(emotional)

I never killed anyone before you
know. You fuck-wit. You know,
(A beat)
I always wondered what it would be
like, killing someone...

Another prolonged silence.

STIV (CONT'D)
(Emotional)
Somebody will find them. It will be
on the NEWs, the fucking National
NEWs.
(Shaking his head in
disbelief)
Where did you tell your folks we
went yesterday?

BOB
Didn't tell them nothing. Never do,
she isn't interested, and I don't see
my old man much these days.

STIV
(Thinking...)
OK look, anyone asks, we hunted
BIRKRIGG FELL for rabbit yesterday,
all day till dark. Don't give any
details. Don't ever deviate. We
never saw nothing. Heard nothing.
We never go back there again, ever.

(A beat, continuing in a
slower more thoughtful tone)

People like that, they get killed you
know. Killed by other people who
are like them. Same as they are you
know. There's no reason for anyone
to suspect us, we are just local guys,
lived around here forever.
(A beat, looking at Bob)
You OK with that Bob?

Bob looks across at his friend, the person who killed for him,
wondered if he could have done the same. The hold each other's
gaze for a long moment. For some vague reason, he thinks his old
fiend Stiv, looks different.

DISSOLVE TO:

INT. WALNEY ISLAND DIVE CENTER. A DIVING EQUIPMENT HIRE BUSINESS. DAVE'S OFFICE. MEDIUM SHOTS AND CLOSE

The phone rings.

DAVE
Dave Geddings, who?
(Listens for a beat)
No, nothing at all here. We rang you
guys as per the rules, that's all we
know. Its been 36 hours now.
(Listens)
OK, will do.
(Remembering...)
Oh yes, one thing. A guy was here,
black Range Rover, well heeled. He
said he was looking for his mates.
(Listens)
No, didn't get a number, it looked
new ish.
(Listens)
Yes, I'd know him again, sure.

Dave hangs up, thinking. He pulls out a map of the area, tracking his finger around the coastline. Mike comes into the office, drops down into a battered office chair. He regards Dave for a beat.

> MIKE
> (Thoughtfully)
> I don't think those guys went out
> along the coast you know, they
> went out along Salthouse Road,
> People don't go that way to the
> wreck.
> (A beat)
> There's nothing else to dive on along
> the Ulverston road, is there? There's
> no depth. Maybe they went up to
> the Lakes...but then they'd probably
> have gone along the other road.

Dave looks at his partner, not really seeing him, his thoughts ranging over parts of his past life.

> DAVE
> Those guys were up to no good
> Mike. I'll bet on it. I have a gut
> feeling. Whatever, we are down
> £500 quid's worth of kit for £120 hire
> charge.
> (Looking up at Mike, a beat)
> Do you reckon they are both dead?

                                              DISSOLVE TO:

BBC TV, NATIONAL NEWS HEADLINES. 'INTERNATIONAL CRIME COMES TO CUMBRIA'.

TODAY TWO MEN WERE FOUND SHOT TO DEATH ON ROUGH GROUND NEAR ULVERSTON, A SMALL MARKET TOWN IN CUMBRIA. THE MEN, BOTH BULGARIAN NATIONALS, HAD USED DIVING EQUIPMENT TO RECOVER A STASH OF ASSAULT RIFLES HIDDEN IN A WATER FILLED MINE SINKHOLE.

30 ASSAULT RIFLES AND 1000 ROUNDS OF AMMUNITION WERE RECOVERED AT THE MURDER SITE, ALONG WITH EXTENSIVE DIVING EQUIPMENT WHICH HAD BEEN HIRED LOCALLY. BOTH MEN HAD BEEN KILLED 'EXECUTION STYLE' WITH SINGLE SHOTS, POINTING TO WHAT POLICE BELIEVE TO BE PROFESSIONAL HITS. THE INVESTIGATION CONTINUES, LOCAL CRIMINAL INVESTIGATORS COOPERATING WITH SPECIAL BRANCH OFFICERS AND INTERPOL. POLICE ARE INVESTIGATING POSSIBLE LINKS TO AN ARMS FIND SOME 16 YEARS AGO IN 1994.

CUT TO:

INT. WALNEY ISLAND DIVE CENTER. A DIVING EQUIPMENT HIRE BUSINESS. DAVE'S OFFICE. MEDIUM CLOSE

                    DAVE
          I fucking knew it!

Dave hits the desk hard with his flat hand. Documents, tools and bits of equipment jumping. He and Mike are sat in the clutter with chipped mugs of tea, watching a small, battered TV with a dusty screen.

                 DAVE (CONT'D)
          We'll never get our stuff back now, it
          will be 'evidence'.

Dave and Mike's eyes meet across the debris on their desk. Mike's eyes drop away.

CUT TO:

INT. BOB'S HOUSE. A TERRACE IN A NARROW STREET. ULVERSTON. MEDIUM AND CLOSE

Bob leans in towards the big TV, eyes wide, pale. He flicks the channel, gets the same story again on Channel 4. Dials his cell phone.

                    BOB
          You watching this?

                    STIV
          Yep. Fucking Interpol, Special
          Branch! Bloody hell.
                    (A beat)
          Put the phone down Bob, you
          hearing me? I'll come round.

                                                            CUT TO:

WIDE AND CLOSE

Stiv parks in the crowded street near Bob's house. Knocks and is
admitted by Iris.

                    IRIS
               (Concerned smile)
          Stiv are you OK? Not your usual self?

                    STIV
          No, I'm good Iris thanks. Bit tired.

                    IRIS
               (Flirty smile)
          Hmm, you young lads should have
          plenty of energy, I still do.
                    (Meaningful look...)

Stiv blushes, ducks his head, uncomfortable with the fact that
Iris finds him so transparent. He shuffles along the corridor; Bob is
alone in the front room as usual.

                    BOB
          Stiv, you OK.

                    STIV
               (breathless)
          Bob look don't ring me about this
          stuff. I don't know what these guys
          can pick up on mobiles... I've heard
          they can put trigger words into the

system, then if anyone uses one,
they home in on that call. If you
want to talk from here on, we'll do it
face to face eh.

                    BOB
          (Looking from the silent TV to
          his friend)
I didn't know I had a mate who was
an international hit man...
          (Smiles ruefully, turns to Stiv,
          emotional)
Do you sleep? I haven't slept since--
-can't think about anything else.

                    STIV
          (Looking anxiously at the
          door into the kitchen)
Can she---

                    BOB
No, she's OK mate.
          (Pause)
We wait it out now, I guess. Do
normal stuff eh?

                    STIV
Totally!

                                        DISSOLVE TO

EXT. ULVERSTON STREET. DAY

WIDE TO MEDIUM

Stiv is heading home. A police car passes, indicating right at the
top of the the street. Stiv, alert, watches, heart rate quickening.

He approaches the top of the street, slows. The POLICE CAR
has stopped by his house two hundred yards away, brake lights

flaring. He waits. Two uniforms get out, looking at street numbers, consulting notes. One officer stays by the car, the other knocks on his door.

The police car is stationary for several minutes, while the officer at his door waits, then returns to car leaning in conferring, then gets in. Finally, the police car pulls out into the street and slowly drives away.

Stiv waits, a tight feeling across his chest. He crosses the road, walks on past his house, walks to the junction at the bottom of his street, no sign of the police car. He stands there for a beat, then pulls out his cell phone.

                    STIV
                (Cell phone)
        Bob, where are you? Home?

                    BOB
        Yes, what's up?

                    STIV
        Police at my place, 5 mins back.
        How the fuck---?

                    BOB
        You are joking-- (A beat) Shit, they
        have just pulled up outside.
                (Pausing...panicked)
        I'm gone.
                (Phone clicks)

                    STIV
        Bob, don't---

Stiv walks back along his street to his house. Nonplussed. He passes a black Range Rover among the usual jam of parked cars, many of which he recognizes. The Range Rover is strange but not a big deal. As he passes, he sees a man in the driver's seat. The man is making a call and ignores Stiv's curious glance.

CUT TO:

INT. STIV'S HOUSE. KITCHEN

His Mother Mary is cooking. She notes Stiv's entry and automatically puts the kettle on, rummaging for the biscuit tin.

> MARY
> What did you two do? Police were here asking for you, and Bob as well. Didn't say much, asked me to let them know when you came home.
> (A beat)
> Shall I ring them now? I said I would.

> STIV
> It's ok. Yeah, ring them. I'll go to them maybe. Dunno what it's about though.

CUT TO:

EXT. ULVERSTON STREET. DAY

Stiv walking briskly, takes a call.

> BOB
> (Voice on phone)

> It's me. I went out the back. I'm back home again now. They are onto us, aren't they? We are fucked big time.

                              STIV
          Don't know mate. It doesn't look
          good. I'm going to them now at the
          Ulverston nick, try to bluff it out, see
          what they know.

                              BOB
          You are fucking mad! You---

                              STIV
          What choice do we have? We live
          here. Sooner or later--- Anyway I'm
          doing it. So, hold your nerve the way
          we said the other night. OK---

One hundred meters back, Stiv is being slowly tracked by a black
Range Rover.

                                                         CUT TO:

INT. ULVERSTON POLICE STATION. DAY

Stiv approaches a desk officer.

                              STIV
          Hello,
          (Nervous smile)
          My name is STEPHEN PARRY, Stiv.
          Some of your guys came to my
          house earlier looking for me. They
          spoke to my Mother.

                                                         CUT TO:

Stiv is asked to wait on a rickety plastic chair. Presently an un-
remarkable, casually dressed man (40s) appears.

                    DI JOE WILSON
          Hello, I'm Detective Inspector
          Joseph Wilson, you are Stephen
          Parry, right.

                    STIV

          Stiv---

Stiv and DI Wilson shake hands. The officer indicates that Stiv
should follow him and turns back into a larger room with several
other people working on computers at cluttered desks. He kicks
out a chair by an overloaded desk.

                    DI JOE WILSON
          Coffee? Its instant, sorry.

                    STIV
              (ignoring the offer of coffee)
          What's all this about, some police
          came to my house earlier.

DI Wilson pulls a large box file over and flips the top open.
Consults inside.

                    DI JOE WILSON
          Routine.

          We are following up the recent
          murder that everyone is talking
          about. Biggest thing to take place in
          Ulverston for many a year.
              (Consulting a document)
          We have micro searched the whole
          area where the two murders took
          place and there are a couple of
          things that I need to clear up with
          you, if that's ok
              (Looks up. smiles)

Stiv is controlling his emotions as best he can. He is walking new
ground, he has only ever read about this stuff, and seen it on TV.

                                STIV
          If I can help---

                         DI JOE WILSON
          Thanks.
                    (squaring documents, then
                    facing Stiv)
          Both parties were slain with small
          calibre slugs, 22's. Both slugs went
          on through, lost at the moment.
                    (A beat)
          But we found this

DI Wilson slides over a transparent plastic envelope to Stiv. Stiv
regards it with shock. Fighting down his reactions. Inside the bag is
22 CALIBRE BRASS SHELL. His shell.

The Police officer watches Stiv closely as he leans down to
examine the shell, noting that Stiv doesn't actually touch the
plastic bag.

                                STIV
                    (thoughtfully)
          Looks like a 22. Probably Winchester
          Triple X

Stiv looks back up at DI Wilson. The Detective doesn't pick up the
shell, he holds his stare to Stiv, indicating with a gesture for Stiv to
elaborate.

                         STIV (CONT'D)
          Dunno what else to say, they are
          middle of the road rabbit ammo.
          Not too fast so they don't damage
          the rabbit too much.

                         DI JOE WILSON
                    (Picking up the shell,
                    turning it)
          You know about this sort of stuff then
          Stiv?

                                STIV
                   I do. Lots of of folks around here do.
                   Rabbit shooters and all, grew up
                   with it. I buy Triple X's from Fawcetts
                   at Lancaster. Got maybe 250 or so
                   in my gun safe at home. It's a ways
                   down to Lancaster, so I buy them
                   1000 at a time. Lasts me a month
                   or two then. It's all on my license,
                   above board.

DI Wilson is silent, thinking. He extracts another document from
the file, slides it over to Stiv. Stiv's confidence is now returning
somewhat.

                           STIV (CONT'D)
                        (Briefly looking at the
                           document)
                   Yep, that's mine. It's all up to date.
                   You can see there that I can buy
                   1000 at a time. Last purchase 3
                   months or so back.
                           (traces his finger along the
                           document)
                   Right here...

Stiv slides the copy of his Firearms License back to the Detective,
who places it back in his box file.

                           DI JOE WILSON
                   Well, interesting, thanks Stephen, or
                   Stiv, can I call you that? Only thing
                   left, can you tell me where you
                   were on the afternoon and night of
                   16th, and any witnesses who might
                   corroborate---
                           (a beat)
                   We are checking all local Firearms
                   Certificate holders as a first sweep

                                        DISSOLVE TO:

EXT. ULVERSTON STREET OUTSIDE POLICE STATION. DAY

VIEW THROUGH WINDSHIELD OF THE RANGE ROVER TO FRONTAGE OF POLICE STATION, PULLING BACK TO REVEAL THE SIDE VIEW OF A MALE, HANDS ON THE WHEEL.

Stiv emerges from the Police Station 100 yards away, he walks to the right, pulling out a cell phone as he goes.

FADE TO BLACK

EXT. BIRKRIGG FELL, OVERLOOKING ULVERSTON. DAY

Stiv and Bob are sitting against a rock looking down at the town center network of streets.

                    STIV
          So, what do you think? Did they ask
          about me?

                    BOB
          Yep, asked about the 16th. I stuck
          with our story.

          To be honest the cop didn't labour
          the point. He asked what ammo I
          used normally. I told him Winchester
          Triple X's from Fawcetts.
                    (A beat)
          He also had a copy of my Firearms
          Certificate. That was it really. Asked
          how often you and me go out with
          rifles, stuff like that.

Stiv was silent, thinking it all through.

                    STIV
          They don't have the slugs, so they
          can't match any rifling to my gun.

I reckon they will move on to other
stuff now.

The paper talked about an
INTERNATIONAL HIT... no mention of
any local connections. We just need
to stick with our story, tough it out.
Never deviate.

                    BOB
OK, will do mate. It's hard though
Stiv, I'm still not sleeping. I lie awake
all bloody night, then I'm knackered
next day. Awful.

Bob glances across at his friend bemused. Stiv seems lost in
thought but is smiling to himself.

                                                    CUT TO:

EXT. BIRKRIGG FELL. DAY.

A mile away, Daniel Laidlow stashes his binoculars and powers
up his window. The Range Rover is parked in a small stand of trees
off a farm track. From his position he can see Bob and Stiv sitting
against a rock.

Daniel has shadowed the police's local investigations and has
noted their interest in the two young men who were both shooting
enthusiasts. Both had appeared to cooperate with the police,
voluntarily attending interviews. The police hadn't followed up so
most likely it was dead-end.

Daniel was in trouble. The murders of his men at the sinkhole had
meant he hadn't taken delivery of the assault rifles, so was unable
to pass them onward to his client. A large amount of money was
involved. He was angry and perplexed and not a little scared
that his deal had gone sour, and day by day, becoming even
more concerned for his own safety if indeed his men had been
professionally assassinated.

The two young men he was watching couldn't possibly have killed both his men. They were two local lads, and from what he could find out, had always lived locally. He just couldn't compute it. His guys were both pros', and they had both been taken out with two single shots. It didn't make any sense.

CUT TO:

Telephone ringing. OS

INT. ULVERSTON POLICE STATION. DAY

DI Joe Wilson's phone rings on his overloaded desk.

> DI JOE WILSON
>
> Wilson
> > (A beat)
>
> Boss.
> > (A beat)
>
> OK, at the moment we don't have much. Both slugs went on through. The shots were both kill shots, accurate and effective. Head and heart. No finishing off shots, so the shooter was confident that he had done the job.
> > (a beat)
>
> He or she shot from the rocks opposite, a range of around 30-35 meters, a scope with a night-sight - not technically difficult shots, even in low light. They were probably quick shots because both bodies were close together with no evidence of being moved afterwards. Quick and accurate.
>
> Some local shooters have been checked out, but they are young lads, zero record and difficult to imagine how they had any sort

of motive or involvement in arms
dealing.

We have no evidence of an
international or professional hit,
but I think that's where we need to
focus now.

The guns were obviously bound for
somewhere, probably Ireland again
like last time, so a buyer and a
supplier are both out of pocket and
will be upset about that to say the
least.
(a beat, thinking)
Yep, Northern Ireland is the most
obvious destination from this area,
and it wouldn't be the first time,
but things have been quiet there
now for about 16 years now. You'll
remember the last time?
(Listening)
No, I was a young rookie back then.
I wasn't directly involved in the
investigation, but I was on duty at
the crime scene a few times. Same
set of sinkholes, but further along.
(listening)
Well, we are still guessing at this
stage.

Boss, we are nowhere with this. We'll
keep pitching.
(Listening)
OK, will do.
(Hangs up)

Wilson puts his feet up on his desk and leans back, his chair
precariously balanced, his eyes closed in concentration.

DISSOLVE TO:

EXT. WALNEY ISLAND DIVE CENTER. A DIVING EQUIPMENT HIRE COMPANY

WIDE TO MEDIUM

A police van pulls up outside Dave's battered tin gates. Dave and Mike wander over as the driver opens the rear doors.

> DRIVER
> Dive tanks, winch, spotlight and all
> sorts of other stuff for you. Originally
> hired from here, yes?

> DAVE
> Brilliant.
> Didn't think we'd see this stuff again.
> Put it over here.

They pile the equipment into the Dave's dilapidated office and after checking against his hire list, he signs the receipt form.

> DAVE (CONT'D)
> You guys any nearer solving this
> then, are you able to talk about it.

> DRIVER
> Can't say much. Sorry. Investigations
> on-going. OK then-

The driver slams the van doors, nods briefly to Dave through the window, and drives away. Dave watches him go, turns back into his office, looking at the equipment.

> DAVE
> Mike, we need to get the residual
> pressure out of these tanks, they
> could be dangerous. We have no
> idea how they might have been
> chucked around or dinged.

They carry the equipment to the DEPRESSURIZING AREA, connecting pipes carefully, consulting gauges.

                    MIKE
          Look at this Dave, this gauge is
          broken.

Dave and Mike bend over the PRESSURE GAUGE which has indeed been broken.

                    DAVE
          It must have taken quite a blow
          Mike, that's toughened glass 8mm
          thick. You'd have to hit it with a
          fucking hammer to break it.

                    MIKE
          Hey, look at this Dave
                    (Probing the broken
                    glass in the centre of the
                    pressure gauge with a small
                    screwdriver)

Mike adjusts the light to shine onto the gauge. He probes carefully, finally teasing out a grey blob of lead from the shards of glass.

                    MIKE (CONT'D)
          It's a SLUG mate, a fucking bullet.
          Pretty bashed around, but that's
          what it is.
                    (Looking up at Dave)
          Better ring those cops, they'll want
          to see this.

Dave picks up the phone, pauses, looking at his partner, replaces the handset.

                    DAVE
          Something I've been meaning to
          say to you... We have been mates' a
          long time now.
                    (Making full eye contact)
          You have been a bit off the last few
          days, not your usual self. Since that
          guy in the range Rover was here in
          fact.
                    (a beat)
          Anything you want to talk about
          mate...? Did you know him?

                                        FADE TO BLACK

Phone rings. OS

INT. ULVERSTON POLICE STATION. DAY. DI WILSON'S DESK

Wilson sits, feet flat to the floor, head down, thinking. His phone
rings.

                    DI JOE WILSON
                    (Picks up phone)
          Wilson.
                    (listening)
          So, no good huh. So, what do you
          have? Hang on...
                    (Gets his notebook, writing)
          OK, so it's a Winchester Triple X, 22
          cal. 40 grain slug. No rifling marks
          recovered - too much damage.
          Anything else you can tell me?
                    (listening)
          OK, well thanks for that. There's
          another slug out there somewhere,
          maybe we'll have better luck next
          time. OK.

Hangs up. Re-dials

Boss, yeh, its Joe.
The slug doesn't tell us anything
useful. Too mangled, sorry.
          (listening)
Well, we don't have much right now.
I'll admit that international hits don't
usually use 22 Cal rifles, but maybe if
the shooter was operating out of his
area...
          (a beat)
OK Boss will do.

                                        FADE OUT

**INT. WALNEY ISLAND DIVE CENTER. A DIVING EQUIPMENT HIRE
COMPANY. DAVE'S OFFICE.**

Both men are sitting in office clutter with mugs of tea. Mike is
reflective.

                    MIKE
Sorry mate. It's a weird time I guess,
being connected to this murder and
stuff.
          (A beat, thoughtful)
Probably nothing, but a few years
back after leaving the PARAs I ran
with some pretty dodgy characters.
We had dived on some wrecked
ships over in Northern Ireland, jobs
for cash, you know.
          (a beat)
Mostly, it was guns, sometimes
bigger stuff - mortars etc. Other
times it was just packages, all sealed
up in plastic. We didn't ask too many
questions. Got paid, went on the
piss, forgot about stuff, you know.
          (a beat)
Then, I came back here, met my
Mrs, and sorted myself out. Never

                                                          45

got involved in any other dodgy
stuff,
  (a beat)
Well, until...

                DAVE
          (Staring at his partner, hands
          flat to the desk)
What the fuck are you going to tell
me mate... bloody hell, I never knew
any of this!

                MIKE
          (Shaking his head)
No, nothing like this stuff mate, fuck
me, I never killed anybody.
          (A beat)
16 years back, two guys turned up
at my place. They were looking for
a diver for a couple of nights work.
No questions etc. £500 quid cash in
hand. As usual, I was skint, I ripped
their hand off.
          (A beat)
They wanted some to sink some steel
boxes into the sinkholes out along
the coast road.

                DAVE

Mike---

                MIKE
No, let me finish, please.
          (A beat)
There were six boxes, steel, fucking
heavy, unmarked. All sealed up.
I'm guessing guns or similar. Same
as Northern Ireland way back. We
couldn't have just tipped them into
the sinkholes, they had to be taken
down. Otherwise, anything could

have happened. No-one really
knows deep these buggers are.
                (A beat)
So, we lowered them down with
winches, stashed them well down
on ledges mainly. Took us all of two
nights. Then on the second night, we
had stashed five of them, working
in the headlights, and we saw blue
lights along the 590.
                (A beat)
We panicked. Piled into the trucks,
doused the lights and drove like
fucking maniacs down to the
beach, then, luckily the tide was
out, right hammered fast along the
sand to Greenodd, then up onto the
A590 and away. We left the last box
unopened where it was on the side
of the sinkhole.

Dave, caught up in the story, leans back into his chair, eyes wide
with concentration.

                MIKE (CONT'D)
Well, as you'll probably remember,
the Police made a big deal of
it. Some of them probably got
promoted. They jumped to the
easy conclusion that we had been
recovering a box of guns out of the
sinkhole. They had then scared us
and we ran off, leaving it.
                (Grinning ruefully, shaking his
                head)
There was a bit of investigation then,
a few questions asked etc, but no-
one ever came near me. I never
got paid of course, so I was £500
out of pocket, but that was it. We
heard later that POLICE DIVERS had

been down looking, but they must
have been crap, cos' they never
reported anything else being found.
The whole investigation was hailed
a major success for the cops, foiling
a stash of guns that were ultimately
bound for the 'TROUBLES' over there
in the old country.

                    DAVE
Bloody hell Mike. I'm saying nothing
mate, I worked years as a RIG
DIVER, I was involved in a whole
mass of stuff that I wouldn't want
investigating. Diving is what it is...

          (Grinning)
we go places where normal people
don't go.

Dave gets up, makes more tea. Drops back down into his chair,
thoughtful.

                    DAVE (CONT'D)
So, where are we? FIVE BOXES OF
GUNS have been lying in fucking
sinkholes along the Coast Road for
the past 16 years, and nothing has
happened since, until now.

                    MIKE
That's about the size of it mate. I've
never even spoke of it to anyone.
Too scared, not only of the Police,
but probably more so of the fucking
bastards who were involved from
the other side. Some very serious
hard men Dave.
          (Shudders...)

I mean men who would take you
down without a second thought,
they would not hesitate.

DAVE
Well, my old mate. Thank fuck we
have nothing to do with that stuff
anymore.
(Grins)
We are innocent bystanders to all
this now. Its water under the bridge
now, long gone.

Dave leans back, takes a drink from his mug. Looks across at his
partner.

MIKE
(Earnestly)
Dave, you don't fucking get it do
you? Its not over, its starting up all
over again...
(A beat)
That guy who was here the other
day, in the Range Rover... Daniel
Laidlow, I know him - knew him! He
was one of them back then. He's
older now, but I knew him straight
away!
(A beat)
I'd know him anywhere. He was the
one who hired me back then, 16
years back. I don't think he knew
me, but I fucking knew him.
(A beat)
This isn't over Dave, not by a long
chalk.

Dave regards his friend across the cluttered desk. He is unusually
pale and clearly frightened.

                    DAVE
        Shit Mike! Do you reckon he might
        have recognized you? It's been 16
        years mate. Bloody hell, you were
        with IRIS in those days, Young BOB
        would have been what, maybe 8?

                    MIKE
        Yeah, I guess about 8.
                (Thoughtfully)
        Iris never knew any details, but
        Laidlow came round the house a
        couple of times. She never said, but
        I think she was scared of him big-
        time, although he was always polite
        and quiet spoke with her.
                (A beat)
        I remember he brought her some
        flowers once...

                                        DISSOLVE TO

Later...

INT. DAVE'S DIVE WORKSHOP, WALNEY ISLAND.

Dave and Mike are stashing the returned diving equipment and
checking for any other damage.

                    MIKE
                (Puzzled, fiddling with
                equipment)
        Dave, I'm right, this equipment
        hasn't been in sea water, it stinks.
                (sniffing)
        Or a lake either... Its definitely
        stagnant water.

        Look at this grease all over the
        harness, I reckon this is off the guns,

this is heavy grease. The same sort
they use on the underwater valves
on the rigs. It withstands long-term
submerging to protect metal.

Dave glances over at his long-term buddy and partner. The
seriousness of the situation hitting both men simultaneously.

                    DAVE
          So, what do we really know? There
          are still boxes of guns submerged in
          sinkholes along the coast road from
          16 years back.
                    (A beat)
          Someone, this Laidlow guy, has
          come back for them, hired some
          BULGARIAN divers to go after them,
          and someone else shot them.
                    (A beat)
          That's it. I wonder why he waited all
          these years...?
                    (A beat)
          What we don't know is, who shot
          these two guys. That's big stuff!
                    (Thinking)
          We don't think Laidlow
          recognized you.
                    (A beat)
          We also don't know if any of the
          other boxes have been recovered
          do we. You lost one box 16 years
          back, then presumably, another
          box is with the cops now, that leaves
          another FOUR BOXES still down
          there...
                    (A beat)
          Say 30 guns to a box, with ammo,
          120 guns. Fuck, that's a lot of
          firepower mate...

Mike is silent, thoughtful. Picks up his iPhone, googling.

                    MIKE
          Shit, a single assault rifle with 100
          rounds is worth approx. £4k on the
          BLACK MARKET, could run as high as
          up to £12k each in hot spots.
                    (A beat)
          There could be upwards of three
          quarters of a million quid's worth of
          stuff in those holes.

Both men are silent, considering...

                    MIKE (CONT'D)
          I guess we have to assume that
          Laidlow won't go away. The other
          guns are in several sinkholes along
          the coast road.

                    (A beat)
          Oh shit!

                    DAVE
          What---

                    MIKE
          Iris, I just hope she doesn't run across
          him, Laidlow I mean. She would
          know him instantly. And she hasn't
          really changed much. He might
          know her... put it together
                    (A beat)
          Its a long shot, there's no real reason
          that she would meet this guy. Fuck...

Dave gets up, searching through drawers, comes up with a local
Ordnance Survey Map. Spreads it out over the clutter of his desk.

                    DAVE
                    (Tracing his finger along
                    the map)
          Where are they Mike?

                    MIKE
              (Getting up, coming around
              the desk to bend over
              the map)
          Several Dave, along here, and here.

                                              FADE OUT

INT. ULVERSTON POLICE STATION. DAY. CONFERENCE ROOM

A dozen officers are assembled in the conference room. All are
seated around a large table, cluttered with files, coffee cups,
car keys, cell-phones and electronic tablets. There is an air of
frustrated tension in the room.

          ASSISTANT CHIEF COMMISSIONER FREDERICK JENSEN
                    (Standing)
              Ok, well thanks everyone,
              particularly the intel report from
              Interpol and the attendance of
              INSPECTOR JEAN LAFITTE from Paris.
                         (Nodding across the room at
                         an elegantly dressed officer
                         sitting slightly away from the
                         table)
                         (Gestures to his right)
              DI Wilson, can you sum up please.

DI Joe Wilson gets to his feet, laboriously gathering a stash of
documents together.

                    DI JOE WILSON
              Right Sir.
                    (A beat)
              To sum up, these are the facts so far.
              The crime scene yielded two male
              bodies, both shot with 22 cal single
              shots. 30 ARMALITE ASSAULT RIFLES
              in 30 cal, and 3000 ROUNDS OF
              AMMUNITION. All in working order.

(Looking around the room)
The guns are probably a post-script
from a crime back in early 1994.
There was an incident where a
crate of assault rifles was recovered
en-route to terrorists engaging the
CONFLICT IN NORTHERN IRELAND. At
that time no other guns were found.
Clearly there was a further stash.

(Clearing his throat)
Our divers have been down again in
the past week and we are satisfied
now that nothing else is hidden in
the sinkhole.

(A beat)
A TOYOTA LAND CRUISER with
WINCHING GEAR, was there, along
with various professional level diving
equipment. The vehicle was stolen a
week ago in the Manchester area,
and the diving equipment had
been hired locally from Walney Dive
Shop.

(Shuffling papers)
The two men were Bulgarian by
birth, legal immigrants, had lived
in the North London area for past
twenty years. Both men held legit
EN/ISO Standard 24801-2014 level 2
Autonomous Diving Certificates up
to 18M.

(Checking documents)
Their names were Antoni Penkar
39, and Marko Zlatko 41. Both born
in Sofia. Neither men had criminal
records.

(Referring to another
document)
One 22 Cal bullet has been
recovered, badly damaged, so
has not yielded any useful intel.

Both shots were taken from rocks
on the opposite side of the sinkhole
at a range of approx. 30 - 35
meters. We also have a 22 Cal
shell, which may have been there
prior, we don't know. There are 18
FIREARM CERTIFICATE HOLDERS
in the Ulverston area, 12 of them
hold 22 Cal rifles, 10 of them shoot
Winchester Triple X cartridges
supplied from Fawcetts of Lancaster.
     (A beat)
All Certificate holders have been
interviewed - no leads or follow-ups
are planned. We don't think there is
any local connection. This is almost
certainly international crime linked
to activities in Northern Ireland.
     (DI Wilson looks around the
     room, receiving confirmatory
     nods from several
     colleagues)

ASSISTANT CHIEF COMMISSIONER FREDERICK JENSEN
Thanks Joe.
     (Looking around)
Comments...

There is an exchange of glances around the room. The
Frenchman stirs, flicks imaginary lint from his suit and languidly
rises to his feet, confident and self-assured.

INSPECTOR JEAN LAFITTE - INTERPOL
My thanks to you Assistant Chief
Commissioner, and to...
     (Consulting his notes, then
     nodding to DI Wilson)
DI Wilson, who is leading this
investigation.
     (A beat)

From INTERPOL's perspective, we
have little to add to what has
been said already. This is clearly
a PROFESSIONAL HIT using fairly
quiet small calibre ammunition.
The assassin was confident and felt
no need to use a 'coup de grace',
particularly on the second shot,
where in all probability, the wound
was not immediately fatal.

> (A beat)

The assassin was most likely
engaged to take down the two
men and clear the area, because
there was no attempt to recover the
rifles, which in fact, would be worth
a considerable sum on the black
market.

> (Glancing around the room,
> then addressing ACC Jensen
> and DI Wilson)

I would suggest that local
inquiries are concluded now, and
investigations on National and
International levels continue. I will
continue to work with colleagues
in London and Paris, and I would
be grateful if DI Wilson could act as
local liaison.

> (Faint smile around the room,
> shooting his cuffs)

I am happy for the crime scene
to be cleared, but files left open.
Thank you.

ASSISTANT CHIEF COMMISSIONER FREDERICK JENSEN
> (Standing)

Thank you, Inspector Lafitte, we are
grateful for Interpol's support.

> (Addressing everyone)

OK that's it for now colleagues.
Locally, our work is done, but we will
remain at National and International
colleagues' disposal.

The formal part of the meeting over, Chairs scrape back, keys
retrieved, cell phones consulted, officers disperse.

CUT TO:

EXT. DAY. ARRAD FOOT FELLS, CUMBRIA, OVERLOOKING THE A590 NEAR GREENODD

Daniel Laidlow sits in his Range Rover overlooking the A590. He
can see two-way traffic streaming past Greenodd below him,
silent with distance. He raises a set 12-50 binoculars and watches
a police van negotiating a rough track connecting the sinkhole
copse to the main road about two miles away. It looked to him
like they were closing down the crime scene, which made little
sense to him. The sinkhole is hidden by trees, but he knows exactly
where it was located.

On the seat next to him, his cell phone trills.

> DANIEL
>
> Yep
> > (Listening)
> Nothing I can do right now. It's a
> crime scene. What the fuck do you
> expect that I can just trundle up,
> get the guns and drive off into the
> sunset. You are out of your fucking
> mind, you moron.
> > (Listening)
>
> I know, get off my back. I didn't
> expect any of this situation. I'm as
> gutted as you are.
> > (Listening)

Look, someone took out my guys.
My guess is that they gambled the
other crates not being found. Or
maybe they were discovered and
had to bugger off quick, I don't
know.

They will be back, for sure. I'm
looking down at the site right now.
The police are closing down the
crime scene. The local cops are
bumpkins, totally out of their depth,
they are no-where.
                (Listening)
Yes, I'm gonna stay around here for
a while. See what pans out. Keep
the faith brother, we go back a long
time, I never let you down yet, did I?

The line is cut abruptly. Daniel throws it impatiently on the
passenger seat. Below him, the police van finally pulls off the
rough track and onto the 590, merging with flowing traffic -
picking up speed towards Ulverston.

FADE TO BLACK

EXT. DAY. SUNNY. BOOTH'S SUPERMARKET CARPARK. ULVERSTON

The car park is three quarters full. Iris passes through the checkout
and heads for her battered Focus parked out on the edge of
the parking area. As usual the parking spaces are too small, and
the supermarket trolley barely fits between vehicles. Iris carefully
negotiates her shopping trolley between a farm pickup truck
and black Range Rover, deciding if she was going to scratch
something, then she would be better veering towards the pickup.

She draws level with the Range Rover door, the window slides
silently down.

DANIEL
Hello Iris, long time.

Iris is shocked. She recognized the faint Irish lilt in the voice, but from where? Daniel lifted his RAY BANS and smiles lazily. Memories flood back.

DANIEL (CONT'D)
The years have treated you well my darlin' You are as beautiful as you always were.

Iris is transported back 16 years in a milli-second.

IRIS
(Flustered)
Daniel, is it you? I thought---

DANIEL
You thought I'd been put away, yes.
(Disarming smile)
Well, its true. They caught up with me and threw me into the deepest hole they could find. But you know me Iris, I'm a survivor. And now, here we both are...

IRIS
(Still shocked, recovering)
Daniel, I ---

DANIEL
Oh, sure now, it's OK. Don't be worried Iris. I wasn't looking for you directly. I'm here on a bit of business, but by God, it's nice to lay eyes on you again.
You must have a 'Fountain of Eternal Youth' hidden away somewhere
I think, you are still the same, not changed a jot. How do you do that?

Tell me, are you still with Nick, was it?
No, Mike, I think?

                    IRIS
Mike, yes. No, we split up years
back. You know how it is...

                  DANIEL
And you had a boy didn't you, he
must be grown into a man now?

                    IRIS
BOBBY yes. He is still with me.
            (Hesitating)
Look Daniel, its nice to see you, but
I'm a bit late you know. Doing stuff...

                  DANIEL
Hey Iris, I'm sorry. Here's me going
on as usual.
            (Disarming smile again)
Forgive me indeed. You must be
away please. Hey...
            (Rummaging)
Look, I have a card somewhere. It
would be great to get together for
a drink sometime. Catch up, you
know? We have a history Iris.

Daniel holds out an embossed card which Iris takes. She puts it
away in her purse, smiles and negotiates her shopping through
the narrow gap to her FORD FOCUS. She looks back once and
Daniel waves with a small hand movement.

                                        CUT TO:

EXT. ULVERSTON STREET. DAY

Daniel cruises the big ROVER gently, watching Iris's Focus
negotiate Ulverston's narrow cobbled streets. She passes through

the main shopping area, stops briefly at the lights, then crosses the 590 and into narrow streets and rows of residential terraces.

Daniel holds back, finally pulling into a parking space as Iris parks her Focus 100 meters ahead. He watches as she unloads her shopping bags, disappearing into a terraced house and closing the door.

Daniel sits very still. He has been here before as he watched the Police Car check out one of the young men several days before. It was the same house - interesting. He sits there a long time watching, but there is no other movement.

FADE OUT

45 INT. ULVERSTON POLICE STATION. DAY. DI WILSON'S DESK

Joe Wilson sprawls at his desk regarding the clutter with distaste. He is in the process of closing down the crime scene at the sinkhole and ensuring that all files and evidence is quickly accessible whenever the phone might ring for National and INTERNATIONAL COLLEAGUES. He is vaguely relieved not to be in the vanguard of the investigation, but nonetheless is quite determined to place the best professional support to his colleagues as/when required.

Something occurs to him and he consults several files, then picks up the phone, dials.

> DI JOE WILSON
> Hello, DI Joe Wilson here from
> Cumbria. Is it possible to speak to DI
> Sean O Flynn please?
>> (Waits, while reading
>> snatches of files)
> Yes, hello Sean, Joe Wilson...It's been
> a while, How are you?
>> (Listens, smiling, vaguely
>> impatient to get to the point
>> of the conversation)

Sean, I'm going over the files
from '94, the guns in the sinkhole,
remember? (Pause) Yes, that one.
            (Listens)

I'm looking at the list of arrests, both
here and with you. If you recall,
there were a couple of names
that eluded us here, but they went
down for other related crimes
several months later with you. One in
particular, DANIEL JAMES LAIDLOW.
            (Listening, waiting)
Yes, that's your man. We knew that
Danny was a player. He had a local
girlfriend here for a while.
            (A beat)
We couldn't pin him down, then
you got him for possession of an
unregistered firearm and second
degree - good result!
            (Listening, writing notes)

Yes, Daniel was a fixer, never got his
hands dirty, too smart for that.

So, he went down for 15 years all-up
in HMP MAGILLIGAN --- what?
            (Sitting up, registering
            surprise)
Did he now... When? Interesting.
            (A beat)
No Sean, nothing mate. Listen, I'll
come back to you. That was useful.

Hangs up, re-dials.

            DI JOE WILSON (CONT'D)
Boss, it may be nothing... a
quick one.
            (A beat)

Danny Laidlow was released from
HMP Magilligan a week ago. If you
recall he...
(Listening)
OK, yes, that's your man.
(Laughs)
No, there's no reports of him here,
but we should keep an eye peeled.
We had nothing on him back then,
but he was pulling strings for sure.
(Listening, jotting notes)
Will do Boss, cheers.

CUT TO:

INT. DAY. WALNEY DIVE SHOP

Amid clutter, the desk phone rings.

DAVE
Dive shop, Dave here.
(Listening)
Hi Iris, yep he's here, I'll get him.

Dave leaves the handset on the desk and goes to the door,
shouting across the yard.

DAVE (CONT'D)
Mike.
(Makes a phone signal to his
ear, then as Mike enters...)
Iris.

Mike grimaces, drops into his chair, picking up the handset.

MIKE
Hey babe, you ok?
(Listens, sits up)
Fuck! When?

                    (Listening, frowning, gestures
                    to Dave to stay put)
          What did he say?
                    (Listens, cups his hand over
                    the handset, mouths to
                    Dave)
          Daniel...

Dave drops back into his chair. The two men make eye contact
while Mike continues the call.

                    MIKE (CONT'D)
          So, how did you leave it?

                    (Listens)
          OK, look, its probably nothing Iris,
          stay cool...
                    (A beat)
          No, I didn't know. Listen love, play it
          safe, if you see him again, don't say
          much and listen a lot. All right, ring
          me if anything.
                    (Then, sits bolt upright...
                    listening)
          What! When? Fuck me Iris, why
          didn't you say before? Is BOBBY OK?
                    (Listens for several beats)
          OK, yes, OK. Ring me.

Dave waits as Mike slams down the handset. Gets up, paces
around the room. Sits down again.

                    MIKE (CONT'D)
          Laidlow, he's still here. Saw Iris
          outside Booths the other day. They
          talked.
                    (Seeing Dave's reaction)
          No, it was ok, nothing said. She said
          he was very pleasant in fact. Shook
          her up a bit though.
                    (A beat)

Police were round the house.
Wanted to speak to BOB, his mate
Stiv as well. He went round to the
Police Stn to see what they wanted.
Turned out they spoke to everyone
who held a Firearms Certificate.
That was it! Neither BOB nor his mate
knew anything, obviously. They said
it was routine that all Firearms Cert
holders were eliminated as a first
sweep.

> DAVE
> (Thoughtful)
> Hmm, makes sense, I guess.
> (A beat)
> Look mate, let's just play this
> careful and cool. We are all clear
> bystanders here. Laidlow is obviously
> up to something, but we have no
> involvement with him.
>
> Iris is good, she won't step out of
> line. Don't worry mate.

A silence descends over the workshop, both men thinking over
the events of the past few days.

CUT TO:

INT. DAY. BOB'S HOUSE

Stiv is welcomed in as usual, but today Iris is pre-occupied and
quiet. Stiv does a double take as he passes her in the doorway.

> STIV
> You OK Iris?

                    IRIS
          Yeh, I'm good Stiv, top of the
          world. You?
                    (Smiles her usual sexy smile)

Stiv, as always, blushes in spite of himself, ducks his head and
heads through to the front room

                    STIV
                    (Nodding back towards the
                    front door)

          She OK?

                    BOB
          Yes, she's ok, I think. What's
          happening? Anything?

                    STIV
          Nothing.
                    (Drops into a chair, looks at
                    the silent TV screen)

          Haven't heard a thing, other than
          it looks like the cops have closed
          down the crime scene at the
          sinkhole. The sign at the top of the
          track where it joins the 590 has
          gone. I've been tracking the NEWS,
          and nothing has been reported for
          a couple of days now, weird huh---

                    BOB
          Yeh, weird.

                    STIV
          Fuck me Bob, you are a bundle
          of laughs today, shall I go out and
          come in again?

                              BOB
                    Sorry Stiv, been a bit pre-occupied
                    lately.

                              STIV
                    (Nodding back towards the
                    front door)

                    Occupational hazard is it?

They both laugh ruefully until Bob jumps to grab the TV control,
hitting VOLUME.

                              BOB
                    NEWS Stiv, here we go...

TV NEWS:

IN THE LATEST TWIST FROM THE DOUBLE MURDER IN CUMBRIA,
LOCAL POLICE ARE CO-OPERATING WITH INTERPOL. IN
A JOINT STATEMENT ISSUED EARLIER TODAY, ASSISTANT
CHIEF COMMISSIONER FREDERICK JENSEN ADVISED THAT
INVESTIGATIONS INTO THE DOUBLE MURDER WERE CONTINUING,
NOW FOCUSSING IN LONDON AND PARIS WITH THE HELP OF
INTERPOL COLLEAGUES. IT IS THOUGHT THAT THE ASSASSINATIONS
ARE LINKED TO AN INTERNATIONAL ARMS DEAL.

EVEN THOUGH THE ARMS TRADE TREATY HAS BEEN IN PLACE FOR
NEARLY FIVE YEARS, ILLEGAL GLOBAL ARMS TRADING IS STILL
ON THE RISE, AND THIS IS A STARK REMINDER THAT THERE IS STILL
MUCH WORK TO BE DONE. THE VOLUME OF INTERNATIONAL ARMS
TRANSFERS HAS GROWN STEADILY SINCE 2003, TO REACH ITS
HIGHEST LEVEL SINCE THE END OF THE COLD WAR.

ACC JENSEN WAS CONFIDENT THAT THIS LOCAL INCIDENT WAS
AN ISOLATED CRIME LINKED BACK TO THE FOILING OF AN ILLEGAL
ARMS TRANSFER TO THE IRA IN THIS AREA 16 YEARS AGO. IT
WAS THOUGHT AT THAT TIME THAT ALL THE FIREARMS HAD BEEN
DISCOVERED, BUT IT NOW SEEMS THAT A SMALL NUMBER OF GUNS
HAD LAID IN THE SINKHOLE SINCE THEN.

POLICE DIVERS HAVE NOW SEARCHED THE SINKHOLES AGAIN, AND
NO OTHER DISCOVERIES HAVE BEEN MADE.

OTHER NEWS....

> BOB (CONT'D)
> (Shutting off the VOLUME)
> Well, that's it then. Looks like we are
> in the clear mate. How do you feel
> about that?

> STIV
> (Deep breath)
> Yes, looks like it mate. Thank fuck
> for that. Look, don't relax yet, no
> loose talk about anything. Our story
> holds, yes?

> BOB
> Totally!

CUT TO:

EXT. DAY. BOB'S HOUSE. A TERRACE IN A NARROW STREET.

Daniel Laidlow notes Iris's FOCUS as he parks in the narrow street.
The Range Rover's locks pulse as he walked to her front door, and
knocks.

> BOB
> Coming...
> (Opening the door,
> non-plussed)
> Yeh?

> DANIEL
> (Disarming smile)
> I'm looking for Iris please. Is she
> about? I'm Daniel.
> (Smile widening)

I'm guessing you'll be her son to
be sure. It's BOB, or BOBBY, isn't it? I
guess you won't remember me, but
we met a long time back when you
were a wee lad.

                    BOB
            (Unsmiling)
Don't know who you are mate.
Don't remember ever meeting you.
            (A beat)
My Mother is out at the shops I think,
she'll be back in a bit. Maybe you
want to wait?
            (Steps back to close the
            door)

                    DANIEL
            (Stepping slightly forward)
Hold on now, are not going to invite
me in Bob? Not very neighbourly to
leave me out on the doorstep is it.
            (Smiling, open hands
            gesture)

Maybe I could come inside and
wait for her, you could make me
some tea?
            (Steps forward into the
            doorway, forcing Bob to
            give way)
That's very kind of you, thank you.
Two sugars for me. You wouldn't
have any digestives, now would
you? I'm very partial to digestives.

Bob is taken aback but stands to one side as Daniel enters. He
goes along the corridor, turning left into the small kitchen.

                    DANIEL (CONT'D)
Well, Bob, this is very nice. It will be
a pleasant surprise for Iris when she
returns.

                    BOB
Tea did you say?
          (Rummaging with kettle and
          cups)
There are some biscuits somewhere
here.

Daniel wanders confidently into the front room while Bob is boiling
the kettle. Stiv is sprawled on the settee non-plussed, having
heard the exchange at the door and kitchen.

                    DANIEL
Well now, who have we here? My
apologies to you sir, I didn't mean to
barge in on you. I'm Daniel.
          (A beat)

Yourself?

                    STIV
          (Flustered)
Er, I'm Stiv, Bob's mate.

                    DANIEL
          (Disarming smile, moving
          forward with outstretched
          hand)
Well, how do you do Stiv, Bob's
mate.
          (Taking Bob's hand, then
          holding on longer than
          expected)
I see that you like to watch TV with
no sound. It's one of my favourite
things you know, putting on the
sound ruins it completely.

Bob comes in with mugs of tea and a packet of chocolate biscuits. They all sit. Daniel completely at ease. The two younger me feeling very uncomfortable.

>   DANIEL (CONT'D)
>   Well lads, this is all very nice, very
>   nice indeed.
>   (Tasting his tea)
>   Oh yes, nice and weak. Just the way
>   I like it.

The front door opens and Iris breezes in carrying plastic bags. She immediately sees Daniel down the corridor. She is shocked.

>   DANIEL (CONT'D)
>   Iris, its yourself at last. Just in time,
>   come and join the tea set.
>   (Smiling, rising to his feet)

>   BOB
>   He just came in Mother...

>   DANIEL
>   Aw, now Bob, it wasn't so. You
>   kindly invited me in to wait for you
>   Iris, offered me tea and biscuits,
>   introduced me to your friend Stiv
>   here, and we've all been watching
>   TV together, with no sound...
>   (A beat)
>   Now Iris, you are here as well. Here
>   we all are.
>   (Sitting back down again,
>   smiling up at Iris)

>   IRIS
>   Daniel...
>   (Still flustered)

Its just a bit of a shock you know, Booths, then here.

BOB
(Seeing his Mother's
discomfort, rising to his feet)
Mum, if you want this guy chucked
out, just say the word. I didn't invite
him in...

DANIEL
(Immediate mood change
to quiet threat, making eye
contact with Bob)
Hey, sit down sonny, nobody is being
kicked out here, that's not nice...
(Looking up at Iris)
Are they Iris?

IRIS
(To Bob)
It's OK Bob.
(To Daniel)
No of course not. Its nice to see you
Daniel. Please sit.

They all sit. Stiv has watched the exchange with an increasing
sense of alarm with a TINGE OF JEALOUSY. It is immediately
obvious that Daniel and Iris have some sort of history. Daniel is
charming but also incredibly dangerous, his mood changing
instantaneously when he sensed a threat from Bob.

He looked across at Bob, catching his eye.

STIV
(Placing his cup on the table)
Well, thanks for the tea. I should be
going, stuff to do you know.

Stiv comes to his feet. Daniel and Bob both stand simultaneously.

DANIEL
It was good to meet you Stiv, really
good.

(Holds out his hand)

                    STIV
Yes... bye then.
                    (Takes Daniel's hand
                    awkwardly)

Bob accompanies Stiv to the door, they exchange meaningful glances as Bob closes the door.

                    BOB
            (To Stiv)

I'll be in touch...

Bob re-enters the front room to sit down. He catches a look from Iris.

                BOB (CONT'D)
Mother, I need to go out for a bit,
won't be long.

Iris nods briefly, her face set. Daniel doesn't acknowledge Bob's presence at all. Bob leaves the house.

                                        CUT TO:

INT. DAY BOB'S HOUSE. FRONT ROOM

                    IRIS
            (Turning a furious face to
            Daniel)
What the fuck Daniel? This is my
fucking house, and that is my son.
You can't just enter our private lives
and threaten us.
            (A beat)
Nobody has seen you for years, then
you just turn up.

DANIEL
(Disarming smile)
Oh, come on now Iris, don't be
angry. I'm so happy to see you. And
you look so...

IRIS
(Angrily)
Fuck off Daniel!

DANIEL
(Palm's outwards)
But you do! Seriously, you have
not changed a bit. I have, I bet
everyone else has, but you...
(Shaking his head in
disbelief)

And Bob,
(Gesturing)
he was just defending his Ma, like
any good son should do. I don't hold
that against him, for sure, I used to
do it myself. Mo one ever thr...

IRIS
(Flatly)
What do you want Daniel?

DANIEL
Well, I was hoping that we all might
get on you know Iris, that's a start at
least.
(A beat)
Where is your husband these days
Iris, that would be Mike isn't it. I take
it that you are not together now.

IRIS
Mike and I split years ago. He lives
his own life now, we live ours.

DANIEL
(Looking crestfallen)
I'm truly sorry to hear that Iris. To be
sure I am. I liked Mike you know, and
you as well. Would you have Mike's
contact number by any chance? I'd
like to speak with him. Maybe a bit
of joint business we could do...

Iris looks from Daniel, then to the window and the backyard
beyond. Her thoughts are scrambled. She was sexually attracted
to Daniel, as before, but he is truly a frightening person. Brutal
violence seethes below his easy Irish charm, milliseconds away at
any moment.

IRIS
(Resigned)
Look, I'll give you his number Daniel.
He works at Walney Dive Shop. I
have no choice really do I...
(A beat)
But please, don't threaten my son
again, ever. If Mike ever got to know
about that, he would kill you.

Daniel notes the information, recalling the two men that he spoke
to recently when he made inquiries about his hired divers. So,
the second man was Mike Kramer, he had changed a bit, and
Kramer had recognized him that day, he was sure. He smiles to
himself; people change over 16 years.

DISSOLVE TO:

EXT. ULVERSTON STREET. DAY. NEAR BOB'S HOUSE

Daniel makes his goodbyes to Iris, His EASY IRISH CHARM finally
making her smile again as he takes his leave. He stands for a
moment on the pavement outside the house, looking up and
down the street. It is his habit and had saved him from harm
several times over the years. The street appears deserted.

He strolls casually the 100 meters or so to his Range Rover, reaching for his keys as he approaches. As he closed on his car, he becomes aware that two young men are leaning against the vehicle.

                    DANIEL
                (Easy smile)
        Now then boys, it's a beautiful day
        is it not. Are you admiring my car
        then? It's not for sale right now.

                    BOB
                (Quietly, standing away from
                the car)
        I didn't like the way you spoke to
        me back there Mister, so I'll be quite
        plain so there's no misunderstanding
        between us.
                (A beat)
        I don't like you very much, and I
        think my Mother is scared of you for
        some reason. I don't want you round
        here anymore, and I don't want you
        seeing my Mother anymore.

Daniel considers the information with a serious expression, looking from Bob to Stiv. Both young men have moved away from the car and are standing facing him.

Daniel smiles winningly, at ease with himself, turning imperceptibly towards Stiv.

                    DANIEL
                (To Bob)
        Sorry, we were just introduced, Its
        Bob isn't it, and...
                (Turning to Stiv)
        Its Stiv, yes? I guess Stiv is short for
        Stephen maybe, is it?
                (The turning back to Bob)

Bob, I want to watch something
very closely, It might help you
understand, and maybe learn
something about people and life.
(A beat)

I'm not any expert you'll understand,
but my old Dad used to always say,
a picture is worth a million pages
of written words. He was very wise,
my Dad.
(A beat)
Are you watching this Bob...?

Daniel pivots, leaning forward and dropping his left shoulder. He
hits Stiv a crushing blow to his sternum. There is a sickening sound
of something breaking deep in his chest. Stiv collapses to his
knees as if pole axed.

Daniel reaches out, grabbing Stiv's shoulder, stopping him from
falling.

DANIEL (CONT'D)
Now Bob, just in case you didn't
quite catch that...

Daniel's second blow is high and to the right of his first. Again,
a sickening sound of bone breaking. Stiv is now on the edge of
consciousness, still held upright by Daniel.

Bob was shocked and awed by the ferocity of Daniel's attack on
his friend. He stands, helpless, eyes darting between Stiv's chalk-
white face and Daniel's solicitous expression.

DANIEL (CONT'D)
Now Bob, give me a hand here
would you. Stiv isn't feeling too well
you know. We need to get him
sitting over here a bit so he's not
blocking the pavement.

Despite himself, Bob involuntarily helps Daniel manoeuvre Stiv to the side of the pavement, leaning his back against a wall. Stiv head sagged down...

>   DANIEL (CONT'D)
>   (To Bob)
>   Here now, support his head. That's it.

Bob is now holding Stiv in an upright position as he sits against the brick wall. He looks up at Daniel.

>   DANIEL (CONT'D)
>   Now hear me Bob, Stiv will need a
>   bit of rest for a day or two. But he's a
>   well set-up lad, he'll be all right.
>   (Looking very concerned)
>   He has sustained an injury to his
>   sternum, I think. There's a cartilage
>   attaching his ribs to the breastbone
>   in the middle. I suspect that is now
>   detached. If its bandaged up tight
>   for a day or two, it will be fine.
>   (faint smile)
>   It'll hurt like a bugger though,
>   particularly if he coughs. Also,
>   (A beat)
>   he has a broken collar bone on the
>   right side. it would be a good idea
>   to get a doctor to take a look at
>   that, but don't be too worried, they
>   will just strap him up for a couple of
>   weeks. People break collar bones all
>   the time.

Daniel steps back, benevolently regarding the two young men, both now sitting against the wall. He looks up, and down the street. It is quiet. Down on the pavement, Stiv is panting, he turns helpless pain-filled eyes up at Daniel, his mouth twisting in pure hatred.

DANIEL (CONT'D)
(Disarming smile to Bob)
Well Bob, I hope you found my little
demonstration useful and instructive.

We could have shouted threats at
each other for ages and made an
unpleasant scene on the pavement
outside your Mother's place, but this
was much easier and quicker don't
you think. And no messy blood or
black eyes either.
(Fumbling for keys)
Do you know, I'm just terrible for
losing my keys. Anyway, good luck
to you Bob. Mind you look after your
friend Stiv.
(Opening the car door)

I'll be seeing you both then, soon...

The Range Rover eases out its parking place and into the street,
Daniel raising an casual hand in farewell. From their sitting
position, both young men watch the car glide silently down the
street, then brake lights flaring red, it turns to the left and out of
their sight.

FADE TO BLACK

EXT. DAY. THE SINKHOLE

The Police pool car crunches along the 2 MILE TRACK connecting
the A590 to the sinkhole crime scene. A few remnants of YELLOW
AND BLACK BARRIER TAPE are attached to trees, but the crime
scene, once a hive of CSI activity, is now deserted.

DI Wilson exits the car, walking over to the muddy patch where a
few days before, TWO BODIES and a stash of ILLEGAL GUNS had
laid. The tree-shaded water is still and black, streaks of oil and

grease catching the subdued light in rainbow colours. There are footmarks everywhere, evidence of the CSI team's intensive work.

DI Wilson stands gazing into the water, then turns to gather up the last few strips of yellow/black isolation tape. On an impulse, he walks away from the sinkhole in the general direction of GREENODD. The copse continued several hundred meters, and soon another sinkhole appears. Along this copse there are seven sinkholes in total. All are now deserted and still.

At the turn of the century local miners had dug down to impossible levels to mine tin. The extent of the MINE WORKINGS was uncharted and the total lack of health and safety legislation at that time meant that seams of tin had simply been followed until they were exhausted with the minimum removal of spoil along the way. As seams petered out, the miners simply transferred their undisciplined attention elsewhere. Wilson knows that the top surfaces of the sinkholes were like icebergs, with potentially HUGE UNDERWATER CAVERNS spreading in all directions below the surface, possibly even connecting somewhere below his feet.

Police divers had made, in his opinion, SUPERFICIAL SEARCHES, but their Police's own rules prohibiting dives any deeper than 18 meters in good visibility, he knew that in reality, these sinkholes had not been searched deeper than 10 meters.

Wilson walks back to his car, takes a cursory look around the area, then carefully drives back along the track back to main road.

CUT TO:

INT. DAY WALNEY DIVE SHOP OFFICE.

Dave is working at his desk. Phone rings.

> DAVE
> (On phone)
> Dave, dive shop...

                    DI JOE WILSON
                    (On phone)
                Dave Geddings please.

                        DAVE
            Speaking.

                    DI JOE WILSON
            Hello, Mr Geddings, this is DI Joe
            Wilson here, Cumbria Police. I'm
            investigating the double murder
            locally here. I wonder if I could
            come over and talk to you. I'm free
            now if that's ok. Could be with you in
            20 mins or so.

                        DAVE
            Sure, that's ok. I'm around

                                                    CUT TO:

EXT/INT. DAY. WALNEY DIVE SHOP

DI Wilson's pool car parks in front of the Dive Shop's corrugated
sheet gates. Wilson negotiates the clutter of diving paraphernalia,
rusting equipment and vehicles, finally making his way the office
building. Dave Geddings gets to his feet from behind a desk
overloaded with paper, air valves, hand tools and other general
disorder.

                    DI JOE WILSON
            Mr Geddings, I'm DI Joe Wilson,
            Cumbria Police. Thanks for making
            the time to see me.

                        DAVE
            No problem. How can I help you? Its
            Dave by the way.
                    (Indicating a chair)

                    DI JOE WILSON
Dave, yes thanks. I'm Joe if you are
happy to be informal.

                        DAVE
Can I get you some tea, I'm having
some.
                (Rummaging with a kettle
                behind him.)

                    DI JOE WILSON
I'm OK, thanks.
                (Consulting a notepad)
I gather there's two of you here, a
Mr Michael Kramer?

                        DAVE
Mike is around somewhere; I think
he's in Barrow picking up supplies.
Be back any minute.

                    DI JOE WILSON
Right, good.
                (Consulting notes)
As I said on the phone, I'm working
with colleagues investigating the
double murder near Ulverston
couple of weeks ago. We have
now closed the CRIME SCENE at
the sinkhole, but our investigations
continue.
                (A beat)

The closing of the crime scene has
thrown up a couple on interesting
possibilities that I'd like your reaction
to Mr Geddings, sorry Dave.

Dave indicates him to continue while he stirs his tea.

DI JOE WILSON (CONT'D)
As you may know from NEWS
REPORTS, our divers have searched
the sinkhole and have not
recovered any other guns or any
other related equipment.
(A beat)

From my own perspective, and
not casting any aspersions on our
Police Divers, I'd like another opinion
on that. It seems to me that you
and your partner may be more
equipped to take a more extensive
look-see down there, than our guys.
(Shrugging)
They are a bit restricted with
equipment, but also our H+S regs
stop us from deeper than 18M.

DAVE
What do you have in mind
Detective? Joe - sorry.
(Taking a drink of tea)
You want us to go down there, see
what we can see.

DI JOE WILSON
(Nodding)
That's about the size of it Dave. I
would just feel that we had made
sure that we don't get a re-visit of
this situation in another few years,
you know some else looking for
'treasure'.
(Smiles)
Of course, you would get your usual
rates, whatever, for the work, Just Bill
me. And you know, do it in your own
time over the next couple of weeks. I

realize this has come out of the blue
for you.

                    DAVE
I see.
          (Thinking)
Can I have a discussion with my
partner and come back to you.
On the face of it, the job seems
interesting enough, but we are quite
busy with our existing workload. Can
I ring you?

               DI JOE WILSON
No problem.
          (Getting up)
Right, I'll get out of your way, thanks
for seeing me at short notice.
          (Stops briefly at the door)
Oh, by the way, your partner Mike
Kramer, he wouldn't be related to Iris
Kramer by any chance would he?

                    DAVE
Iris is Dave's Ex. They split several
years back.

               DI JOE WILSON
OK, right. Its always good to get
relationships right isn't it.
          (A beat, thinking)
And so Dave will be young Bob's
Father then?

                    DAVE
That's right. Bob still lives with Iris in
town. They all get on OK these days.
No problem with Bob is there?

               DI JOE WILSON
Well, yes, thanks for that Dave.

> (Smiles reassuringly)
> Oh no, we had young Bob in to
> check his Firearms Certificate, usual
> stuff. All was Ok. Its just me getting it
> all straight in my head.
>> (Turning back to go out the
>> door)
> Right, well thanks Dave, that was all
> very useful. You'll come back to me
> directly once you have spoken to
> your partner, right?

                    DAVE
> Will do.

                                        CUT TO:

INT. DAY. STIV'S HOUSE

Stiv is lying on a settee propped up with cushions. Next to him a table with books, and iPad, cell phone and TV control. He is channel hopping. The doorbell chimes.

                    STIV
> What...

Bob enters, grins.

                    BOB
> Hello mate, how the hell you doing?

Stiv is looking at the usual silent TV, he indicates his bandages with a grimace.

                    STIV
> How the fuck do you think I'm
> doing? I'm fucking sore is what I
> am. That bastard knew what he was
> doing didn't he...

(Painfully hauling himself
more upright on the settee)
You know Bob, what I did
to that fucker, (pause) you
know, those fuckers, who
were going to do you, I'm
going to do it to him. I'm
going to fucking kill him.
(Muttering, looking at the TV)

Kill him...

BOB
(Guilty look)
It's my fault Stiv, I had no idea how
handy he was. Bloody hell talk
about a shock.
(Shaking his head)
It was in my head to give him a
good pasting after the way he
spoke to me and my Mother, in
our fucking house. He's something
else mate, he's not like anyone I've
ever seen around here. Talk about
handle himself...
(Shaking his head)
Didn't even put him into first gear.
Scary or what... I didn't tell Mother
about it at all. I just said you had
fallen off a wall, you know, like we
agreed.
(A beat)
She might have wanted to go to
the Police you know. She would
have definitely told my Dad, then
fuck knows where this might have
ended up.
(A beat)
It could have ended up with my
Dad getting done as well. You know

what he's like if there's a fight... has
to get involved...

                    STIV
               (Bitterly)
I don't want anyone else fighting my
battles Bob. I'll do my own thanks.
This will NEVER happen to me
again; I totally guarantee it. Fucking
guarantee, it!
               (A beat)
That fucker is going to die!

Then catching Bob's look.

               STIV (CONT'D)
I mean it Bob, I've done two
bastards, I might end up going
down for them in the end. So, I might
as well go down for him as well. No
fucking problem.

                    BOB
Oh Stiv, come on mate, I feel
seriously awful about all this, first I'm
the reason you commit two murders,
then you get the shit kicked out of
you, again, all of it because of me.
               (Looking emotional)
And I'm supposed to be your mate.
Bloody hell.

                    STIV
               (Looking at his friend, also
               getting emotional)
Sorry mate don't mean to kick off.
It's just I sit here all fucking day and
go over stuff in my head. Over and
over. He shouldn't have been able
to take me like that, I used to fancy

myself as a bit of a mover... Not any fucking, more do I?
            (Straining painfully into a new
            position)
Anyway, you are out and about. What's happening out there? Anything?

                    BOB
I can hardly dare to say it Stiv...
            (Looking at the TV)

                    STIV
What---

                    BOB
            (Shaking his head, looking
            away)
    I---

                    STIV
What the fuck Bob, I'm bloody dying here, tell me for Gawd's sake.
                    BOB
It's my Mother Stiv. She's only seeing that Daniel.

Stiv stares at his fiend, incredulous.

                    STIV
What the fucking hell do you mean Bob? Seeing him?
            (A beat)
You mean 'SEEING HIM' Like they are a couple. Er, like, she's shagging him?

                    BOB
Yep, she is seeing him, and shagging him. He came round the other night, like nothing had happened. Spoke

to me like I was a old mate, like I'd
known him for ever. Brought her a
great big FUCK-OFF bunch of roses
and wine, chocolates, the works.
            (A beat)
She was like, WOW! Being courted
again, all that stuff. Later on, he took
her out to the Bay Horse Pub down
by the Bay. Big expensive meal as
the sun went down. All that romantic
stuff.
            (A beat)
Earlier today, I came back home,
and he was just coming down
the stairs with a towel wrapped
around him. Went into the kitchen
and made some tea, took it back
upstairs, asked me if I wanted some.
I could hear them laughing up
there, the pair of them.

Bob's monologue tails off. The two young men fall into a
depressed silence, both looking at the silent TV.

FADE TO BLACK

EXT. DAY ULVERSTON STREET

Stiv is parked in his Mother's car, 100M along from Bob and Iris's
house. Looking through his car mirror and along the street he can
see Daniel's Range Rover and he also has a clear view of Iris's
front door. Stiv is still in a lot of discomfort, but gradually improving.
The street is deserted as usual during the daytime. After 5pm
the street fills up, and by 7pm all the parking places are taken, a
testament to the poor quality and irregularity of public transport.

Stiv has sat there for more than 2hrs. No real reason that he could
clearly articulate, other than the burning deep seated anger that
he felt towards Daniel. Up to the point of his violent encounter
with the Irishman, he was consumed with guilt and fear relating to

killing the two divers at the sinkhole. He had no second thoughts about why he did it, he was certain that he had saved Bob's life by his actions that day.

Since being beaten by Daniel however, his feelings had changed radically. He now continually replayed the moments of shooting the two divers with an exultation that was almost sexual in its intensity. He pictured Daniel sinking to a sitting position with alarm, fear and shock playing across his features, his fluttering hands searching for the source of the sudden massive pain in his chest. He, Stiv, watching this play out in high definition - slow motion, jacking a new shell into the chamber of his firearm, stepping forward into the light so that his victim could see his killer clearly as he gasped his last few wracking breaths.

Stiv's reverie ceases instantly as Daniel steps out of the front door of Iris's house and into the late afternoon sunlight. Daniel pauses, looking carefully up and down the street, his eyes tracking along the parked vehicles. He looks towards where Stiv was parked. Daniel appears to focus, standing very still. Stiv is transfixed, watching Daniel with a feeling of rising alarm, he then freezes as Daniel starts walking his parked car, rather than towards his own Range Rover as Stiv would have expected.

Iris's front door opens, and she steps out into the sunlight. She is wearing a housecoat hugged closely around her shapely figure. In the near distance Stiv watches her exchange some smiling words with Daniel. Daniel turns to face her, and some sort of light-hearted conversation takes place. Stiv starts his car and pulls away immediately, watching the in mirror as Daniel's silhouette recedes in the distance, aware that he had turned and was tracking Stiv's car to the end of the street.

CUT TO:

EXT. STIV'S HOUSE. DAY

Stiv pulls in and parks in front of his house several minutes later. He sits there in the car a few moments, heart thumping. Then he starts the car again and parks it at the back of the house by the allotments. He enters the back of the house, immediately walking through the house to peer up and down the street from the front window.

CUT TO:

INT LATE AFTERNOON. WALNEY DIVE SHOP

Dave and Mike are in the office facing each other across the cluttered desk. Both have tea. Mike is dismantling a brass air valve assembly.

DAVE
So, what do you think?

MIKE
(Concentrating on his task)
We can't really refuse it can we. Its
the Police. What reason could we
give? To be honest, I don't want to
touch it. I'd rather stay clear.

DAVE
I was thinking about our
conversation a few days ago. You
reckon there is still some stuff down
there. This could be an opportunity
for us mate, we could maybe...

MIKE
No Dave...

DAVE
Wait a minute Mike, think about it.
(gathering his thoughts)
What about we take a look, just like
he asked us to. That's it, just do as
he asked, bill him, take his money.
What's wrong with that?

(Leaning back, placing his feet on
the waste bin, looking across at
Mike)

Mike stops tinkering with the valve assembly, hands flat to the
desktop, raising his eyes to his old friend and partner.

                    MIKE
          Mate, I know for fucking certain
          there are more boxes down there.
          I know it! There are spread across
          several sinkholes, more than 20M
          down. Not easy you know, hauling
          them motherfuckers up. Then
          getting them away.
               (A beat)
          Two men just died doing it. Who shot
          them? We don't know Dave.
               (A beat)
          How do we know that whoever did
          that, seriously doesn't want those
          boxes to see the light of day? Or
          even...
               (Thinking)
          .. maybe they are waiting for us
          idiots to complete the job, for us to
          do the donkey work for them, either
          way, we could be dead meat mate.

Dave spins his old office chair around to the window facing
across his yard. The sky is set in battleship tones from the sou'
westerly that cut in earlier. In the distance he can see rows of
terraces decked in grey stone, chimneys marching diagonally
into a downward curve to the shipyard. After a long moment, he
tunes back to his friend.

                    DAVE
          Hmm, maybe you are over-thinking
          this Mike.
               (A beat)

Look, we take a look, get paid for it
anyway. Whatever we find, we keep
it to ourselves. Simply tell DI Wilson
that we saw nowt
            (A beat)
Then, only then, we talk about what
we do next. Which may be nothing -
How's that?

Mike goes back to tinkering with his valve assembly. Dave drinks
his tea, brooding, watching his partner thoughtfully.

                                                    FADE TO BLACK

INT. LATE AFTERNOON. IRIS'S BEDROOM

Iris and Daniel are in bed. They have made love and are now
relaxing with mugs of tea. Iris is propped up with all the pillows.
Daniel is sitting on the bed, gazing thoughtfully out of the window
towards the allotments. Daniel's cell phone trills.

                        DANIEL
            Danny...
                        (Listening, glancing back at
                        Iris)
            Not now!
                        (Sharply)
            Stop fucking hassling me. It will all be
            sorted, but it will take a bit of time. I
            told you. Softly catches monkey you
            know.
                        (Listening, then quietly)
            I don't respond well to being
            pushed, nor to being spoken to with
            disrespect. You would do well to
            stand down from me and treat me
            gently.
                        (Softly)
            Think of me as a fragile ornament,
            precious and expensive. Break

me and sharp bits of me may be
difficult for you to deal with...

Behind him, Iris shifts in the pillows, her fingers trailing down
Daniels's spine. He frightened and fascinated her in equal
measure. His uncompromising strength and strange twisted
integrity and sense of honour made her feel protected, but at the
same time, she knew that Daniel made choices where he walked
a dangerous path on the edge of the law, with the dark abyss of
organized crime close by and ever present.

                    DANIEL (CONT'D)
          You are aware that I have a
          situation here. It was not one of my
          making. I sit here not knowing who
          has played a hand in this situation.
                    (A beat)
          So rather than spending your
          precious time hassling me, get off
          your fucking ass and find the people
          who took down my boys.

Daniel turns, catching Iris hand in his, smiling reassuringly at
her, pushing her playfully back into the pillows, holding her eye
contact as he spoke.

          Do not ring me again unless
          you bring me new and/or useful
          information. Other than that, your
          input is not required or welcome
          here. Now, tell me that you
          understand that.
                    (Waiting)
          OK.
                    (Hangs up)

Daniel drops his cell phone and rolls on top of Iris, tickling her. She
squeals in pleasure.

                                        CUT TO:

EXT. DAY. ALLOTMENTS

Deep in the afternoon shade of the allotments, Stiv hears Iris's muted squeals of pleasure from 40M away. He looks up at her window, using his high-power telescopic sight as a monocular. It is impossible to see inside, and he settles back into his hiding place, watching.

FADE TO:

EXT. WALNEY ISLAND DIVE CENTER. DAY.

WIDE:

Dave and Mike are loading equipment into a 4*4 and a battered Transit. The equipment is extensive and includes spare dive bottles, winch, cabling floodlights and other tools.

CUT TO:

EXT. AERIAL SHOT. THE COPSES AND COASTAL AREA ON THE SINKHOLES

The Land Rover and Battered Transit turn off the A590 onto the rutted track leading to the Sinkhole copses. The aerial shot widens to show more of the alluvial plain and the beach beyond, white lines of surf curving inwards.

CUT TO:

EXT. THE SINKHOLE. DAY.

Wide, then Medium.

The Land Rover and Transit are parked, tailgates to the side of the sinkhole. Dave and Mike are setting up the dive. DIVING EQUIPMENT is all around, cables and HALOGEN FLOODLIGHTS set up, SHORT WAVE RADIOS and WINCH being tested. Mike is already dressed in full NEOPRENE WET-SUIT, spare tanks in a cluster near the edge of the water.

> MIKE
> (Busy with equipment)
> This is weird mate, don't like it much.
> Did you ring the Cops?

> DAVE
> No, I'll ring them later when we report back. We don't want them looking over our shoulder, do we? Or indeed, anyone else

> MIKE
> Quite...
> > (Looking ruefully at the black water)
> They say there could be more than seven miles of ABANDONED SHAFTS down here. Old train tracks, ore carts, old shovels and steam-powered jack hammers, as well as GUNS.
> > (Wolfish grin at his partner)
> Are we fucking mad or what? I'm getting too fucking old for this 'Journey to the Centre of the Earth' stuff.

Mike switches on his GO-PRO CAM and THROAT MIKE, floods his mask and drops into the water. Its a shaft with vertical sides, so he is immediately treading water. He shakes out and frees up cabling to his PORTABLE FLOODLIGHT.

> MIKE (CONT'D)
> (Treading water)
> Can you switch me on mate?

Dave fiddles with equipment and Mike's floodlight comes on, dazzling, even in daylight. Mike immediately directs it downwards.

Both divers are acutely aware that this is ADVANCED DIVING with zero natural light. Even at 28 feet, with halogen, the light only illuminates approx. 4 feet ahead. Ascents and descents are tricky and require clear focus on gauges to AVOID DISORIENTATION.

                    DAVE
              (Voice raised across the
              water)
        Mike, I know you know this, but just
        saying anyway...

        Take it easy mate. We are just
        looking right now. I'm told there are
        some very odd lava-like spires down
        there, no one knows quite what
        they are. They look a bit like STONE
        CHIMNEYS, sometimes 20 foot long.
        Don't touch them motherfuckers.
        They are like RAZORS.
              (A beat)
        I really do not want to do a rescue
        today please Michael.

Mike raises his thumb and disappeared into the black water leaving a swirl of bubbles. Dave watched the cable slip easily downwards over the edge of the sinkhole. He spun full circle on his heels, looking around the copse in the muted afternoon light filtering through the trees, there was no sign of anyone.

                                              CUT TO:

INT. THE SINKHOLE SHAFT. UNDERWATER. MIKE DIVING.

Mike, feeling that familiar sense of being airborne, slowly drops down the vertical shaft. At first, the water is clear, the halogen lighting up the VERTICAL RAGGED SHAFT wall 20 feet away from him. As he drops, watching his gauge, the shaft of light shortens progressively. He can see old tools here are there, embedded into the wall. A section of metal ladder. Silver shreds of old dynamite packaging clinging here and there, swaying like living creatures.

His TEMP GAUGE indicates 55 degrees and falling. The cold spreading through the neoprene, slowing down his thinking, his movements.

> MIKE
> (To Dave, through the throat
> mike)
> Thought I would remember, I don't.
> (A beat)
> Nothing yet.

CUT TO:

EXT. THE SINKHOLE. DAY.

Dave jumps as Mike's voice crackles in his earpiece. By now his peripheral vision had closed down to a 10 feet circle of bubbling black water.

> DAVE
> Loud and clear Mike. Take it slow
> and easy.

CUT TO:

EXT. WALNEY ISLAND DIVE CENTER. LATE AFTERNOON.

Daniel's Range Rover crunches the gravel outside the Walney Dive Shop, his window sliding silently down. The CORRUGATED IRON GATES are clearly locked with chain and padlock. High above the fence a CCTV CAM looked unblinkingly at him, a tiny red pilot showing in the fading afternoon light. Clearly there is no-one home.

He sits there for several minutes, deep in thought, his eyes raking the yard, the workshop and office. Then, shifting in his seat, looking around at other neighbouring industrial units, noting other CCTV cams. Eventually he starts the big car, window sliding upwards, peripheral sounds muting, bumping over the kerbside, swinging wide across the deserted dock service road.

The black Range Rover accelerates away, receding into the monochrome distance, sudden bright red brake lights pulsing briefly.

CUT TO:

EXT. THE SINKHOLE. DAY.

An eternity passes. The black water circle that filled Dave's world, suddenly heaves as if alien life was bursting forth. Mike is suddenly there, glistening, water cascading from his mask in explosions of light.

DAVE
(Angry)
Fuck you Mike, no word from you
for the last nine minutes. I wanted a
running commentary you twat!

MIKE
(Pushing up his facemask)
I'm good, no problem. Nothing to
report.
(Grin flashing)

DAVE
Is that a joke? If it is then I don't
appreciate your crap sense of
humour.
(Pulling in cables)
What are you doing? Coming in?

MIKE
Yep, haul me in David, we have
other sinkholes to do before we go
home tonight.

Dave throws a rope past Mike, the coil splashing behind him. Mike's fist closes on the rope and Dave slowly hauls him to the edge of the sinkhole, first taking his tanks and floodlight, then finally reaching down to clasp his hand, breaking him free of the water's suction, springing upwards onto the edge of the sinkhole.

CUT TO:

EXT. STREET NEAR IRIS'S HOUSE. DAY

Daniel's car parks near Iris's terrace. Daniel exits, standing for a moment looking both ways, lights pulse and the electronic sound of the car burglar alarm locking reaches faintly to where Stiv watches through his rear-view mirror. His car now a safe 200 meters away, facing away. Lessons learned.

CUT TO:

INT. WALNEY ISLAND DIVE CENTER. DAY. THE OFFICE

Dave sprawls in his usual chair. Opposite him, Mike drinks tea, fiddling with a GO-PRO camera and USB cable.

> DAVE
> (On phone)
> Hello, yes, can I speak to DI Wilson
> please, thanks.
> (A beat)
> DI Wilson, Dave Geddings.
> (A beat)
> I'm good. We went down.
> (A beat)
> Nothing I'm afraid, not a dickey bird.
> We did all the other holes too. Sorry.
> (Listening)
> I know, well your guys didn't find
> anything either did they. I think
> you've had what there is old mate.
> We went down 22 meters. No sign of
> any bottom, God knows how deep
> that thing is. If anything is deeper
> than that, then it might as well be
> on the moon. We don't have the

resources to recover it, even if we
had found it.
(Listening)
Well, the weight of a SUBMERGED
CRATE is a lot more than if it was in
open air. I won't bore the shit out of
you with Archimedes principles, but
its fucking heavy. Too heavy for our
equipment at that depth.
(A beat)
We didn't find shit anyway.

Mike and Dave lock eyes across the cluttered desk.

DAVE (CONT'D)
OK, well I guess that's it. Do you
want something in writing to justify
my invoice?
(A beat)
OK then. Cheers.

Dave hangs up. Mike is checking their security cams before
connecting the GO-PRO Cam to his LAPTOP. He suddenly reacts.

MIKE
(Surprised)
Look at this!
DAVE
What...

Dave gets up, walks around the desk to bend towards Mike's
laptop, scrutinizing the screen. Mike leans back with a resigned
expression.

DAVE (CONT'D)
(Looking at the laptop
screen)
Well, fuck me...
MIKE
It was a matter of time I guess.

                    DAVE
            (Leaning back, exhaling)
        What time was he here?
                    MIKE
            (Checking at the bottom the
            screen)
        Let's see, yes, at 1435pm, yesterday.
        We were at the sinkhole.

Dave returns to his side of the desk, throwing himself down in his
seat. Speaking to no-one in particular.

                    DAVE
        So, Mr fucking Laidlow, what the hell
        do you want?
                                        FADE TO BLACK

**INT. INTERPOL HQ. 200 CHARLES DE GAULLE 69006. LYON. FRANCE.
INSPECTOR JEAN LAFITTE'S OFFICE.**

Aerial and wide shots

Lafitte's office is located in a CLASSICAL BUILDING overlooking
the RIVER SEINE, 200 meters from Notre Dame to the East, to the
West he can see the entrance to the Pompidou Centre on Sainte
Chappelle.

Today Laffite takes no pleasure from the view. He is not amused,
as usual, by the 30-minute queues to view the exhibits, the street
music and show biz atmosphere in the huge milling courtyard
below his window.

Inspector Jean Lafitte walks a circle around his FRENCH OAK DESK
before dropping into his chair. He is baffled. A RED NOTICE that
simultaneously alerts police Worldwide to locate and provisionally
arrest a fugitive pending extradition, surrender or similar legal action
has come up totally blank for the two murders in Cumbria, UK.

One by one, his leads from colleagues around the carefully nurtured
NETWORK OF CRIMINALS AND INTERNATIONAL POLICE FORCES

have dried up. The dozen 'possibles' of staring heads displayed on his office wall, have all checked out with alibis, or unavailable, or in prison, or dead. All have red felt X's drawn from corner to corner.

His desk is clear apart from a Jacob Jensen handset, he speaks to it.

> INSPECTOR JEAN LAFITTE - INTERPOL
> Call DI Wilson, Cumbria Police.
> > (A beat, then connecting)
> Hello, DI Wilson, Joe, this is Jean
> Lafitte, Interpol.
> > (Listening)
> Good afternoon my friend, I hope
> you are well. I call to give you news,
> or indeed, the lack of it, of my work
> towards the two assassinations that
> we are both engaged in.
> > (A beat)
> I am very sorry to report that I have no
> leads on the assassin, either singular
> or plural. My TEAM started here with
> 12 possibles. All of which have now
> checked out as 'c'est pas possible'.
> > (A beat)
> No good Joe, I am afraid.
> > (Listening)
> Yes, I am surprised and disappointed
> and not a little puzzled. These were
> EXECUTIONS, both single shots
> with no 'Coup de Grace' This is a
> very singular and unique crime
> signature that pertains to very few
> international assassins. My list is
> exhaustive, and right now I have
> nothing in terms of any new leads.
> > (A beat)
> I am proposing, from Interpol's
> perspective, to provisionally list the
> crimes as 'Unsolved - on-going - No
> suspect Identified'. I am so very sorry
> my friend, I realize how unsatisfactory

this must be for you. Maybe things
will change, I do not know.
(Listening)
Conclusions? Well, I think there are
maybe two.
(A beat)
(1) this is a NEW ASSASSIN with
zero record. This person has no
international footprint to date, but
it is likely that this person will strike
again. He, or she, will very valuable
to some people, so we shall surely
meet with this person's work again.
(A beat)
My second conclusion is more
difficult. That these murders were
not committed by a professional at
all. Hence my eliminated list of PRO's
coming up ZERO.
(A beat)
Maybe we are over-thinking this Joe,
maybe the killings were personal
to either the Bulgarians themselves,
or to the person who hired the
Bulgarians to recover the guns from
the, how do you say... the Sinkhole.
(Slowly, developing his
theme)
The guns were not taken, and it seems
the shooter had enough time to do
that, so maybe the guns were of no
interest to him. This means of course,
that the killings themselves were the
primary goal for the assassin, and the
crime was timed to possibly 'send a
powerful message' to someone.
(Listening, several beats)
Well, yes, OK, we will hope.
Thank you for your kind words my
friend. Good luck and stay in touch.
Keep the faith, Goodbye.

Lafitte requests Edith Piaf's 'La Vie en Rose' from his handset. Leaning back in his swivel chair, pivoting back to gaze at the place where the spire of the Notre Dame had once reached impossibly into the evening sky.

FADE TO BLACK

INT. WALNEY ISLAND DIVE CENTER. DAY. THE OFFICE

Mike closes his laptop with snap raising a triumphant grin to Dave opposite.

> MIKE
> So, what are you thinking?

> DAVE
> I'm thinking that you made a right
> twat out of me. You sat there while
> I rang the Cops and told them we
> had found nothing.
> (Indicating the laptop)
> Then this... What do I say to them
> now...? that I made a mistake? What
> would they make of that?

Both men exchange glances as a vehicle pulled up outside their gate. Dave spins his chair, looks, then turns back to Mike.

> DAVE (CONT'D)
> Daniel Laidlow...

CUT TO:

EXT. WALNEY ISLAND DIVE CENTER. DAY.

Daniel takes his time parking and making noise as he clatters the through the iron gates. He has no intentions of creating a surprise entrance, which could then have an unpredictable element. He knocks on the wall before entering the open door of the office.

CUT TO:

INT. WALNEY ISLAND DIVE CENTER. OFFICE. DAY

Daniel enters the office. Both men are seated on each side of the heavily cluttered desk. Both look at him.

>   DANIEL
> Good afternoon gentlemen, I'm
> so pleased to catch you both in
> residence.

>   DAVE
> Mr Laidlow, this is a surprise.

>   DANIEL
> Oh, I'm sure you played back your
> CCTV the other day. This is my
> second attempt to see you both.
>   (Addressing Mike)
> Mike, do you remember me? We
> worked together some years back.

>   MIKE
>   (Flatly)
> Not the way I would describe it. I
> wasn't paid. But yes, I do remember.

>   DANIEL
>   (Acknowledging with a nod)
> Yes, I agree, it was not a satisfactory
> outcome for any of us Mike. But to
> be honest, there was no intention to
> defraud you.
>   (Disarming smile)
> Do you mind if I sit?

No-one replies. Daniel dumps equipment from a chair and sits to the side of the desk, seemingly at ease. He looks pointedly at their mugs of tea, but neither man offers hospitality.

                    DAVE
          The last time you were here, you
          asked about the TWO BULGARIANS.
          I take it they were working for you.
          Have you spoken to the Police yet?
          I imagine they would be pleased to
          meet you.

Daniel ignores Dave's comment. He addresses Mike directly.

                    DANIEL
          I'll be blunt with you, my guns are
          down that hole, I can't get them
          out, you can.
                 (A beat)
          You probably even remember
          where they are, because you put
          them there 16 years ago.
                 (A beat)
          Bring them up, load them into a
          van - £100k.

Daniel sits back, fixing Mike with a hooded stare. At no point does he address Dave.

                    DAVE
          I think...

Daniel holds up a hand in Dave's direction, silencing him.

                    DANIEL
               (Looking at Mike, but
               addressing Dave)
          I'm talking to him. His decision.
                 (A beat)

You don't know where the stuff is, he
does. I know his capability; I don't
know yours.
(Then turning to face Dave)
Please, I am not disrespecting you
Mr Geddings. Mike and I have
unfinished business from 16 years
ago. An unfulfilled contract you
might say, on both sides.

Daniel stands abruptly.

DANIEL (CONT'D)

Four crates, out of the hole, in a van.
£100k cash in your hand. That's it.

He bends, scribbling something on a slip of paper, slides it
forward. Nods briefly to both men and leaves the office. Moments
later the sound of a car pulling away. The office is silent, both men
looking at the SLIP OF PAPER showing white on the dusty desk.

Eventually Dave reaches over, pulls the slip of paper towards him,
he looks at it, then slides it across to Mike. The paper has a cell
phone number, and beneath it was written:

'I'm with Iris'

FADE OUT

INT. NIGHT. WALNEY DIVE SHOP. OFFICE

Later.

Dave and Mike are still there late into the night. It is several hours
since Daniel's ultimatum.

MIKE
Dave, I need this you know.

DAVE

I know you do. But it isn't a simple
dive is it? Two men died doing
what he has asked us - you, to do.
The Police are breathing down our
necks.
(A beat)
Someone is out there Mike, they
could be watching us even as we
speak. Two shots, two dead men,
probably in a few seconds. They
didn't even take the guns, they just
killed those two Bulgarian divers, just
like that.

MIKE
(Agonized)

£100k, one hundred thousand
pounds Dave, the job could take
three hours. After we load them into
the van it's up to him then.

DAVE
(Exasperated)
Mike, I told the Police there was
nothing there, you know that. So,
if we are caught, we go down, for
what, ten years maybe. Ten fucking
years.

MIKE
(Flatly)
I'm going to do it.
(A beat)
You can step back Dave. I'll walk
away from our partnership; I'll say
that we fell out or something. I'll
take any heat from the Cops about
misleading them if we are caught.

I'll say I found the stuff but didn't let
on. That you had no idea.

In a sudden violent movement, Dave throws his mug against the
wall, it shatters. He spins his chair to face the yard. The lights of the
terraces blurring in the light rain. Somewhere in the distance a
ship's horn hooted, a long-drawn-out wail, eerie and forlorn.

FADE TO BLACK

EXT. NIGHT. BOB'S HOUSE. A TERRACE IN A NARROW STREET.

Bob closes the front door and stands for a moment on the step
listening to Iris's tinkling laughter. He hears Daniel say something,
then Iris laughs again, louder this time.

He walks around to Stiv's house. It is lit up, the flickering of a TV
screen somewhere in the house brightness. He knocks, enters.
Stiv is sprawled in his usual place. He doesn't smile, just gestures
vaguely as Bob entered.

BOB
Hey mate... you OK?

Stiv grunts something unintelligible, fiddling with the TV control.

BOB (CONT'D)
You haven't been round, thought I'd
say hello.

STIV
Is he still there with Iris?

BOB
Yep, still there.

STIV
What does she see in that fucker?
He's...

110

                    BOB
            (Standing abruptly angry)
Bollock's mate! I just got here, now
I'm fucking going. I came out of the
house for some fucking peace from
them two, not to sit here and talk to
you about them.
                    (Turning towards the
                    corridor)
I'll see you...

                    STIV
            (Making eye contact for the
            first time)

Sorry mate, come on, sit down. Do
you want tea? Don't take any notice
of me.

Bob hesitates, then drops back into his seat. They both look at the
silent TV for a few minutes.

                    BOB
            (Slowly, still looking at the TV)
You know you said you had the idea
that you wanted to kill Daniel...

Stiv, looked from the TV to Bob, his attention caught by something
in his voice.

                    STIV

            Go on...

                    BOB
            (Thinking it through)
You might think really weird, but I
want to kill the fucker as well Stiv. I
want my life back how it was. My
Mother fucks him and feeds him,
laughs with him, but she's scared
shit-less of him you know.

(A beat)
I catch her eye sometimes, she looks
at me, then away. It was OK before
him you know. We got on OK, her
and me.

Stiv switches off the TV with the handset. The room was silent.

> STIV
> (Shifting in his chair, eye
> contact)
> You are serious, aren't you? This isn't
> a joke?

> BOB
> That day when you shot those two
> divers, it still plays clear in my head,
> they were alive one minute, then
> they were dead. They didn't even
> speak. I have thought about it ever
> since. It's on my mind the whole
> time. At first it did my head in, but
> now, I'm OK with it you know.
> (A beat)
> It's like I've come to terms with it.

Both men were silent for several minutes.

> STIV
> Just supposing then, how would you
> do it?

> BOB
> (Triumphantly)
> I know exactly...

> STIV
> (Incredulous)
> You know...? Fuck off you twat! What
> do mean - 'know'...
> (A beat)
> Really?

BOB

Yep, I know. It would work as well.
(Sitting up)
We, well, you, already killed two
people. Got away with that didn't
we. It was bloody weeks ago now.
(A beat)
It's our secret mate, we will always
have that, you and me. Till we die.
(A beat)
I want to do it this time, not you. I
want to know what it feels like. And
then we are both equal, you and
me. I want to kill that fucker so bad.
Never had a feeling like that before.

STIV

(Warming to his friend)
I know. Me neither. Its all I think
about as well. I wake up thinking
about it in the night. It was like slow-
motion you know; I saw dust fly off
his jacket when the slug hit him.
(A beat)
I've been watching him you know -
Daniel. He doesn't know, well, at
least I don't think he does. Been
trying to work out how to do it for
days now.

BOB

Don't try to work anything out Stiv, I
told you, I know.
(Leaning forward, eyes
shining)
The Sinkhole.

Stiv watches his lifelong friend turn into someone he hardly
recognized as they sit there in his front room. The moment is
surreal, and he feels as if he was floating above them both,
looking down.

                    BOB (CONT'D)
We kill him, weight him, and drop
him into the sinkhole. No-one knows
how deep them motherfuckers are
Stiv. Hundreds of feet, deeper than
any divers can go. Vertical sides.
We do him exactly like you did them
two Bulgarians. Shoot the bastard
from the rock's opposite.
          (A beat, leaning back)
He's got something to do with those
Bulgarians you know, My Mother
said so. I reckon those were his guns,
and there's more stuff down there.
He will go back there for them, haul
them up, when he does, we will
be waiting, we shoot that fucker,
tie him to the crate, and drop him
in. Nobody is ever going to search
those sinkholes ever again.

Stiv stares at his friend, his face clearing, a slow smile emerging for
the first time in weeks. Both young men lean back in their seats,
putting feet up onto the coffee table.

Stiv indicates a can of beer on the table, Bob smiles. The TV is
switched back on, silent.

                                          FADE TO BLACK

EXT. STREET OUTSIDE BOB'S HOUSE. NIGHT

Bob takes his time walking home. He is in no rush to be back in
the company of Iris and Daniel. As he approaches the house, the
front door opens violently and Daniel is silhouetted, a black figure
against the bright lights of the corridor. Bob stops, rooted.

He hears Iris's raised voice from inside, then Daniel...

114

DANIEL
(Angrily)
Well fuck you too Iris. I do not need
this...

Daniel leaves the door open and marches off to where his car
is parked. Bob watches as the car security pulses, headlights
flaring, red brake lights briefly on, and the big car surges away,
soon lost from view. The street is still again. Bob stares at the
bright rectangle of light framed by the front door of his house. Iris
doesn't appear.

After a long moment, Bob steps towards his front door. The street
remains quiet.

CUT TO:

INT. IRIS'S HOUSE. NIGHT.

Bob enters, closing the front door quietly, standing in the corridor.

BOB
Mother... are you ok?

IRIS
In here.

Bob goes into the front room. The coffee table is on its side, and
something is broken into glistening shards by the TV. Iris is sat on
the floor against the far wall. She is hugging her knees, her skirt
around her hips, shapely thighs chalk white against the dark
carpet. She is crying, a smear of blood on her cheek.

BOB
(Kneeling in front of her)
Mum...

Iris jumps visibly as he touches her arm. She looks at him, eyes
wide, tear streaks and mascara smudged where she had wiped it
away.

                    BOB (CONT'D)
                    (Emotional)
          Mum, what the hell happened? Are
          you hurt? What has that bastard
          done to you?

                    IRIS
                    (Looking fearfully towards
                    the door)
          Has he gone Bobby? Has his car
          gone? Go lock the door please Bob.

Bob goes to the front door, opening it and looking both ways. The
street is quiet. He locks the door, returning to Iris with a teacloth,
she is still on the floor. He gives her the cloth, she dabs has face
with it, looking away from him.

                    IRIS (CONT'D)
          We had a row. I guess it got out
          of hand. I slapped him and he
          reacted. I shouldn't have done it.
                    (Looking at Bob)
          It was my fault Bob, really. I hit him
          really hard.
                    (Smiling tearfully)
          You know what I'm like love,
          don't you?

Iris reaches a hand to touch Bob's face.

                    BOB
                    (Evenly, looking at Iris, tears
                    in his eyes, trembling)

          I'm going to kill that fucker Mother. I
          mean it, he is going to fucking die.

Iris strokes her son's face, smiling gently at him. Bob looks at his
Mother, he thought she was the most heartrendingly beautiful
and vulnerable creature he had ever seen.

IRIS
(Lovingly)
Bobby, my darling. I love you so
much. You have been my constant
you know. My rock. It's been hard for
you, I know that.
(Dabbing her eyes)
You lost your Dad years back, I know
he's still around, but you stayed with
me, and I love you for it.
(A beat)
You've been the man of the house,
and sometimes I've felt like the child.
(A beat)
God, what a mess. I'm sorry Bob.

Iris leans forward and hugs her son, pulling him towards her,
holding him tight. They stay like that a long time.

CUT TO:

**AERIAL SHOT OF DARK STREET, ZOOMING BACK, WIDENING TO
SHOW ULVERSTON TOWN AREA.**

FADE TO BLACK

EXT. DAY. FELLSIDE LOOKING DOWN ON THE A590.

Wide Shots, then Medium and Close Ups.

DI Wilson sits in his unmarked pool car with a sandwich and
binoculars. Below him the relentless traffic surge along the A590.
Two miles ahead he can see the dark green smudges of copses
shielding the sinkholes from view. Beyond, is the curve of the Bay,
white lines of surf breaking every few seconds. Somewhere further
out, lost in the soft white mist where sky and land merged, lay the
busy towns of Lancaster and Morecambe.

Wilson loved this spot. Even before the Sinkholes murder, he would
bring a sandwich and gaze into the distance, losing himself in the

epic grandeur of the landscape. Now however, it had changed. The murders had happened, and it was all different. His eye was drawn to the wooded copses where once tin miners had scratched and clawed their way into the depths of the earth to make a living for their families.

Out there somewhere was a shooter. He, or she, had come to this quiet town on the edge of the National Park and sullied the timeless beauty of this place with an extreme act of violence. The men that were killed were also engaged in violence, even though, on this occasion, they had become the victims. A small part of DI Wilson's sense of justice felt that a status quo of some sort had been achieved. Had the rifles been sent onward to their destination, many more people might have died. Perversely, the shooter had probably saved lives, and was now being hunted.

Wilson reflects on his conversation with Lafitte, his French colleague. 'Unsolved and On-Going'. He pictures the file being slotted into a grey metal box, and closed, maybe never to be opened again in his lifetime. The quietly spoken men in suits transferring their febrile attention to the next thing, and then the next after that. The SHOOTER doing normal things, paying bills, maybe taking kids to school, filling a car with fuel, watching the news. Wilson shakes his head, the reverie blurring his vision, the landscape swirling in a liquid mix of muted colour and texture.

Wilson focuses his binoculars on the line of copses far below. Tracking along, imagining the black still water beneath the tree cover, below that, a rippling surface of dark glass, caverns of looming vertical walls dropping away, deep into the earth, cold, silent, motionless, once a world of noise and activity, now held in suspension like the yolk of an egg in albumin.

Wilson leans back, closing his eyes momentarily, allowing reality to flood in. He stows his binoculars, checks his cell phone for messages, starts his car and edged onto the single lane road that eventually joined the A590 at Newlands, then back to Ulverston.

CUT TO:

EXT. AERIAL SHOT OF COASTAL AREA, ZOOMING UP. WIDENING TO SHOW ULVERSTON TOWN

CUT TO:

INT. DAY. WALNEY ISLAND DIVE CENTER. OFFICE.

Mike is alone in the office. The phone rings.

> MIKE
> Dive shop, Mike.
> (Listening)
> Bobby, you ok?
> (Listening, then sitting up,
> alert)
> What! Is she ok? What happened?
> (Listening)
> OK. Look mate, stay out of it. This
> is her life, her decisions. She is your
> parent, not the other way around.
> Obviously, I don't want her to get
> hurt, but you know what she's like,
> she just lashes out. It sounds like he
> hit back. At least he stopped and
> walked away.
> (Listening)
> So, you haven't seen him since?
> Well, stay cool son, it will work out.
> (A beat)
> How's Stiv, he ok? You guys been out
> with the guns?
> (Listening)
> OK then, be cool, you hear me...
> OK, bye.

Mike hangs up, staring at the handset. Dave enters carrying tanks, rubber hoses and brass connectors. He drops them onto a workshop bench along the back wall, drops down into his usual chair.

DAVE

What's up mate look like you lost a
quid and found sixpence.

MIKE

Iris and Daniel had a fight. Looks like
he whopped her one.

(A beat)

Bob rang. He's pretty wound up. Not
a lot I can say is there... it's a ringer
for how me and her used to carry
on. Don't know how Bob made it
through all that.

(A beat)

Looks like she landed him one first.

DAVE

Best for Bob to stay out of it I reckon.
This is the story of Iris's life.

(Catching Mike's look)

Sorry buddy...

Mike lets the jibe go. It is true he reflected. There is a silence,
then...

MIKE

I rang him. Daniel, I mean.

Dave looks up, watchful, silent, waiting.

MIKE (CONT'D)

It's now £120k. He went up £20k if
we do it Friday night after dark. I
told him I'd talk to you, but I told
him - yes.

Dave remains silent. He spins his chair to stare out of the window.

MIKE (CONT'D)

By 'we', I mean me really. You do
not have to be in this mate, I accept
that, and respect it.

120

I'll pay you the £20k to use the
equipment etc. I'll do it!

> DAVE
> (Softly)
> Fuck you Mike.
> (A beat)
> Fuck you...
> (Facing Mike, hands flat to
> the desktop)
> You know I can't just leave you to
> do this on your own. Its a night dive.
> You need someone up top who
> knows what they are doing. You get
> in trouble down there, some needs
> to know how to get you out - without
> killing you in the process.

Both men are silent for several moments.

> DAVE (CONT'D)
> Right, we have stuff to do, we better
> get started. We have two days to
> get our shit together.
> (A beat, lazy grin to his
> partner)
> Ring him to confirm.

CUT TO:

EXT. DAY. STIV'S HOUSE. FRONT ROOM

Stiv and Bob are in their usual positions, feet on the coffee table.
There is an air of tension.

> BOB
> (Disgusted)
> He's back. They are both lovey
> dovey again. Like it never fucking
> happened. I can't stand it. Can't

bear to even look at the bastard. He
knows I hate him, but he couldn't
give a shit. Smiles at me as if I'm
stupid. My Mother needs her fucking
head looked at.
(A beat)
Fucking house is full of flowers, roses.

Stiv is silent. He watches Bob, knowing something else is coming.

BOB (CONT'D)
Something is happening. Not sure
what, but he is picking up a van
tomorrow, a big Transit, high top. She
is taking him to pick it up, then she's
driving the Range Rover back.
(A beat)
He's not hiring this van; he's getting
it from someone he knows out of the
area.
(Looking at Stiv)
I reckon this is it mate. He's getting
the rest of his stuff out of that hole.
The van, get it?
(A beat)
I heard him telling her that he will
leave the Rover here, she can use
it for a few weeks, then he'll come
back for it. Then he wants her to
go with him, away somewhere,
probably overseas.
(A beat)
She won't go... She's stringing him
along. It suits her at the minute.

STIV
What's your plan?

BOB
Its Wednesday today, they're getting
the van tomorrow, so I reckon he's

getting his stuff Thursday night, or
Friday. He'll be gone by weekend.

Bob arranges several items on the coffee table to represent the
sinkhole and surroundings. Pointing with a pen, Stiv leans forward.

                    BOB (CONT'D)
          Here is the sinkhole, here, the rocks
          where you shot the Bulgarians
          from. Here is where I was. Here was
          their 4*4.
                    (A beat)
          We stake the place out from
          tomorrow. Two shooting positions,
          you as back-up. I'll shoot. You only
          shoot if necessary - but you won't
          need to, OK?
                    (A beat)
          I think he's probably got the crates
          up near the top already. All he has
          to do is haul them out and load
          them into the van. We shoot the
          fucker, drop him down the hole tied
          to one of his crates. One of us takes
          his van and dumps it somewhere.
          That's it. Job done. We collect any
          ejected shells, wear gloves.
                    (Smiling triumphantly at Stiv)
          Same as last time, but now we know
          what we are doing eh? - Pros..

Bob throws down his pen with a flourish, leans back. Stiv looks
at the make-ship sinkhole layout on the coffee table for a long
time. Finally, he too leans back, looks at his old friend with the
beginnings of a faint grin.

He nods.

                                        FADE OUT:

EXT. AERIAL SHOTS. DAY. FELL-SIDE AND COASTAL REGION HIGH ABOVE THE SINKHOLE.

Friday dawns grey over Morecambe Bay, the largest continuous inter-tidal area in the whole of the UK. The Bay is fed by five mighty rivers, opening out into 120 square miles of sand and mud flats. Vast areas are covered at high tide, then exposed like a micro desert when the tide is low.

Hills, valleys and channels, an entire alluvial landscape emerges from the sea each day, transforming the entire environment every few hours, fascinating for visitors and tourists, but for the peoples of The Bay, rooted in the South Lake-land landscape, just another day.

Walney Island has an ethereal ground mist creeping white against its hips. The harbor and dock area, normally industrial and drab, take on a mystical eerie aspect. The vast bulk of moored ships like primeval creatures sleeping. The arms of tower cranes reaching skywards 'luffed' in their parking positions, pointing diagonally upwards, their hook blocks tethered, black cables hanging still as death, disappearing impossibly into whiteness.

Ulverston Town was stirring, unfurling, the streetlights along Queen Street dying in the daylight. The alleys, ginnels and yards still deserted, apart from some locals here and there who have been up for hours tending their allotments. A dog is barking somewhere up on The Gill, and an early train from Grange over Sands, small with distance, creeps silently along the aqueduct, disappearing and re-appearing in the mist.

CUT TO:

EXT. THE SINKHOLE. DAY.

Bob and Stiv have spent an uncomfortable night lying in the rocks overlooking the sinkhole. As the light filtering downwards through the tree cover increases, they stand with some effort, stretching painfully, stowing their rifles in gun-slips and collecting shooting paraphernalia together.

STIV
Well, its tonight then, I guess.

BOB
Yep... gotta be. No point in hanging
around here all day. Come back
later on huh?

CUT TO:

EXT. WALNEY ISLAND DIVE CENTER. YARD

Dave and Mike are up early. They are loading the black Transit
van with equipment. There is little communication between
the two men. They understand their craft perfectly and have
worked together for years. Each does their part without effort or
discussion.

CUT TO:

INT. IRIS'S HOUSE. DAY

Iris rolls into the middle of the bed, fiddling with her cell phone.
Daniel is in the shower. On the bedside cabinet, his cell phone
rings, vibrating sideways. He appears, gleaming wet, white fluffy
towel around his muscled waist.

DANIEL
Danny.
(Listening)

Tonight.

Daniel hangs up, grinning down at Iris, nodding. She looks
pensive. He flicks moisture from his hair at her and she pulls the
duvet over her, laughing.

CUT TO:

EXT. ULVERSTON POLICE STATION. DAY

DI Wilson parks his pool car, blipping the security button on the keyring. He presses his plastic Warrant Card over the digital entry screen and the door swings open. He moves forward, glancing back as two other colleagues quickly enter before the door closes.

He walks to his desk, passing the conference room on his right. Through the glass wall he can see the first shift receiving their instructions. Uniforms, taking notes, concentrating. In the 'bullpen' several officers are at their desks, the TV screen showing the early morning news, and a small cluster of colleagues in the coffee area getting their first fix of the day.

CUT TO:

EXT/INT. INTERPOL HQ. 200 CHARLES DE GAULLE 69006. LYON....

Inspector Lafitte is collecting a latte and croissant from the street stall outside the entrance. Balancing his cardboard tray, he negotiates the entry security system, smiles at the beautiful girl at reception, nudges third floor on the glass lift, and looking out across the city, rises silently through the building.

Across the boulevard, construction work continues on Notre Dame, and the first tourists wander into courtyard in front of the Pompidou Centre.

CUT TO:

EXT. DAY. ULVERSTON CENTRE

DI Wilson is buying sandwiches in Greggs. He pays, takes the paper bag and heads back to his pool car. As he crosses the pavement a white Renault Kangoo Van pulls to the kerb. Something alerts his interest, and he stops to watch the refection in Ross's Estate Agency window, his back to the street.

126

A beautiful dark-haired woman gets out of the passenger side of the van, her movement lithe and feminine. She stands at the open door for a few minutes talking to the driver. It is Iris. Mike Kramer's ex-wife. Wilson is intrigued, he knows her. She hasn't changed much in the 16 years since he last saw her. But it isn't just Iris that has caught Wilson's interest, it is the driver.

Wilson moves to stroll past the van on the opposite side so that Iris doesn't recognize him. He knows the man instantly and immediately averts his face, passes the van and as he walks away, takes the number.

Wilson passes the Coronation Hall on his left, dropping onto the kerbside bench as a series of connections suddenly explode in his brain.

Daniel Laidlow is in town, he is linked back 16 years to the IRA guns recovery from the sinkhole - not proven.

Iris is Mike Kramer's ex-wife, in a van with Laidlow.

Mike Kramer recently dived in the sinkhole, searching for guns, and was paid for the job by Cumbria Police.

DI Wilson watches from a distance as Iris slams the van door, waves coquettishly at Laidlow, and walks away towards The Gill. The Renault Van indicates into the traffic flow, and pulls away, tires rumbling on the cobbles.

CUT TO:

INT. ULVERSTON POLICE STATION. DAY

Wilson sprawls at his desk, deep in thought. Daniel Laidlaw's face stares out of his computer screen, with text scrolling down the left dialogue box.

Laidlow has had minor police records, but nothing until being sent down for illegal possession of firearms, and second-degree murder of an informant. Wilson knew that he had been linked to

Iris Kramer 16 years ago, even though she was married to Mike at that time.

Laidlow could be back in Ulverston to take up with her again, or back here for another reason entirely. Wilson stared at Laidlaw's electronic face until it blurred into a teeming mass of pixels.

He looks around the office, he is alone, he reaches for his phone...

FADE TO:

EXT. NIGHT. FELLSIDE OVERLOOKING A590 AND SINKHOLE

Wilson is sitting in usual place on the fellside, the lights of Ulverston clustered to his right. The 590 is busy as always, fast moving traffic, trucks jostling for position, headlights flashing, two miles over towards the coastline, the area of the sinkhole was unlit, totally black.

Wilson is playing a hunch, old instincts that gave him no peace. He is resolved to stay up all night, tomorrow is Saturday - a day off. He pours himself a coffee from a flask, hunching back into his seat, watching.

CUT TO:

EXT. NIGHT. THE SINKHOLE

Stiv and Bob are sitting with their backs to the rocks across from the sinkhole. Both have rifles and are dressed in their usual cammo clothing.

Both are quiet and reflective, exchanging glances from time, privately daring each other to be the first to call the whole thing off. Neither does.

CUT TO:

EXT. NIGHT. A590 FROM ULVERSTON TOWARDS GREENODD

Daniel drives the Renault Kangoo along the frenetic 590 towards Greenodd. He keeps pace with the traffic, then indicates right to take the unlit rutted track to the sinkhole.

Daniel has a packed suitcase with him on the floor of the van, and a travel bag on the seat next to him. The travel bag contains among other things, a large amount of cash, and a Glock 17, with two loaded magazines.

CUT TO:

EXT. NIGHT. FELLSIDE OVERLOOKING A590 AND SINKHOLE

DI Wilson spots the vehicle indicating right to take the track to the sinkhole. He watches as the headlights move away from the heavy traffic, laboriously negotiating the otherwise dark scrubland.

Wilson starts his own vehicle, taking the road downwards towards the 590.

CUT TO:

EXT. NIGHT. A590 COAST ROAD FROM BARROW TO ULVERSTON

Dave and Mike are running later that they planned. Mike has spent 30 minutes trying to ring Bob, his son, to check if he was OK. Since the phone conversation, Mike had felt pangs of guilt about his estrangement. He always assumed that Bob was OK, but now worried that he has overestimated Bob's coping skills.

Dave is silent, concentrating on driving. His face illuminated by the dashboard glow.

CUT TO:

EXT. NIGHT. THE SINKHOLE

Daniel reaches the sinkhole. He reverses the Renault to the edge of the black water. Leaving the headlights on and engine running, he gets out, walking around the rear of the van, looking around. He is the first.

He checks his watch, they are late. There are no messages on his cell phone.

CUT TO:

EXT. NIGHT. THE SINKHOLE

Stiv and Bob hear Daniel's vehicle as it bumps slowly towards them. Both ease up the rocks and watch as the van reverses up to the side of the sinkhole. The van lights cast a flickering glow across the water.

A man's black silhouette stands motionless behind the van for a few moments, then disappears out of their sight. Both young men recognize the silhouette immediately. It is the man they had come to kill, Daniel Laidlow.

CUT TO:

EXT. NIGHT. THE TRACK TO THE SINKHOLE

DI Wilson drives with side lights as far as he dares. Then parks his unmarked pool car behind scrub off the side of the track. He goes forward in the darkness with a small, hooded torch from the car toolkit.

CUT TO:

EXT. NIGHT. A590 FROM ULVERSTON TOWARDS GREENODD

Dave and Mike have made good time. They are late but are confident that they have adequate time to get the job done. Dave indicates right and pulls onto the dark track to the sinkhole.

CUT TO:

EXT. NIGHT. THE SINKHOLE

Daniel is tense. They are clearly late. He walks away from his lit-up van, retracing his steps along the track towards the 590. He stops in the darkness; he can hear a vehicle coming towards him. He listens intently, nodding to himself, It is them.

He walks back towards his headlights shining in the trees.

CUT TO:

EXT. NIGHT. THE COPSE NEAR THE SINKHOLE.

DI Wilson stands stock still in the darkness. Daniel Laidlow passes within several feet of him, heading back towards his van. Wilson thinks it through, if Laidlow is to be charged, he has to be in possession of the guns. Otherwise, he has nothing.

Wilson edges towards the sinkhole.

CUT TO:

EXT. NIGHT. THE TRACK TO THE SINKHOLE

Dave and Mike spot Daniel's headlights. They are shining towards their vehicle as they approach, so they assume that Daniel has reversed up to the edge of the sinkhole.

Dave stops his vehicle.

                    MIKE
        What are you doing? You need to
        get close so we can use the winch.

                    DAVE
        I know, I'll just take a look first.

Both men exit their van, walking towards the headlights.

                                                    CUT TO:

EXT. NIGHT. THE SINKHOLE

Daniel sees Dave and Mike arrive and walk towards him lit by the
Renault headlights. He throws up a hand in casual greeting, then
walks towards the rear of his van to open the doors.

As he stands looking out across the water, a survival instinct deep
inside his psych is triggered. He stares into the darkness, suddenly
alert and spooked. Adrenaline surges and his heart rate rapidly
increases.

His eyes search, sweeping along the darkness above the black
water, vague shapes of rounded boulders, tangled branches. A
flare of white light blossoms silently.

Daniel shudders, taking a step backward as he feels a violent
impact to his chest. He squares his feet, looks down at his chest,
his hands searching, but can see nothing. He walks a few steps,
then inexplicably, his legs give way and he sits down with his back
to the Renault.

                                                    CUT TO:

EXT. NIGHT. THE SINKHOLE

Fifteen feet away, DI Wilson flattens himself to the ground behind
some scrub. He has clearly heard a single shot from somewhere in

the darkness in front of him. His own survival instincts trigger as he burrows closer to the ground in the darkness.

CUT TO:

EXT. NIGHT. THE SINKHOLE

Dave and Mike hear the shot but cannot see Daniel at that moment. The shot makes no sense to them. Independently, they both assume that Daniel has shot at them. Both men flatted to the ground in panic.

CUT TO:

EXT. NIGHT. THE SINKHOLE

Daniel pulls in ragged breaths and watches as two men materialize out of the darkness and make their way towards him. Both carry rifles. He knows now that he has been shot in the chest. He feels no pain yet, but his breathing is laboured and his legs feel leaden and unresponsive.

The two men appear, lit in the crimson rear light of the Renault. They stop several feet away from him. He recognized them both.

>   DANIEL
> Well boys, this is strange place for us
> all to meet up.
>   (A beat, a faint smile on his
>   lips)
> Out hunting, are you?

>   BOB
> Fuck you Daniel.

>   DANIEL
> And its Stephen over there, Stiv.
> Come to settle a score with old
> Danny here, have you?

133

> (Lifting his head to look
> square at both men)
> Well come on my lovely boys, get
> the job done. It's my time, I guess.
> It was always going to be a bullet
> for me.

Bob shoots Daniel in the chest again from six feet away. Daniel doesn't speak again. He settled against the back of the Renault, his feet twitched several times, then he is still.

Stiv and Bob stood facing him, both still.

CUT TO:

EXT. NIGHT. THE SINKHOLE.

15 feet away, DI Wilson hugs the ground, not moving, breathing the scent of earth and alluvial mud.

CUT TO:

EXT. THE SINKHOLE. NIGHT.

30 feet away, Dave Gedding and Mike Kramer rise shakily to their feet. Both had seen what happened and were deeply shocked. Mike walks forward.

> MIKE
> Bob, what the fuck have you
> done son...
> (Horror etched in his face)
> You've just killed a man, shot him.

Mike sinks to his haunches, staring at his son lit red in the rear lights of the Renault.

Dave, up on his feet, walks shakily over to Daniel, checking his carotid artery.

                    DAVE
        He's dead.
              (Quietly to Stiv and Bob)

        Put the guns away lads. There's no-
        one else to shoot here now.

Both young men lower their rifles. They walk to nearby rocks and
sit with their backs pressed against the rounded surface. Both are
transfixed by Daniel. Alive until moments ago.

DI Wilson works his way carefully back and away from the
immediate area. Now lying very still.

Dave goes over to sit with the two young men.

                    DAVE (CONT'D)
        So, what's the plan lads? I assume
        you have one. You weren't just
        passing, were you?
              (To Mike)
        Get the fuck over here Mike, work to
        do I think.

Mike, looking dazed and emotional, gets up from his kneeling
position and comes over to the rocks to join Stiv, Bob and Dave.
Both Stiv and Bob are very calm, almost arrogant.

Dave looks carefully at both of them.

                    DAVE (CONT'D)
        Time to talk lads, we have a
        situation here. One that I have never
        confronted before.
              (Several beats)
        Look guys, we have to take some
        actions here. Decisive actions. Life
        changing actions. None of our lives
        will be the same after this.

Stiv and Bob exchange glances.

                    BOB
        We are not sorry for any of this you
        know. That fucker deserved to die,
        and I'm glad.

                    STIV
        Me too. He beat the shit out of me,
        and Iris as well. She was scared
        of him.

                    DAVE
        Well, at least we are now talking.
                (A beat)
        Lads, no one doubts that this guy
        was a bad man. That falls a long
        way short of killing him for it.
                (Looking at Mike for support)
        Mike, what's your take on all this.

Mike is clearly still in shock. This has been compounded by Stiv
and Bob's total lack of remorse.

                    MIKE
        Who fired the shot, the first one I
        mean?

                    BOB
        It was me, this time. My turn.

Dave reacts.

                    DAVE
        This time...
                (Several beats)
        I hardly dare ask...
                    STIV
        It was me, the first time.
                (A beat)
        I shot both of the Bulgarians. They
        were going to kill Bob. Shoot him in
        the head.

Dave and Mike are both shocked into silence. Hidden in the scrub, DI Wilson, hearing every word, is also shocked.

                    BOB
          We were coming home from
          shooting. We saw lights here and
          crept up. The Bulgarians were
          hauling a crate of guns up from the
          sinkhole.
                    (A beat)
          They spotted me. Pulled me out from
          the rocks over there.
                    (Indicating)
          They talked between themselves,
          decided to kill me... chuck me in
          there
                    (Indicating again)
          Just like that.

                    STIV
          I was still over there by the rocks.
          Saw it all. They were gonna shoot
          him in the head.
                    (A beat)
          I had my rifle, what the fuck was I
          supposed to do? I had no time to
          think about it.
                    (Looking defiantly around,
                    voice raised)
          Well... what would you fucking do?
          What would anyone do? Anyway,
          I'm not sorry... I did what I did.

                    MIKE
          But you shot both of them...

                    STIV
          So, you clever shit. I should have only
          shot one of them eh. That would
          have worked, wouldn't it...?
                    (Looking away, disdainful)

Everyone falls into silence.

CUT TO:

EXT. NIGHT. SCRUB NEAR THE SINKHOLE

Hidden in the scrub, DI Wilson lowers his face onto his hands. He can taste the earthy alluvial mud, salty and primal, he draws the scent deep into his lungs, then exhaling with a shudder.

CUT TO:

EXT. THE SINKHOLE. NIGHT.

Bob is sitting with his back against rocks, Stiv sitting next to him.

> BOB
> Stiv saved me. I would have been dead. I'd have been buried by now, but for him. Neither of us slept for days on end afterwards.
> (A beat)
> We have been in hell. In fucking HELL!
> (A beat)
> I wanted to make it OK for Stiv, I couldn't undo it could I? So my way of making it OK was to shoot the fucker who beat us, and beat my Mother. That's it.

The two young men exchange glances. Nodding to each other, confirming their resolve.

> BOB (CONT'D)
> Ring the cops. Let them sort it out. We are up for that, eh Stiv?
> (Looking at Stiv)

                    STIV
        Yep, ring them. Do it. Me and him,
        we shot three guys, we admit it.
        We're not gonna deny shit.
                    DAVE
        Fuck lads...
                (Deep breath)
        We can't just sell you out to the cops...
                (Looking at Mike)
        Mike...
                    MIKE
                (Flatly)
        Nobody is ringing the cops. Given
        the circumstances, I'd have done
        what you did.
                (A beat)
        Well, maybe not shoot Daniel, but
        the first two.

Dave becomes decisive. He gets to his feet, pacing. Everyone
watches. Finally...

                    DAVE
                (To Stiv and Bob)
        Have you got passports with you?

                    STIV
        Shooters always carry passports,
        along with Firearms Certificates. Its
        normal practice. I have mine in my
        pack.

                    BOB
        Yes, I have mine too.

                    DAVE
        Right. Get your stuff together.
        Everything into Daniel's van. Both
        rifles into the hole, now!
                (Rounding on everyone)
        NOW! Do it!

Everyone moved at once. All the two young men's packs are stowed in the Renault van. Both reluctantly surrender their rifles to Dave, who throws them into the center of the sinkhole.

Dave rummages in Daniel's packs and holds up wads of bank notes.

> DAVE (CONT'D)
> You two are heading to the ferry now. When you get there, dump this van. Get different transport. Book into a small hotel somewhere in the country and get in touch.
>> (Eye contact with both young men)
> We will sort this.
>> BOB
> What about...
>> DAVE
> I told you. We will sort this. Now move.

FADE TO:

EXT. NIGHT. A590

Ten minutes later, the Renault van is indicating right into the traffic of the A590.

CUT TO:

EXT. SCRUB NEAR SINKHOLE

DI Wilson creeps away silently, disappearing into black darkness.

CUT TO:

EXT. THE SINKHOLE. NIGHT.

Dave and Mike weight Daniel's body and tip him into the sinkhole. They pace the area, finding Bob's two ejected shells, these also pitched into the black water. Daniel's packs and the rest of the money is thrown into their van, and they drive silently back towards Barrow.

FADE TO BLACK

FADE IN:

EXT. DAY. CAEN. FERRY TERMINAL. FRANCE.

The Brittany Ferry Ouistreham, noses into the landing ramp at Caen after the 7 hour crossing from Portsmouth.

CUT TO:

EXT. UPPER DECK OF FERRY

Stiv and Bob watch from the deck above the stern loading gate as the ferry docked in a maelstrom of metallic noise and engine rumbles. They await their call as trucks and articulated lorries took the first priority to unload.

Both men are excited and scared in equal measure. The events of the past weeks have been momentous. Since leaving the sinkhole, there had been no opportunity to review or discuss their situation. They are both in free fall. Both expect to be captured in a flashing display of blue lights at any moment, but miraculously, even though ticketing had taken a long time, they had boarded Brittany Ferries with no problem, and now they were almost in France.

Finally, it is their turn to drive their van off the ferry and through the customs checks of France. They join the long queue to the checkpoint, passports at the ready.

CUT TO:

EXT. DAY. CAEN CUSTOMS CHECKPOINT

As they moved closer to the checkpoint, both men are tense, but everything seemed quite normal. Two customs officers are routinely checking vehicles, then waving them through with bored expressions.

They draw level with the customs check. Passports are taken. They waited. Stiv is looking through the windscreen when there is a polite tap on his side window. An elegantly dress male, 50's, indicates for him to open his window.

> INSPECTOR JEAN LAFITTE - INTERPOL
> Mr Stephen Parry? And I assume My
> Michael Kramer?

Both men look at the Frenchman. He smiles widely, taking a step back and bowing slightly.

> INSPECTOR JEAN LAFITTE - INTERPOL (CONT'D)
> Welcome to France gentlemen. I am
> so very happy to see you both.
> > (Stepping back, hand
> > outstretched)
> I am Inspector Jean Lafitte of
> Interpol.
> > (Opening the passenger side
> > door)
> Please gentlemen, would you care
> to accompany me.

After initial hesitation, both men exit their van, expecting to be cuffed and arrested. Lafitte, however, leads them to an unmarked Citroen, where he opens the rear doors with a flourish.

> INSPECTOR JEAN LAFITTE - INTERPOL (CONT'D)
> Please...
> > (Getting in the front
> > passenger side, speaking
> > over his shoulder)

We have a short car journey
gentlemen, Please bear with me.

CUT TO:

EXT. CAEN CITY. DAY. AERIAL AND WIDE SHOTS

Lafitte signals his driver, and the car sweeps silently out of the
busy harbour and onto a smooth dual carriageway, then silently
picks up speed, moves over to the fast lane. Lafitte studies the
two young men closely in his mirror. He picks up a slight tension,
but surprisingly, they both seem calm and resigned to whatever
happened. They don't speak.

The Citroen sweeps into the City, the driver negotiating the busy
streets expertly. Lafitte remains silent. Eventually the car turns right
into a vast underground car-park, pulls up by an illuminated lift
door. Lafitte exits the Citroen, indicated for them to follow him.

CUT TO:

INT. HIGH TECH OFFICE BUILDINGS. CAEN CITY. FRANCE

The lift rises through concrete, then long corridors, another glass
lift, exposed to a vast cityscape, offices to right and left, finally
a room with a long polished table, chairs around. Lafitte sits and
indicates for them to join him. The door opens and a beautiful
but unsmiling woman places a tray of fresh coffee and croissants
on the polished table in front of them. She glances at Lafitte and
immediately withdraws.

Lafitte crosses his legs, brushes imaginary lint from his immaculate
trousers, leans forward and takes a coffee and a croissant,
delicately pulling off a piece and chewing thoughtfully. He
indicates the tray...

INSPECTOR JEAN LAFITTE - INTERPOL
Please...

                         STIV
          I don't understand. What's going
          on? Are we arrested?

          INSPECTOR JEAN LAFITTE - INTERPOL
                    (Smiling)
          Well, that depends on the discussion
          we are about to have gentlemen.
                    (A beat)
          Certainly I can see that you would
          have an expectation that you would
          be arrested.
                    (A beat)
          But life can be extraordinary at
          times. Please have some food,
          coffee, I feel terrible eating alone.

Both men pull a coffee towards them.

          INSPECTOR JEAN LAFITTE - INTERPOL (CONT'D)
          That's better.
                    (Smiling, a beat)
          Gentleman,
                    (Looking from one to
                    another)
          I am in a interesting position today.
          Your life is at a T junction, you may
          turn left, or right.
                    (A beat)
          You both have demonstrated that
          you have very unique and special
          skills.
                    (A beat)
          These skills are in demand by
          powerful individuals, and now
          you both have an opportunity
          to develop your existing skill-set
          beyond your wildest dreams.

Warming to his task, Lafitte leans forward looking earnestly at his
two guests.

INSPECTOR JEAN LAFITTE - INTERPOL (CONT'D)

This opportunity comes with its opposite, a threat. This my friends, is always the case, in this life.

(A beat)

The refusal of the opportunity immediately invokes the possibility of you both going to prison for a very long time, and the loss of your liberty.

(A beat)

I know as country men, you would take that very hard.

The opportunity my friends that ~I am empowered to place before you, is to become professional assassins.

(A beat)

Becoming Assassins is an opportunity to gain money, power, respect, and maybe for some, to be feared, where fear is currency. You have shown that you can kill with surgical precision, without hesitation or mercy. This is very rare in humans.

(A beat)

Assassins date back as far as recorded history. They are determined, courageous, intelligent, resourceful, and physically active. They also have the ability to carry through a set of agreed actions to a conclusion, and live with the consequences.

(A beat)

Both of you already have some of these qualities, you can be trained in the rest.

Both young men are sitting agape at Lafitte. They are astonished, but surprisingly controlled. Lafitte, exuding self-confidence and elegance, leans back, awaiting a reaction.

                    BOB
              (Incredulous)
          How can you possibly know
          anything about us? We are in
          France, this stuff happened in
          England, some of it only yesterday?

          INSPECTOR JEAN LAFITTE - INTERPOL
              (Leaning back, hands
              outspread)
          It is my job to know these things. I
          am a policeman. I have access to
          investigative resources that you can
          only guess at.
              (Smiling indulgently)
          Before I reveal more, I would like to
          know your reactions to what I have
          told you...

Stiv and Bob exchange glances.

                    STIV
          How does this work? You can't
          just let us off. You said you were
          a policeman for Interpol... I don't
          understand any of this.
              (Shaking his head in
              astonishment)
          We are just lads from Cumbria,
          normal folk really, but we got into
          something that escalated out of
          our control. None of this has been
          planned.

Bob nodded his agreement.

INSPECTOR JEAN LAFITTE - INTERPOL
The reason I am saying these things
to you is because of the very fact
that you are not normal at all. You
are both a very long way from being
normal. I accept that you got into
something extraordinary, then the
situation rapidly escalated in such
a way that life-changing decisions
were forced upon you with no time
for thought.
(A beat)
But those decisions were taken,
and now the consequences exist.
Everything brings us together today
in this room.
(A beat)
But believe me, we would not be
here if you were two 'normal lads
from Cumbria. Whatever happens
here, You will never be 'normal'.

BOB
(Glancing at Stiv, then to
Lafitte)
I want to do this, yes. I really want to!

STIV
Yes, I do too.
(A beat)
So, tell us... how did you know?

INSPECTOR JEAN LAFITTE - INTERPOL

I will briefly explain how this will
work, and things will become
clearer.

We will take your van and
possessions, we will put you in a nice
country hotel for a couple of weeks,

then you will go home to Cumbria,
that's it! We will furnish you with a
story to ring your parents so they do
not worry, then...
            (A beat, smiling)
You will return home, carry on your
life as if nothing has happened.
Accounts will be opened for you
both, and a substantial salary will
be paid into a Swiss Bank. From time
to time, you will do very specialized
work for me. This work will involve
detailed planning, then the rapid
and efficient execution of a human
target somewhere in the World.

This work may take place anywhere.
You have become 'International Hit
Men' my young colleagues.
            (Smiling broadly, leaning
            back)
Congratulations!

                BOB
But what about my Father, and
Dave Geddings? They know...

    INSPECTOR JEAN LAFITTE - INTERPOL
Ah Yes, the ubiquitous divers.
            (Hands spread)
We will keep those two on a 'loose
leash', to use an English colloquialism.
They already have aided and
abetted significant events, but they
will inevitably go further. They will not
be able to resist it.
            (A beat)
After a week or two, they are bound
to return to the sinkhole, haul out the
rest of the guns, and make a deal
for themselves.

                    (A beat)
          We will ensure that they are given
          the space, and the confidence
          to do this. No-one will bother, or
          investigate them, but by allowing
          this to happen, we will know for
          certain, that their silence will be
          secured, and indeed, ensured.

Lafitte, pours more coffee, treats himself to another croissant,
delicately tearing it into small fragments. The two young men
watch him, fascinated, increasingly excited.

Lafitte finishes his coffee, mopping up the crumbs with a wet
finger, then stands decisively.

          INSPECTOR JEAN LAFITTE - INTERPOL (CONT'D)
          OK, we are done here!
                    (A beat
          When the time comes to travel
          somewhere to undertake work on
          my behalf, you will be contacted
          by a local 'Handler'. He will give
          you basic instructions and arrange
          travel etc.
                    (A beat, watching them both
                    carefully)
          Your 'HANDLER' gentlemen, is
          Detective Inspector Joseph Wilson
          of Cumbria Police.

                                        FADE TO BLACK

EPILOGUE

Several weeks later.

EXT. DAY. BIRKRIGG FELL. CUMBRIA.

Stiv and Bob are walk through light brush with rifles. Two rabbits hang from their belts, another two and they will head home. Stiv's cell phone rings.

> STIV
> (Glancing at the screen,
> frowning)
> Stiv...
> (Listening)
>
> OK.
> (Checking his watch)
>
> Will do.

Stiv hangs up. Bob looks at his friend.

> STIV (CONT'D)
> (Holding Bob's gaze...
> Joe Wilson. Wants to meet. ASAP.

                                        FADE TO BLACK

TITLES AND CREDITS.

PART TWO

INT. PARIS INTERPOL HQ. INSP. JEAN LAFITTE'S 2ND FLOOR OFFICE - MORNING

INSPECTOR JEAN LAFITTE (56), fingers steepled to pursed lips, sits at his desk staring sombrely down into a sunlit circular courtyard below his 2nd floor office...

At the far end of the courtyard are beautiful wrought iron gates decorated on each half with the coat of arms of the Republic of France, beyond them the Place Beavau where streams of traffic from the Faubourg St Honore and Avenue de Marigny hoot and swirl around the hips of the energetic policeman directing them theatrically from the centre of the square.

On the edge of LAFITTE'S view, at the main gates of the Interpol Compound two GENDARMES stand immobile, SUB-MACHINE GUNS slung from their shoulders, looking impassively at the World through the high impact resistant steel gates.

Though not easily ruffled, LAFITTE is tense on this autumn morning as he peels a SLIP OF PAPER from his LUIS XIV WALNUT DESK and regards it for confirmation - '2.00pm Ministry' is written in his own elegant handwriting. He slides the SLIP into his breast pocket, clears his throat as he reaches for his TELEPHONE HANDSET.

> JEAN LAFITTE
> Eric please.

The PHONE SCREEN flares, recognizing his voice, then flickers bringing a DIAL TONE and VIBRATION from the HANDSET.

> CHAUFFER (O.S.)
> Sir?

> JEAN LAFITTE
> Have Eric bring the car to the inner
> door. Thank you.

LAFITTE shrugs into an immaculate BLUE PIN-STRIPED SUIT JACKET, pockets his CELLPHONE, checks his appearance in a LONG MIRROR by the door and shoots his cuffs as he stalks the room...

CUT TO:

123 EXT. PARIS STREETS - MORNING

WIDE AND AERIAL

A CITROEN DS19 swings out of the Interpol HQ gates and along the Place Beauvau to the Square de la Place Etienne Parnet. Gives a DISCREET BLIP from its horn prompting the POLICEMAN in the centre of the square to halt traffic, allowing the CITROEN enough space to swing out and pass through the narrow archway to the...

CUT TO:

124 EXT. INTERIOR MINISTRY OF FRANCE - CONTINUOUS

Two GARDES REPUBLICANS stand immobile in sentry boxes but move white gloved fingers to safety catches of their RIFLES as the OFFICER OF THE DAY bent to check the identity of LAFITTE in the rear seat.

He nods and the sentries relax, The chain across the portico was dropped to the ground and the CITROEN gently CRUNCHES over the chain, moving smoothly across a hundred feet of tan coloured gravel to the classical facade of the Palace.

The CITROEN circles clockwise and pulls up at the entrance. LAFITTE'S door is opened and he exhales as he steps up the granite steps.

CUT TO:

INT. INTERIOR MINISTRY OF FRANCE, HALLWAY - CONTINUOUS

The CHIEF USHER greets LAFITTE with a nod.

> CHIEF USHER
> Monsieur Lafitte.

LAFITTE nods back and follows him off down the hall, passing beneath a VAST CHANDELIER as the USHER makes a brief and inaudible call on his CELLPHONE as they ascend a double granite stairway. Keeping a majestic, unhurried pace.

CUT TO:

INT. INTERIOR MINISTRY OF FRANCE, UPPER FLOOR - CONTINUOUS

The USHER leads LAFITTE across a vast landing overlooking the hallway below... Reaching a door on the left and knocking gently...

> AIDE (O.S.)
> Entrez.

The USHER opens the door and steps back allowing LAFITTE to pass into the...

CUT TO:

INT. INTERIOR MINISTRY OF FRANCE, INNER OFFICE TO THE SALON DES ORDNANCES - CONTINUOUS

The door is closed gently behind LAFITTE as a uniformed AIDE rises silently from an ORNATE DESK.

The great south windows on the far side of the Salon stream early autumn warmth across the deep pile carpet and an open window allows the CHIRPING of wood pigeons and the faint MURMUR of traffic along the Champs Elysee.

LAFITTE, his footsteps muted, crosses the vast carpet meeting the AIDE in the middle.

                              AIDE
                    Monsieur Lafitte...

                         JEAN LAFITTE
                    I am expected
                              (Gesturing towards a door
                              beyond)

                              AIDE
                    Of course.

The AIDE crosses the carpet, knocks briefly on the double doors and stands to attention.

                         AIDE (CONT'D)
                Inspector Lafitte Monsieur Le Ministere

A MUFFLED ASSENT (O.S) prompts the aid to step back an inch, smiling briefly at LAFITTE with a short nod. LAFITTE steps past through one side of the double doors and enters the inner sanctum of the French political machine.

                                                        CUT TO:

INT. MINISTER OF HOME AFFAIRS OFFICE - CONTINUOUS

WIDE AND MEDIUM

LAFITTE pauses to take in his lavish surroundings; nothing in the room is simple, nothing without dignity, nothing un-tasteful, exemplifying the absolute totality of French grandeur.

MONSIEUR JACQUES DE FREYN (60's) rises smoothly and greets LAFITTE with elaborate courtesy. Wearing an immaculate CHARCOAL SUIT, handsome and self-assured.

MONSIEUR DE FREYN
Lafitte, welcome.
(Indicating with a gesture)
Please sit.

De Freyn returns to his customary seat, leans back, and places the fingertips of both hands together. He regards Lafitte gravely.

MONSIEUR DE FREYN (CONT'D)
I hope you are well Lafitte; can I get
you something? Coffee, something
stronger perhaps?

JEAN LAFITTE
Nothing Sir.
(A beat)
You wished to see me on a matter of
urgency?

De Freyn breaths in deeply. He spins his chair slightly to gaze upwards at the vast First Empire Tapestry that covers the east wall.

MONSIEUR DE FREYN
Indeed.
(A beat)

De Freyn, still looking at the tapestry, places a finger delicately on a folder, then slides it across the desk towards Lafitte. Lafitte glances at it, but makes no move to take it, keeping his eyes on the Minister.

MONSIEUR DE FREYN (CONT'D)
As you well know Lafitte, we are
both loyal servants to the interests of
France...
(A beat)
There is a small matter I must bring
to your attention.

De Freyn glances at Lafitte, then leans forward, his hand flat on the file between them.

This is a top-secret police report that
arrived this morning. It comes from
the Police Judiciaire of Metz, stating
that a man has been questioned
during a routine raid on a bar. He
had half-killed two policemen in the
ensuing fight. Later he had been
identified as a deserter from the
Foreign Legion by the name of Bulgar
Karienco, Hungarian by birth and
refugee from Sofia in the early 50s.
(a beat)
Karienco is a mercenary, a gun for
hire.
(Faint smile at Lafitte)
You will be familiar with the type, I'm
sure Lafitte.
(a beat)
Karienco has been long wanted for
his connections with series of terror
murders of loyalist notables in the
Sidi Bel Abbes region of Algeria over
the past five years.
(Leaning back)

Karienco is safe. He is going to be
our guest for many years, he knows
that. Unsurprisingly, he wants to
make a deal.
(a beat)
He has revealed a name to us,
which has shed light some otherwise
unresolved issues over the past two
years.
(A beat)
A Diplomat of some standing must
be removed immediately. We are
aware that this person is not acting
alone, and our discussions with M.
Karienco are continuing.
(a beat)

This 'removal' task is now being passed to you Lafitte, and his removal must also necessarily and immediately be identified as a random crime, and the criminals be brought to justice very quickly. Nothing of this should reflect back to our Government in any way. Do I need to elaborate?

               JEAN LAFITTE
I understand Sir.

               MONSIEUR DE FREYN
Good.
          (a beat)
In this file is also an Interdepartmental Memorandum from our permanent office in London. Our target is a guest, with several other Notables, at a Game Shoot in Scotland in three week's time. This is where you should focus your attention for several reasons.

One, it is outside France and indeed outside London. Two, security is practically non-existent. Three, you have acquired some APPROPRIATE SHOOTERS who can operate in this scenario, in the genre they would be classified as 'DISPOSABLE CLEAN SKINS', IE; they have no previous form, no police record, no military record, no motive, and they are not by any stretch of the imagination - Pros
          (Eyes drifting upwards to
          Lafitte)
I am also reliably advised they are especially skilled marksmen.

De Freyn slowly leans back, staring down his long nose at Lafitte through a curdling veil of blue cigar smoke.

> MONSIEUR DE FREYN (CONT'D)
> So, you see Lafitte,
>> (Gesturing with the smoking
>> stub of the cigar)
> you have all of the elements to
> hand to resolve our small issue.
>> (A beat)

De Freyn leans forward to stub out his cigar, carefully grinding out the embers, then leaning back, consults his watch. Lafitte takes the dismissal cue and leans forward, his hands flat to his thighs.

> JEAN LAFITTE
> Thank you, Sir.

LAFITTE stands, looks at DE FREYN for a long moment as he busies himself with papers on his desk seemingly forgetting that LAFITTE is even in the room.

The AIDE silently appears, standing to one side of the desk, hands clasped behind his back, eyes respectfully downcast. The room silent except for the low, constant, MURMUR of traffic (O.S). LAFITTE abruptly turns on his heel, walking past the AIDE, straight through the open door and onward into the Salon des Ordnances without a backward glance.

He marches in a straight line across the wide expanse of carpet, through the slanting shafts of late afternoon sunlight and into the semi-darkness of the outer vestibule. The AIDE hurries to catch up with him, flustered as he calls the Usher on a cell phone.

DE FREYN pauses, looks up from his desk and watches LAFITTE'S exit with narrowed eyes.

> FADE TO BLACK.

> FADE IN:

129 **EXT. PARIS. DRONE SHOTS. EARLY EVENING**

AERIAL

Camera rising past six floors of stone facade, topped by a parapet, then steeply sloping black tiled rooves containing the attics, pierced by rows of 'mansard' windows, then upwards, past ornate brick chimney stacks, rows of squabbling pigeons, finally soaring high above the city, the autumn sun low in the western sky, and the Eiffel Tower casting a elongated finger of shadow towards the maelstrom of silent traffic streaming along the Boulevard de Montparnasse, joined by other relentless traffic streams from Rue D'Odessa and the Rue de Rennes.

DISSOLVE TO:

TITLES AND CREDITS

FADE IN:

EXT. FELL IN CUMBRIA, NEAR ULVERSTON - AFTERNOON

A LATE MODEL LAND ROVER DISCOVERY glides off the fell road onto a viewpoint facing towards Morecambe Bay. Half a mile below the relentless A590 carries its traffic load between Barrow shipyards and the M6. In the background the copse hiding the SINKHOLE that changed BOB and STIV'S lives forever.

CUT TO:

INT. LAND ROVER DISCOVERY - CONTINUOUS

STIV drives with BOB as passenger, both relaxed but the latter with his eyes on the copse in the distance as they come to a stop. STIV with his eye on his ROLEX WATCH.

> STIV
> We're early--

                              BOB
                  What d'you think he wants?

STIV frowns at BOB who's still peering out at the copse in the
distance...

                              STIV
                  Bob?

STIV reaches round and clicks his fingers in BOB'S face bringing
him back around.

                              BOB
                  What?

                              STIV
                  Will you relax?

BOB shakes his head and returns his gaze to the passenger
window. STIV rolls his eyes and checks the REAR VIEW MIRROR.

                          STIV (CONT'D)
                  It's probably a job of some sort.

BOB rears his head and glares at STIV, now smiling excitedly.

                              BOB
                  You reckon..?

                              STIV
                  Make sense wouldn't it? Being all
                  the way out here?

                              BOB
                          (Thoughtful)

                  I guess you are right Stiv. I wonder
                  what...

                    STIV
          we know what don't we. I just hope
          it's something we can do. We are
          not exactly experts are we?
                    (A beat)
          It's exciting though.

                    BOB
          You're like a big kid. Let's see what
          he has to say before we get ahead
          ourselves.

STIV scuffs BOB'S hair, laughing.

                    BOB (CONT'D)
                    (Leaning away)
          Fuck off. Don't you worry about
          stuff? I bloody do. I've been
          dreading the day they would want
          us to do something for the money
          they have been paying.

                    STIV
          Nope, I don't worry, you shouldn't
          either. You'll be fine, I'll take care
          of you.

STIV smirks but BOB ignores him with an eye on the REAR VIEW. A
car is heading towards them on the fell road.

                    BOB
          He's here.

D.I. WILSON pulls in beside them in a BLACK FORD... The trio share
nods and WILSON climbs into the rear seat. They sit sideways on
their seats so they can see him.

                    DI JOE WILSON
          Lads... Nice car,

STIV nods with a grin, but BOB is tense, with his eyes fixed on the FOLDER in WILSON'S hands.

                    DI JOE WILSON (CONT'D)
                         (To both, but holding on Bob)
                    You boys alright? It's been a while...

STIV nods and BOB reluctantly follows suit.

                    DI JOE WILSON (CONT'D)
                    Bob?

                    STIV
                    We're fine! Little nervous but... Ready
                    to do some work. Eh Bob?

BOB nods and reaches for the FOLDER, but WILSON holds it tight.

                    DI JOE WILSON
                    Whoa, in good time Bob. This is
                    serious shit. We have an identified
                    target that we need you guys to
                    take down.

                    You both knew this day would
                    come?

Both boys nod as an air of tension comes over them. BOB takes the FOLDER and reads it with STIV.

                    DI JOE WILSON (CONT'D)
                    We'll go over the outline now, get
                    the feel of things. Then later, we will
                    work up a detailed plan for the HIT.
                    We know the time and location.
                         (A beat)
                    So, some work to do lads.

The car is silent as both MEN read... Bob's eyes rise above the top edge of the folder to meet Wilson's.

                         BOB
          Are you being serious? How the fuck
          are we supposed to--

                     DI JOE WILSON
          In the usual way of these things
          Robert, we walk the ground, devise
          a detailed operational plan,
          execute, and exit. It may have
          escaped you, but this is our business.

                         BOB
                      (To Stiv)
          Stiv, are you reading this?

STIV ignores BOB and continues reading, then goes to the top
page and reads again. Then he fully turns in his seat to look at DI
WILSON.

                         STIV
          Is the Frenchie involved in this?

                     DI JOE WILSON
                  (Nodding gravely, turning
                  towards Stiv)
          He is, yes.

                         STIV
          OK, what's next?

                     DI WILSON
          The HIT is 20 days from today.
          Location is Scotland, a big country
          estate. We will walk the ground in a
          couple of days' time, produce an
          operational plan in 10 days.

                         STIV
          Sounds good.
                  (Glances at Bob)

                                                    163

WILSON nods definitively and takes the FOLDER back before leaving the CAR. Both MEN are fixed on the REAR-VIEW MIRROR as WILSON reverses back out.

> STIV (CONT'D)
> So, here we all are then...

CUT TO:

EXT. FELL IN CUMBRIA, NEAR ULVERSTON - CONTINOUS

The LAND ROVER hums into life, reversing and pulling away, the busy road below and the copse linger as it drives off...

FADE TO BLACK

FADE IN:

EXT. IRIS'S HOUSE. DAY.

Stiv pulls up outside Iris's house just as she is unlocking her door. She has been shopping. She turns with a smile as Stiv slides down his car window.

> IRIS
> Hey boys. Your timing could have
> been better. I've just carried these
> bloody bags back here from town.

Stiv grins as Bob exits the passenger door.

> STIV
> Good for the figure Iris, plenty of
> exercise to keep those looks.

Iris pirouettes with a pout.

> IRIS
> Is it working then Stephen?

164

                              BOB
              Oh for fuck's sake...

                              IRIS
                           (To Bob)

              Language Bobby. I'm your Mother
              you know.
                          (To Stiv)
              Well come on, just cos' you are my
              son's friend, doesn't mean you can't
              fancy his Mum...

Stiv blushes, the banter has gone past the point he can cope with
it. Iris laughs, its all very familiar.

                        IRIS (CONT'D)
              Are you coming in for a drink and a
              digestive then?

                              BOB
              He's busy.
                          (To Stiv)
              You are busy, right?

                             STIV
              Yeah OK. I'll see you Iris.

                          (To Bob)
              Later mate.

Stiv slides up his window. Pulls away. Iris, her hand still on the door
handle, regards her son.

                             IRIS
              I see you are your usual bundle of
              joy then.

Bob hefts shopping bags with ill humour.

                                                    CUT TO:

                                                    165

INT. IRIS'S HOUSE KITCHEN. DAY. CONTINUOUS

Iris busies herself unpacking plastic bags.

> IRIS
>
> Kettle Bob...
> (A beat)
> What's happening Bobby?
> Something has changed since this
> morning. You were happy as Larry,
> now you look like you lost a quid
> and found sixpence.

> BOB
>
> Aw, nothing Mum. I'm OK. Its just
> him, he sometimes winds me up
> with all that banter with you. He
> fancies you something rotten, but its
> all bravado. You make him worse,
> acting like you are sixteen.

Iris pauses surrounded by packages on the worktop.

> IRIS
>
> Come on Bob, I have known Stiv as
> long as I've known you. He's not my
> son, but he is in almost every other
> way. I love him. And I love the way
> he looks out for you. I know its all
> loose banter, but its part of the way
> we all co-exist you know.
> (A beat)
> You know you can talk to me about
> anything don't you Bob. If there's
> something that...

> BOB
>
> There's nothing. Leave it Mother. I'm
> fine.

Bob abruptly turns and leaves the kitchen. Iris looks at the open doorway for several seconds with a worried expression.

NEXT DAY

INT. IRIS'S HOUSE. FRONT ROOM. DAY.

Bob is sprawled on the settee reading GUNS&AMMO magazine. His mobile trills. Stiv's number displays on the screen.

PHONE CONVERSATION

> BOB
> Hi mate, you ok.

> STIV
> Wilson rang. We are heading north
> to Scotland tomorrow Bob. I'll
> pick you 0900 ish. You don't need
> anything.

> BOB
> That's quick... I thought...

> STIV
> Don't think. Nine o'clock
> tomorrow, yeh?

Bob's cell phone screen clears as Stiv hangs. Bob stares at it for a beat, then idly picks up his Magazine. He looks at a page for a few seconds, then throws the magazine across the room.

FADE OUT

FADE IN

EXT. BEDGOWAN COUNTRY ESTATE. SCOTLAND.

Stiv parks the Disco on the public carpark and he, Bob and
DI Wilson exit, entering the small restaurant to the side of the
Mansion's main entrance

CUT TO:

INT. BEDGOWAN ESTATE. SCOTLAND. RESTAURANT

They take a table and order food. Many tables are vacant. Wilson
glances round, then speaks in low voice.

> DI JOE WILSON
>
> This place has been owned by the
> McTavish family since the 1400's.
> 10k plus acres of woodland, main
> house and stables. It was a war
> recuperation hospital during the
> latter part of WW2. The family are
> well connected to many of our
> major political figures, both here
> and abroad.
>   (a beat)
> They are Old Conservatives, so they
> have an agenda of wrecking, or
> at least slowing down the UK's exit
> from the EU, if they can. The family
> also have relatives in the Dordogne
> region of central France.

Stiv and Bob are silent, both slightly overawed by the situation
they have found themselves in.

> DI JOE WILSON (CONT'D)
> We are going to have a look around
> today and scout the area a bit. See
> if anything occurs to you guys as
> to how we might do this. We have

168

around 9 days to come up with a
working plan.

STIV
(Resentful tone)
You do know that we are fucking
amateurs at this. You know exactly
how we got into this situation, and it
wasn't through choice.

DI JOE WILSON
(Gravely)
Oh, I think there have been choices
made Stephen. You are driving a
very nice car, and you've had a
significant retainer salary paid for
several months now, and nothing
whatsoever to do for it. This day was
always going to come...
(a beat, business-like)

Look, both of you have significant
advantages to operate in this
scenario.

For a start, you have no motive.
Nothing drives a homicide detective
crazy like not understanding why an
executive action was taken.

You both have a shooting
background and are country guys
who are at home in the woods, so
working as beaters gives you both
a good reason to be here. Many
beaters follow the big shoots around
the country during the season.
(a beat, harder tone)
Listen, I understand your situation,
if you guys are morally squeamish
about this, then we should abandon

this right now. We'll all have some
nice tea and buns today, and then
go home.

Mind you, our French Master might
not be too pleased, his 'protection'
will be immediately withdrawn, and
I imagine he will want his money
back.

Remember, without his 'protection'
you will be guests of Her Majesty
almost immediately, and lads, I
would be the one who'd arrest you.

There is silence. DI Wilson stirs his tea thoughtfully, then pushes the
plate of cakes towards Stiv.

                    DI JOE WILSON (CONT'D)
                    (Conciliatory tone)
          These scones are wonderful
          Stephen, Robert...?
                                                        CUT TO:

EXT. ULVERSTON PREMIER INN HOTEL CAR PARK. DAY

A black late model Audi 4*4 pulls into a parking place. Michael
O'Leary (Irish, 50s) takes a small hold-all, closes the tailgate,
does a slow turn around, taking in vehicles, passers-by, windows
overlooking the carpark. He glances up at the HOAD LIGHTHOUSE
on the hill above the town, then crosses the open space of the
carpark and enters the building.

INT. ULVERSTON PREMIER INN RECEPTION. DAY

The receptionist greets O'Leary as he breasts the counter.

                    MICHAEL O'LEARY
          Good day to you Ma'am, Michael
          O'Leary. I pre-booked.

170

                    RECEPTIONIST
                (Consulting computer)
        Oh yes, Mr O'Leary, Belfast? Did you
        have a pleasant trip?

                    MICHAEL O'LEARY
        I did so, thank you. Its good to be
        back here in Ulverston again.

                    RECEPTIONIST
                (Busy with documents)
        You know the town then Mr
        O'Leary?

                    MICHAEL O'LEARY
        I do, from many years back. Certainly
        this hotel wasn't here back then.

O'Leary picks up external door key and plastic room entry card
and proceeds to...

INT. ULVERSTON PREMIER INN, ROOM 17. DAY

O'Leary unpacks his hold-all, checks out the room and small
bathroom. Goes to the window, trying the opening sash, finding
it restricted to opening more than 3 inches. His car was parked
below the window, beyond he could see the canal and towpath.
He drops onto the bed, pulling out his cell phone.

                    MICHAEL O'LEARY
                (On phone)
        Its myself. I'm here.
                (Listening)
        No, no-one yet. Just checked in. I'll
        have a ride around the area later
        and get the lay of the land a bit.
        I'm going to talk to the two divers
        first off.

        OK then

O'Leary puts his cell phone away, leans back, then grimaces, rolls over slightly and removes a GLOCK 17 handgun from the back of his waistband. He springs the magazine, works the slide to eject the shell in the breech, leans back and closes his eyes.

EXT. BEDGOWAN ESTATE WOODS. SCOTLAND.

Stiv, Bob and DI Wilson are sitting in a wooded area looking down on a small open field through the trees.

> DI JOE WILSON
> (Indicating with a sweeping
> motion)
> Down there is where the shooters
> will be located. They will be spread
> right along the field approx. 30M
> apart, standing at numbered pegs.
> They will face this wooded high
> ground where we are sitting. The
> beaters will drive game towards the
> guns, so any flying game will take
> off out of the treetops above us. The
> shooters will be looking into the sky
> for targets.
> (a beat)
> Your specific target will be allocated
> Peg 16, which will be close to the
> centre of the field. Special guests
> always get the centre ground,
> easiest shots.

Wilson points to where Peg 16 will be located, turns to Stiv and Bob.

> DI JOE WILSON (CONT'D)
> Thoughts....

Stiv is highly alert, scanning the ground, trees, lines of fire, beater's pathway, positions of other shooters.

                    STIV
        I'll need to step it out, but it looks
        like straightforward shot from here.
        Around 120M. Piece of piss from a
        shooting point of view.

Bob who had been silent and thoughtful, finally spoke.

                    BOB
        How do we get away? The shot is
        easy, I can see that. Remember,
        we will be in the woods with 30- or
        40-armed game shooters, plus
        maybe 50 beaters.
                (A beat)
        A lot of people.

DI Wilson is silent. Bob looks at him. Stiv is thoughtful, looking
around, then he wanders off, poking around in bushes below the
crest of the hill. Looking critically at various angles downrange.
The other two watch. After ten minutes or so, he returns to the
other two men, drops down beside them.

                    STIV
        Listen guys, can I make a
        suggestion... I think I might know
        how we might do this.

DI Wilson and Bob look at Stiv expectantly. He hunkers down,
leaning in.

                    STIV (CONT'D)
        How about this...
                (warming to his task)

        I will take the shot. Bob is backup,
        he will only shoot if I miss, and I
        won't miss. I will lay up in a gillie
        24hrs before, and NOT SIGN UP as a
        beater at all. Bob will be a beater,
        working the game towards and

past me, and watching my back at the same time. I will have the two rifles with me, so that Bob could be searched afterwards if necessary.
(a beat, eye contact)
I'll take the shot when everyone else is shooting as well... that's important.

No-one around here will have any idea what has happened, or even where a shot has come from. There will be lots of shooting noise going on, so the gunshot sound is not an issue, no need for a silencer. I will go for a single upper body shot through his clothes, so it won't be immediately apparent that he has been shot.
(a beat, thoughtful)
We'll need a high velocity, small caliber round. Small entry wound, not much bigger exit. Looking at the angles from here, the round will end up a long way down there in the woods. They'll never find it.
(A beat, thinking)
I reckon a 223, or even a 017 calibre. Flat trajectory, hardly any drop at 120M. With shooting clothes on and a Barbour jacket, it won't be immediately apparent what's wrong with him.
(A beat, grinning)
Nobody will be looking for a gunshot wound immediately will they...?

In the confusion following the shot, I will merge with other beaters and disappear. Bob will stay, acting all confused etc.

> (Looking at both Wilson and
> Bob, smiling triumphantly)
> Even if someone saw me, what
> would they see? A man with a gun
> who looks like everyone else.
>
> That's it, simple. What do you think?

Bob looks at Stiv with wonder. He looks downrange for a long moment, judging angles, then back to Stiv, then he looks at DI Wilson and slowly nods. DI Wilson smiles slowly. Bob looks relieved, and for the first time all day, allows a vague semblance of a grin across his features.

> DI JOE WILSON
> You are my boys!

DI Wilson gets to his feet, he steps forwards and hugs Stiv briefly, beams at Bob.

> DI JOE WILSON (CONT'D)
> You are my fabulous boys!

> CUT TO:

EXT. AERIAL SHOT OF VAST COUNTRY ESTATE, SCOTLAND

Camera lifts from the wooded copse, rising high above a country area, finally showing a motorway network at the edge of the screen.

> DISSOLVE TO:

EXT. WALNEY DIVE CENTER. DAY

O'Leary's noses the big Audi to the front gate of the Dive Centre. He can see Mike Kramer working at a bench in the yard. Kramer looks towards him straightening up as O'Leary exits the car.

                    MICHAEL O'LEARY
          Good day to you Sir, I hope you
          are well. Its Mike isn't it? Do you
          remember me from back in the
          day? We share a name.

Kramer makes no effort to shake the proffered hand.

                    MIKE KRAMER
          I wondered how long it would be
          before you showed up.

                    MICHAEL O'LEARY
          Like the proverbial bad penny, I
          guess Mike.
                    (Looking around)
          It's a nice place you have here. Is
          business good?

                    MIKE KRAMER
          What do you want Mr O'Leary?

O'Leary shrugs with good humour.

                    MICHAEL O'LEARY
          Oh, nothing much.
                    (Grins)
          118 M16 Assault Rifles and 50k rounds
          of 7.62 brass will do for a start. You've
          had £20k cash paid already, and
          I imagine you have been keeping
          Daniel's cash safe for me...?
                    (A beat)
          Did you haul them up yet?

Several meters away, the office door opens, and Dave Geddings
emerges. O'Leary moves imperceptibly where he can face both
men clearly. Dave approaches.

DAVE GEDDINGS
You going to introduce us then
Mike?

MIKE KRAMER
(Eyes on O'Leary)
Mr Michael O'Leary from The
Emerald Isle. This is Dave Geddings,
the Proprietor of this establishment.
(A beat)
Mr O'Leary is here for his guns, and
also some cash money that he
thinks we have been safe-keeping.

DAVE GEDDINGS
Shall we go inside? Tea?

Dave turns and leads the way. O'Leary follows, Mike following
behind.

INT. WALNEY DIVE CENTER. OFFICE. DAY.

The three men sit with mugs of tea. O'Leary is totally at ease,
ignoring the high tension in the room.

MICHAEL O'LEARY
This is nice, thank you Dave. It's
good to meet you both. Daniel
spoke very highly of you.
(A beat)
We have a certain amount of
anecdotal information already, but
it would be good to get your take on
events to date, if you wouldn't mind.

Dave raises his eyebrows at O'Leary, glancing at Mike.

DAVE GEDDINGS
What information do you have
'already'? As far as I know the

police have not been forthcoming,
only to say that investigations are
on-going - mainly overseas.

O'Leary drinks, then carefully placing his cup on the dusty
desktop, leans forward to regard both men with his pale blue eyes
crinkled in concentration.

                    MICHAEL O'LEARY
          I have a whole range of faults, like
          all of us. One of my problems is that I
          have a limited tolerance of hostility.
          It goes against the country Irish
          value system imbued by my family.
                    (A beat)
          I have come here, open handed, to
          complete the work that my friend
          and colleague Daniel started. I will
          do that, make no mistake gentlemen.
          I hope that you believe me.

O'Leary leans slightly forward, his eyes switching from Kramer to
Geddings. He looks around the cluttered room filled stacked with
diving paraphernalia. He gets up and wanders around with the
two men's eyes following him.

There is silence while he pokes here and there. After several beats
he turns to face Geddings and Kramer and stamps his feet down
hard on the floorboards. The sound is hollow, indicating a sub-
floor. He smiles broadly, returning to his seat.

                    MICHAEL O'LEARY (CONT'D)
          I imagine you two lads are tough
          old boys. Ex-paras, used to physical
          hard work, handy in a pub when
          it all goes off on a Saturday night.
          But you are not criminals, you don't
          think like that.

O'Leary points downwards to the floor and grins.

                    MICHAEL O'LEARY (CONT'D)
            Down there, right?

Both men return his gaze, impassive.

                    MICHAEL O'LEARY (CONT'D)
            A hero of mine, Demosthenes, once
            said 'Clouds cannot cover secret
            places, nor denials conceal truth'
                    (A beat)

            Now I would like to work with you
            gentlemen and pay you a fair and
            equitable fee for the privilege.
            I would also like it if you pay me
            the same respect that I give to
            yourselves. Please do not make the
            mistake that many do, and think I
            am an idiot from the backwoods of
            Killarney. I am not that.

O'Leary takes a sip from his mug, leaning back, regarding both
men with a faint smile curving his lips. The room is silent for several
beats, then Dave gets to his feet.

                    DAVE GEDDINGS
            More tea, I think.

Mike Kramer is silent. Dave rinses the cups, makes more tea and
returns to his seat.

                    DAVE GEDDINGS (CONT'D)
            18 guns are down there in the sub-
            floor. Two were left at the sinkhole,
            these are with the police. We were
            paid £20k by Daniel.

                    MIKE KRAMER
            Dave...

Dave holds his hand up palm outwards to Mike, silencing him.

DAVE GEDDINGS
We recovered £180k in cash from
Daniel's van. We have spent £20k
of that, so we have £160k left. That's
down there with the guns.

Mike Kramer throws his mug across the room violently and slumps
in his seat, glaring his anger at Dave. O'Leary ignores Kramer,
nodding gravely at Dave Geddings.

MICHAEL O'LEARY
Thank you, David. I appreciate your
candour.
(To Mike)
Mike, I do understand your slight
annoyance. In your position I would
probably feel the same.

MIKE KRAMER
(Half out of his seat)
Fuck you O'Leary, you...

MICHAEL O'LEARY
(Both hands up, palm
outwards)

I know about your boy, and his
partner, the two young shooters.
(A beat)
Guys, I know, OK! Handy lads,
them two!

Both Mike and Dave react in shock. Mike Kramer settles back into
his seat.

DAVE GEDDINGS
How could you know that? The
police have not said anything...

                    MICHAEL O'LEARY
          I know, and they won't. The two boys
          may fulfil a different destiny. I will say
          no more about that,
                    (Turning to face Mike)

          and I strongly suggest that you do
          not question them.
                    (A beat)

          So, £160k left eh, well you have been
          delightfully circumspect gentlemen,
          I'm not sure I would have had the
          same constraint.
                    (A beat)

          So, my offer is this, you owe me 118
          guns and brass. Keep the money.

O'Leary leaned back, smiling at the two white faces across the
dusty desk.

                    MICHAEL O'LEARY (CONT'D)
          Best to keep things simple, my old
          Dad used to say.

EXT. IRIS'S HOUSE. EARLY DAWN

Bob is outside his house, sitting on a pile of equipment in the pre-
dawn gloom lit by orange streetlight. Presently Stiv's Discovery
draws up next to him, window sliding down.

                    STIV
          Morning.

No reply from Bob. Stiv reaches down to the dashboard and the
tailgate opens. Bob loads his equipment into the rear of the Disco,
gets morosely into the passenger seat, hunkering down.

STIV (CONT'D)
Yes well, good morning Stiv! How
lovely to see you, are you well? Isn't
it a beautiful day. Thank you for
picking me up.

Stiv grimaces at a silent Bob in the passenger seat, releases the
handbrake, indicates and pulls away.

EXT. M6 MOTORWAY NORTH OF KENDAL. DAY

Aerial shot: Disco indicating left, speeding down M6 slipway,
heading north towards Scotland. Camera pulling back to show
motorway signage.

DISSOLVE TO:

EXT. BEDGOWAN ESTATE, SCOTLAND. FRONT COURTYARD

DRONE SHOT, CIRCLING

The vast country estate of Bedgowan is crowded and busy as
an aristocratic shooting party mill around the large gravel area
in front of the main entrance. Parked to one side are dozens of
large 4*4s and limousines with uniformed drivers standing around
in small groups eating and drinking. The larger group of men and
women in the centre of the gravel are dressed in tweeds and
country clothing. They are animated, talking, gossiping. Servants
circulate with trays of food and drinks.

CUT TO:

The camera moves over the roof of the great house. Behind are
stables and outbuildings. Here another smaller crowd dressed
in country clothing is standing respectfully being addressed
by a Head Keeper. They are BEATERS and PERSONAL CADDYS
receiving instructions for the event. The rear courtyard is filled with

4*4s, some with trailers carrying guns, ammunition and assorted equipment.

CAMERA ZOOMS DOWN TO:

EXT. BEDGOWAN ESTATE, SCOTLAND. REAR COURTYARD

Bob is standing in the crowd of beaters. He is dressed in heavy country clothing, carrying a shoulder bag and a shepherd's crook. He looks exactly like everyone else. The Head Keeper is standing in front of a large whiteboard addressing a diagram of the estate, and the organization of the shoot.

Shooter's pegs are indicated on the diagram with coloured flags, Bob focuses on Peg 16 as the Head Keeper begins his instructions.

> HEAD KEEPER
> Thanks everyone, particularly to
> those beaters who have travelled
> from outside the locality today.
> This is an important event, not
> just for Bedgowan, but for the
> UK's corporate business. Several
> international figures from showbiz
> and politics are here today to enjoy
> our shoot, and your contribution is
> part of what makes that possible.
> (A beat)
> Before I get into today's operational
> detail, I know that you all know
> this, but with apologies, I'll repeat it
> again.
> (Eye contact)
> Do not break formation as you BEAT
> towards the guns. The guns will be
> focused in the sky above you where
> their targets will appear. THEY WILL
> NOT BE LOOKING AT YOU AS YOU
> APPROACH.
> (Eye contact)

They do not even think about you.
Their concentration is mainly in two
areas - (1) They want to look good to
their peers and caddies, hit plenty
targets, and thereby survive the
drinks party ribbing afterwards. (2)
The showbiz and politicians all have
their specific agendas, which have
little to do with shooting game in the
woods.
>   (Grim smile, nodding, looking
>   around the group)
Breaking the formation of the
advancing line of beaters is
breaking your contract with
Bedgowan. It can kill you, and
unwittingly cause someone else to
do the deed. So, stay in line please.
>   (A beat)
Right, that said, let's get on with
details. Emergencies, I'm not
expecting any but...

SOUND FADES. Camera rises into drone shot.

CUT TO:

EXT. BEDGOWAN ESTATE. SCOTLAND. COPSE OVERLOOKING PEG 16

Stiv is bedded down in a full Gillie suit. He is totally merged into
his surroundings in light brush. He has been in position for the past
12 hrs. A Sako 223 rifle with a 10-round magazine of high velocity
cartridges is held loosely against his shoulder. The rifle is topped
by a Hawke 4-25*52 telescopic sight. The rifle is dead zeroed at
120M. The image of Peg 16 crystal sharp though the telescopic
sight optics.

The technicalities of the shot have engrossed Stiv and the
nervousness he expected to feel has simply not happened.
Despite being laid up in the same position for hours, he is feeling

fully alert and filled with an excitement and sense of being and purpose that he has never experienced before. The woods are quiet and still with no sign of the mayhem and frenetic activity that is about to take place.

CUT TO:

EXT. BEDGOWAN ESTATE, SCOTLAND

AERIAL SHOTS

The Head Keeper finishes addressing everyone and the Beaters and Caddy's move out of the rear courtyard. They are split into smaller groups, each going to their allocated start positions. All have mobile phones.

The BEATERS and CADDYS board vehicles and a cavalcade of 4*4s stream out into the estate. The cavalcade split into two groups, Beaters heading away to their start points. The Caddy's converging onto the pegged areas where shooters will be positioned. Each peg allocated with its own 4*4 parked nearby, and personal Gun Caddy/Loader.

CUT TO:

EXT. BEDGOWAN ESTATE. SCOTLAND. COPSE OVERLOOKING PEG 16

Stiv watches from his higher ground position as a new Range Rover Evoque parks 20M away from Peg 16. The Caddy exits, walks to the rear and raises the tailgate. The Caddy picks up an Over/Under shotgun and walks to the Peg. He hefts the gun a few times, swinging upwards into the sky above the trees.

Stiv centres his telescopic sight crosshairs onto the Caddy's chest, refocusing crystal sharp. Stiv experiences a massive adrenaline surge, knowing that his preparation and positioning has been good.

CUT TO:

EXT. BEDGOWAN ESTATE. SCOTLAND. FRONT COURTYARD

The Head Keeper circulates the crowd of SHOOTERS as servants collect plates and champagne glasses. He passes out Peg numbers as he circulates, engaging short respectful banter here and there, acknowledging shooters that he knows from previous game-shoots, welcoming new shooters. The hum of conversation has now died down and a sense of expectation is settling over the crowd.

Some of the non-shooting crowd withdraw, waving and smiling as they ascend the steps on the main entrance. The shooters mill around, boarding several large purpose made vehicles to transport them to their shooting positions. Finally, everyone has boarded.

CUT TO:

AERIAL

The large vehicles make their way in convoy from the Main House courtyard and thread their way through copses of trees and open fields towards the PEGGED area.

CUT TO:

EXT. BEDGOWAN ESTATE. SCOTLAND. WOODS

Bob has positioned himself to beat towards Peg 16. He is wound up and tense. He has resisted any casual conversation with other beaters, keeping his responses mono-syllabic and terse. His start-point is several hundred meters away from where he knows Stiv is positioned. He and Stiv have not communicated by mobile cell phone for the past 24hrs on DI Wilson's instructions.

Bob's phone vibrates silently in his pocket, he glances at the Head Keeper's name on the screen. The message 'all beaters move forward NOW!' shows. Bob pockets his mobile and steps forward into low lying brush, beating the bracken lightly with his stick.

CUT TO:

EXT. BEDGOWAN ESTATE. SCOTLAND. COPSE OVERLOOKING PEG 16

Stiv gets his first sight of his target as the Frenchman is dropped off at his peg by the transporter.

The French Politician is late 50s' urbane and aristocratic and perfectly dressed for the shoot. Through the 'scope' Stiv watches light-hearted exchanges between the Target and the allocated Caddy, the Caddy respectful but authoritative. Silent with distance, Stiv watches the Caddy explaining something about the gun, then indicating skywards, sweeping his arm from right to left, momentarily looking directly facing Stiv, his face suddenly sharp in the scope's image.

Stiv jumps involuntarily, then relaxes again with a rueful grin to himself. The Frenchman attentively follows his Caddy's instructions, nodding with approval, then taking the shotgun himself, swings it upwards and across a few times, nodding appreciatively to the Caddy. Stiv knows that the Frenchman will be told clearly to always shoot into the sky, and never horizontally to where a beater might be in the line of fire.

Stiv waits for shooting to begin. His cue is to shoot when all shooters are fully engaging targets, but before the beaters get too close to his position.

CUT TO:

EXT. BEDGOWAN ESTATE. SCOTLAND. WOODS

Bob draws nearer to the Crest of the hill where he knows that Stiv is concealed.

CUT TO:

AERIAL TRACKING ALONG THE LINE OF PEGS

The first game birds of the day begin to rise through the trees, along the line of pegs sporadic shooting begins with white puffs of cordite skywards.

CUT TO:

EXT. BEDGOWAN ESTATE. SCOTLAND. COPSE OVERLOOKING PE...

Stiv is focused. Shooting has started 200M further away down the line of pegs. The Frenchman is rapt with tension - waiting, his gun held at high port, his eyes searching the treeline for his first game bird targets, fluttering dots rising black against the sky. Behind him, the Caddy also watches the treeline, clusters of red cartridges clutched between his knuckles.

The Frenchman shoulders the gun, his first two fast shots merging now into the almost continuous sound of gunshots engaging along the whole line of pegs. He grimaces. The Caddy steps forward as two ejected shells fly backwards, blue cordite smoke curling from the shotgun breech. Two new shells are immediately breech-ed, the gun snapped closed, the Frenchman, breathless, eyes skywards, seeking his next targets.

CUT TO:

SLO-MO SEQUENCE

Stiv's cross hairs are positioned onto the centre of Frenchman's chest. The Frenchman shoots again twice, bringing down his gun, snapping it open, ejected shells flying backwards, he turns slightly towards the Caddy, his chest opening up. The Caddy slips two new shells into the breech, the Frenchman smiles at the Caddy - excited.

CUT TO:

Stiv shoots, the world stands still.

188

The Frenchman pauses, his smile fading. Stiv's small calibre slug has passed through his chest with minimum body shock, destroying his heart, exiting way down the valley. The Frenchman stands still. He looks momentarily at the Caddy, they lock eyes, the Caddy questioning.

CUT TO:

The Frenchman, shock in his eyes, exhales and slowly sinks vertically down into a squatting position. The Caddy shocked, reaches down to support him, taking the open gun from him, a look of concern on his face. Neither of the two men look in Stiv's direction.

END SLO-MO SEQUENCE

CUT TO:

EXT. BEDGOWAN ESTATE. SCOTLAND. WOODS

Two hundred meters to the left of beaters, the Head Keeper pauses, suddenly alert, his face upwards, head to one side. He thinks he heard a rifle shot, a higher pitched crack in the midst of the cacophony of deeper shotgun notes. He shakes his head - doesn't make any sense.

CUT TO:

EXT. BEDGOWAN ESTATE. SCOTLAND. WOODS - BOB

Bob, fully tuned, hears Stiv's shot clearly. He hears it as a fully separated single shot which echoes sharp and fully defined in his ear drums. He stops dead, his eyes on the crest of the hill in front of him. Other beaters 30M to his right and left continue forward without a pause - they don't react. Glancing both ways, heart racing, Bob steps forward again towards the crest staying in perfect line with the beater formation, his stick flailing the brush.

CUT TO:

Stiv exhales, certain of his shot, he immediately ejects his magazine, picking up the spent shell. Glancing around, then rolling to his left he slides his rifle into a gun slip, unzipping his Gillie, cramming it into a shoulder bag. No beaters have yet emerged over the crest of the hill behind him.

Below him, The Frenchman and the Caddy are sitting together on the grass. The Caddy now supporting the Frenchman, looking with concern at his protege's face, reaching for his cell phone. No-one looks towards Stiv. Along the line of pegs, the other shooters are still completely focused on the skyline and targets, the cacophony of shooting continuous - unabated.

Stiv lays in cover, totally still. Beaters begin to crest the hillside behind him. He recognizes Bob coming towards him. He stays put. Below him, the Caddy is now waving an arm, trying to attract the attention of other shooters and Caddies. The Frenchman is now flat to the ground.

The two beaters on each side of Bob see the Caddy waving, but stand with uncertainty, extremely reluctant to break formation and the 'Beater's Protocol'.

By now, several beaters along the line begin to realize that something is amiss, and the line begins to fragment. Some beaters stopping, calling to each other.

After several moments of agonized indecision, several beaters on each side of Bob are making calls on their cell phones, a couple of other beaters commit the mortal sin of breaking formation protocol and run pass Stiv's hidden position, jogging down the slope through the trees down to the pegged open field area where the Frenchman's Caddy is waving. In this confusion, Stiv rises to his feet, glances briefly at Bob, then walks casually away. He is dressed exactly like the other beaters.

CUT TO:

EXT. BEDGOWAN ESTATE. BOB. SHOOTERS PEGS

Bob looks away from Stiv's receding figure and carries on walking downwards through the trees to the open field area and Peg 16. Several beaters and two more Caddies now cluster around the Frenchman who is lying quiet and still on the grass. Everyone is confused. No-one knows what has happened. Along the long line of pegs shooting continues although some of the other shooters are becoming aware that something has happened at Peg 16. Various people begin to make mobile calls.

CUT TO:

EXT. BEDGOWAN ESTATE. HEAD KEEPER

Two hundred meters away, the Head Keeper is frowning, looking quizzically along the line of shooters as the rhythm of shots changes. His phone trills in his pocket.

CUT TO:

EXT. BEDGOWAN ESTATE. BOB.

Bob watches, he is standing apart from the cluster of people around the Frenchman. He also wants to make a mobile call but resists the urge.

CUT TO:

AERIAL SHOT ZOOMING UP

The camera rises up from the cluster of people around the Frenchman's body, clearing the trees and upwards, finally high above the Bedgowan Estate Game Shoot. White puffs of silent gun-smoke still squirting upwards at the extreme ends of the pegs. Clusters of people are converging onto Peg 16 from all directions.

The camera rises further, the Bedgowan Main House complex comes into view. A 4*4 Range Rover leaves the courtyard at speed, racing towards the Game Shoot, and Peg 16.

The camera rises up further until the edge of the screen shows the M6 Motorway system several miles to the west, the main arterial traffic-way linking Scotland and London.

FADE TO BLACK

INT. M. DE FRYN'S CENTRAL PARIS APARTMENT

MEDIUM/CLOSE; MOVING AROUND APARTMENT

M. De Freyn woke early as was his habit. His apartment was one of several in a great house on the Ile Saint Luis, one of two islands in the River Seine. The Ile Saint Luis is located within the 4th Arrondissement of Paris, between Saint Germain des Pres and Le Marais.

Hi role as a senior minister in the French Government took him around the World in the splendour of fast jets and fabulous luxurious palaces, but he was happy to be back in Paris. He was not particularly a morning person, but he preferred to wake up early to enjoy some time to himself before making himself available to the daily intensity of political life.

CUT TO:

FROM BEHIND DE FREYN - THROUGH SALON WINDOW

From his floor to ceiling drawing room window the Seine's grey waters churned at the end of his unruly garden. He could see the Pont la Turnelle footbridge and on the far bank, along the street, his favourite Michelin Starred Restaurant 'La Tour d'Argent'.

CUT TO:

KITCHEN AREA

M. De Freyn enjoyed the company of beautiful women, but not to the extent he wanted to marry one and share his intensely private life. Neither did he employ a personal servant, as did many of his colleagues. With precision, he lit an aromatic candle in a simple silver holder, and prepared a coffee pot of Italian Mocha, black, no sugar. His breakfast was simple, fresh bread with salted butter, and blueberry pancakes. If he had early morning meetings, he would forego breakfast and collect croissants from Le Boulanger de la Tour across the footbridge close by.

CUT TO:

SITTING AT TABLE, CONSULTING DIARIES/DOCUMENTS

Glancing at his cell phone online diary, his meetings on this day were few, but of momentous importance. As he ate, he re-read with satisfaction, the handwritten note from Inspector Jean Lafitte. He had harboured nagging doubts regarding Lafitte, but on this occasion he had delivered his mission impeccably. The problematic diplomat had been removed quickly and efficiently. Another highly placed traitor still had to identified, but for the moment, De Freyn felt satisfied that he had good news to report to Monsieur Le President when they met later in the day.

In the centre of his table, unopened, lay an embossed envelope. His breakfast table's contents had been arranged carefully around it. It bore the crest of the President's Office. De Freyn regarded it gravely. He knew its content, but was savouring the moment to read the text, and run his fingers across the spider like handwritten signature of the most powerful man in France.

De Freyn finished his leisurely breakfast, sipped his coffee, and finally slid the crested envelope towards himself. He broke the bright red waxed Presidential seal and unfolded the single sheet of heavy paper.

The single paragraph of black type and an inked signature was a fait accompli, it placed De Freyn three positions from the pinnacle of French politics.

The 'Minister for Europe and Foreign Affairs'.

The re-shuffle, ahead of the oncoming Presidential elections was not yet announced, his acceptance however was not in any doubt, and it would be ratified later in the day with a brief meeting and a handshake with M. President.

De Freyn leaned forward wetting his fingertips and extinguished the candle, inhaling and relishing the curdling white smoke drifting above the sunlit breakfast table.

FADE TO BLACK:

NEWS BULLETIN (BLACK SCREEN)

A French political figure was shot dead while taking part in a Game Shoot on the Bedgowan Country Estate in Perthshire. The Man, who has not yet been named, was a guest of the McTavish Family and had attended the high-profile Game Shoot Event along with several other members of the British Government and show business figures.

Police have condoned off the area and prevented any aerial photography as an intensive investigation is launched. The British PM has contacted the French President to offer his condolences as an international political storm speculates that this was an assassination hit on British soil.

Our Scottish Correspondent Hamish McLeod is at Bedgowan...

CONTINUOUS

INT. O'LEARY'S AUDI 4*4. CUMBRIA COUNTRY RD, NEAR ULVERSTON. DAY.

O'Leary switches off his car radio, smiling gently to himself. He slows the Audi to a crawl to pass several mounted riders. One by one they acknowledged his courtesy as he passes them. A beautiful blonde smile dazzlingly down at him from her mount and O'Leary is tempted to follow up. He flashes a crooked grin but gradually accelerates away.

CAR PHONE

MICHAEL O'LEARY
Benny, Michael.
(Listening)
I'm OK yes. Did you get the news?
(Listening)
Don't know yet, info is sketchy but
possible it could be our boys. More
later. Is Georgie OK?
(A beat)
OK, Be safe Benny.

O'Leary glanced in the mirror at the receding blonde rider with a
regretful smile playing on his lips.

EXT. IRIS'S HOUSE. STREET. DAY

Stiv's Land Rover indicates and pulls into the kerb. Bob exits,
rummages in the rear and piles his gear by the front door. He
comes round to stand by the driver's door.

STIV
You feeling any better about
stuff now?

BOB
(Acknowledging)
It was good mate. You did good. I'm
not sure I would have pulled it off
like you did. Wilson is over the moon.

STIV
You'll be questioned Bobby, its not
over and done yet you know.

BOB
Yep, I know that. I was a beater,
that's it. I didn't see anything
unusual, I thought maybe he had a
heart attack. I'm solid Stiv, totally.

                                STIV
        And you didn't see me right? Never
        went. I'm down with a sore throat.
        We clear?

                                BOB
        Clear.

Stiv's window slides silently up, and the 4*4 glides away along the
street between the parked vehicles. Bob watches it go, suddenly
tired, he collects his gear by the front door, feeling for a key.

                                                        DISSOLVE:

SKY NEWS (NEWSREEL FOOTAGE)

In other news, the French re-shuffle is gathering pace. In total
there are more than 1200 announced positions from which
candidates have withdrawn, resigned or been terminated as well
as holdovers from the previous administration. The latest Cabinet
Level appointment is M. Jacques De Freyn who will controversially
move to being Minister for Europe and Foreign Affairs. De Freyn,
former Colonel in the Foreign Legion has ruffled a few feathers in
his meteoric rise to being No3 in the French Political machine.

CONTINUOUS: CAMERA PULLS BACK TO REVEAL TV IN LAFITTE'S
PARIS OFFICE.

INT. LAFFITE'S PARIS OFFICE. DAY

Lafitte flicks the TV to silent as the screen shows clusters of
microphones thrust towards De Freyn's limousine door as he exits
at the Elysée Palace. Lafitte watches for several beats, drumming
his fingers, then spins his chair to the window, his eyes, as always,
drawn to the empty sky where the massive Notre Dam spire once
dominated the cityscape.

His cell phone is face up on his empty desktop. His hair lifts on
the back of his neck as he watches the handset intently. It trills,
vibrating sideways.

PHONE CONVERSATION

                    JEAN LAFITTE
        Sir.

                    M.DE FREYN
        My congratulations Lafitte.
        Impeccable!
                    JEAN LAFITTE
        I was just watching Sky News Sir.
        My congratulations to you in your
        new role transforming France's
        ideological journey into the
        unknown,
                    (Smiling)
        ...and surrounded by the unknowing.

                    M.DE FREYN
        Yes Lafitte. Your understanding of
        our task is poetic and as well as
        astute. Enough! We have a new
        objective, but this specific project
        must be brought to its logical
        conclusion now. CLEAN SKINS have
        a 'once only' application, after that
        they are no longer CLEAN.

                    JEAN LAFITTE
        I understand Sir. It will be done.

The handset pulses and the screen clears. Lafitte tosses it irritably
onto his desktop where it slides to a stop, screen still back-lit. He
watches it until the handset dims, finally turning black.

                                                        CUT TO:

INT. ULVERSTON POLICE STATION. PRIVATE OFFICE. DAY

Wilson slumps at his desk with paper cup of coffee, he is alone in
the staffroom. He has dialled a number.

On telephone (burners)

                    DI WILSON
          Lafitte, Joe Wilson

                    JEAN LAFITTE
          Monsieur Joe...?

                    DI WILSON
          Did you get the Scotland Report?

                    JEAN LAFITTE
          Got it yes. All on track my friend. Bob
          Kramer is close to being identified;
          he will quickly lead them to Stephen
          Parry. Then the SWAT move in and
          clean up. Good work Joe.

Wilson is momentarily silent, uncomfortable.

                    DI WILSON
          Look Lafitte,
                    (A beat, stirring coffee)
          I'm very close to all this, and I must
          say, I'm really not happy. First of all,
          killing these two young men was
          never any part of this. Secondly, for
          all sorts of reasons, the SWAT Team
          may not take them down in an
          arrest, it may not be as clean as you
          think.
                    (A beat)
          I live in this town; I know their
          families.

Lafitte was silent for a full minute. Wilson could hear him
breathing, he waited.

                    JEAN LAFITTE
                    (Coldly)
          Detective Inspector Wilson, Joe,

(A beat)
I have no wish to work through
the mechanics of this with you
yet again. Your 'happiness' or
otherwise, in this situation is a matter
of total indifference to me.

You have a lot of experience on
both sides of this, and you and I
have collaborated successfully
over a number of years on several
extremely delicate projects.
(A beat)
The details of how you might do
it - I leave entirely up to you. But the
OUTCOME, the end result, must be
understood, and delivered. Are we
clear?
(A beat, Wilson is silent)
These two young assassins are
DISPOSABLE CLEAN SKINs to be
eliminated by your SWAT Team in
the process of their arrest. They were
recruited for a specific purpose and
do not, under any circumstances,
survive their arrest.

That's it Wilson, this is NOT a
negotiation. The next time we
speak, you WILL report this to me as
a 'fait accompli' - done - achieved.

The line goes dead. DI Wilson is aware that his heart is racing, and
he is deeply angry. He takes several deep breaths.

CUT TO:

DI WILSON'S WARNING

EXT. FELL ROAD OVERLOOKING A590 AND SINKHOLES. DAY

DI Wilson sits in his pool car, dejected. The view over Morecambe Bay is obscured by mist, with banks of rain sweep across the muted grey landscape. Wilson glances at his watch, they are late. Nonetheless, he must wait for them on this occasion.

The Land Rover pulls in beside him, wipers stop and Bob grins across at him from the passenger seat. Wilson composes himself, and exits his vehicle, landing into the rear seat of the Land Rover in a flurry of cold air and raindrops.

> BOB
> Mr Wilson, you OK? Its a shit day, I
> thought we...

> DI WILSON
> (Irritated)
> You are late! I don't have the time to
> sit around here waiting for you two
> to arrive whenever you feel like it.

Stiv and Bob are momentarily taken aback by Wilson's departure from his usual avuncular disposition.

> STIV
> (Quick retort)
> Well, that's OK with me, don't
> fucking wait then. I don't give a sh...

> BOB
> (Concern)
> What's up Mr Wilson? Problem?

DI Wilson was silent for a moment. Both men, their attention caught, turned slightly in their seats to look at him. Wilson, fighting an inner battle with himself was suddenly resigned.

> DI WILSON
> We haven't met up since the
> Scotland job. I've been busy with
> local stuff and also, I have been
> co-opted to do some work with

the Scotland Team as well - you
wouldn't have known that.

Bob and Stiv both reacted with surprise.

                    BOB
          (Grinning from Wilson to Stiv)
     Really, wow, you are working on
     investigating the shooting of the
     Frenchman. That's bloody amazing.
     How did you manage that?

                    STIV
     So, you'll be able to steer them off
     a bit, may be throw a down a few
     false trails etc, to protect us, yeah?
     That's totally brilliant!

          (A beat)
     Sorry I was a bit off with you before
     Mr Wilson.

Wilson ignores Stiv's belated apology.

                  DI WILSON
     It's the Scotland investigation that I
     wanted to talk to you guys about. It's
     not going too well, from your point
     of view, that is. This is why I wanted
     to meet with you both today.

Wilson takes a breath, composing himself.

             DI WILSON (CONT'D)
     Lads look there's no easy way to say
     this, so I'll just get it out there for you,
     then we'll deal with your reaction as
     it comes.

Both young men went silent, exchanging glances, the mood
changing, darkening.

DI WILSON (CONT'D)

You know some parts of this, other
parts I have never shared with you
for all sorts of obvious reasons.
(A beat)
The Scotland hit was brilliantly
done, you were both right on the
money in terms of planning and
delivery. Since then, the issue has
been with me every waking minute
because I am in the dual role of
being your handler, and I am also
a police officer - that is... a working
policeman.
(A beat)
More than that, as an investigating
officer. I have to...

Stiv shifted in his seat, turning fully to Wilson.

STIV

(Flatly)

You are going to tell us now that we
are blown, aren't you? The Scottish
Cops, you...whoever, are on to us.
Is that what you are working up to
telling us? I can tell its nothing good.
(A beat)
Are we fucked? Yes?

Wilson, suddenly silenced, turned slightly to look out across the
landscape into the rolling mist. Bob shifted in his seat, looked
incredulously at Stiv, then at Wilson.

BOB

Is he right? Is he...?
(A beat)
How the hell can this happen? You
and that French guy organized this,
surely you should be protecting us.

We did everything you asked of
us - everything.

The car went silent for several moments.

> DI WILSON
> (Clearing his throat)
> Several other Beaters have asked
> questions about you Bob. You
> were a new guy, they never saw
> you beating there before, that
> sort of thing. It resonated with the
> investigating team, consequently
> there's an APW out on you at the
> moment.

> BOB
> APW...?

> DI WILSON
> An 'All Points Warning'. It's an
> exchange of info with a number of
> different Police sources, a version
> goes to airports, seaports and
> international rail etc.
>
> When they searched the Crime
> Scene, they also found the LAY-UP
> HIDE, where the shot came from. It
> was directly in line with Bob's beater
> path, some people remarked
> that it was all a bit too much of a
> coincidence etc.

> BOB
> But hang on, we knew all this would
> be found out didn't we. We talked
> about it. You said they would be
> able to work out the line of the shot.
> The point is they don't know that I'm
> here in Cumbria, do they? I gave a

false name. You said they would be
looking for a big-time shooter, not
me and Bob.

                    DI WILSON
                  (Doubtful)
They don't know it's you guys, at
the moment... but with the APW
out it's a matter of time. Both of
you guys are on record of being
interviewed previously - and by me
even, you are Firearms Certificate
holders... with a photograph. There
is a standardized search process
here that I don't have any power to
influence.

The car went silent again, then Stiv suddenly stiffened, colour
draining from his face.

                    STIV
I think I get it Bob...He's going
around the houses to make his point,
but I think I can see where this is all
heading...

Grinning savagely at Wilson, then Bob, fist thumping into the side
of the car seat.

                    STIV (CONT'D)
They're not protecting us at all
Bobby!
                  (A beat)
These bastards have used us. They
got us to do the KILL for them, plan
it, everything, kill the FROG, then
they put us in the frame for the
fucking crime. We are then duly
arrested and put away for it, then
file closed - all sorted.
                  (Bitter)

Very neat and tidy. Brilliantly done
Mr fucking Detective Inspector
Wilson and Mr fucking Interpol Frog.
You have played us like a pair of
idiots - simpletons - country lads -
wet behind the ears.

We can shoot, but we are fucking
disposable.
(Bitter grin)
Just like the movie eh, we are
Collateral Damage.

Stiv leans back in his seat, running his hands over his eyes. Bob is
white with tension, looking from Wilson to Stiv.

BOB
(Shaky, slowly, tears forming)
He's not right is he Mr Wilson? Tell me
he isn't right.

Wilson is silent, looking downwards, miserable. The Land Rover
grows silent, everyone lost in their own thoughts.

DI WILSON
(Conciliatory)
Look lads, I'm sorry about all this, but
I'm fucked both ends up here. The
only way I could think it through was
to warn you, then at least you have
some time to get the hell away from
this place.
STIV
(Bitterly)
You are not anywhere near as
fucked as we are, are you Mr Wilson.
In terms of fuckedness, we have
cornered the fucked market - me
and him.

Stiv punches down on the steering wheel twice, wincing, looking at his fist.

                    STIV (CONT'D)
                 (A beat, slower)
            Well Mister, you can pass this back to
            your Frog mate. We go down, then
            we all go down in flames together.
            Put us through court, and I for one,
            will sing like a canary, I'll tell the
            whole story. All of it, then we'll all do
            time together. Maybe we'll all be in
            same nick, that would be good eh.

Wilson looks up at Stiv slowly, shaking his head, mouth twisting.

                    DI WILSON
                 (Resigned, quietly angry)
            You poor miserable twat, you don't
            get it do you? You really have
            missed the point here Stephen. The
            Frenchman is far too clever to permit
            that sort of risk.
                 (A beat)
            You guys will never go through a
            courtroom.

Bob and Stiv are silent for a beat, exchanging glances. Stiv is angry, Bob is emotional.

                    BOB
                 (Voice breaking)
            Well, the only way we don't go
            through a court is that you kill us.
                 (A beat)
            So, how will you - they, whoever, do
            this? Are you going to tell us?

Wilson leans forward, distraught, the pain evident on his face.

                    DI WILSON
            Its very likely you will be taken down
            by a SWAT Team. Professionals with
            heavy weaponry. The story will be
            that you resisted, maybe fired on
            them, and they had no choice but
            to return fire.

Bob is openly crying now. Stiv thumps his shoulder angrily.

                    STIV
                (To Bob)
            Bob, for fuck's sake don't let this
            bastard see you like this. Get a grip
            mate, come on.
                (To Wilson)
            So, you are saying the SWAT Team
            are in on this as well?

                    DI WILSON
            No, they know nothing. They will
            be issued with a 'NO KNOCK'
            arrest warrant to detain 'ARMED
            TERRORISTS', so they will be tooled
            up tight, locked and loaded, ready
            to shoot if they have to.
                (A beat)
            Now look, let's stop this, we are
            wasting valuable time here. I have
            given you guys an opportunity to
            get the hell away from here. I am
            personally taking a serious risk doing
            this - warning you.

Wilson eyes them both, his hand on the door handle.

                    STIV
            Oh well that's ok then, thanks for
            that. Really kind...

DI WILSON
I'm going now, do not wait. Get your
stuff, passports etc, whatever, and
go - NOW, like this afternoon.
I don't really care where or how you
do it, just go - the further the better,
preferably out of UK. Its better that I
don't know anything.
          (Earnest eye contact with
          both)
Good luck lads, and again, I'm
really sorry how this has panned out.

Stiv turns away, facing out through the rain-streaked windscreen,
angry tears in his eyes.

STIV
Good try Wilson, you lousy double-
crossing bastard. I'm not running
anywhere. I'm staying. You and the
FROG are in this up to your fucking
eyeballs, as well as us.

Wilson looks at them both, shakes his head, bites back an angry
retort, and gets out of the car quickly. He reverses his pool car,
revving uncharacteristically, and takes off, disappearing quickly
in the mist. Bob calms himself with a superhuman effort. He and
Stiv sit there silent for a beat.

BOB
          (Exhaling)
Well, what a load of bollocks
that was.

I know what I'm going to do Stiv. I
agree with you, I'm not going to run
anywhere either, I'm staying put
right here.

We need to leave our guns locked
up at all times, so we can never be

challenged while we are carrying them. No hunting, no nothing. We don't give his SWAT Team even the slightest reason to use guns on us.
(A beat)
If we are arrested, we go quietly, then at least we have a chance to have our say. We blow the GAFF when we stand up in court and then everyone goes down. Its all that's left for us now mate. I guess the reality is that we have been on borrowed time ever since we shot those two Bulgarians.

Stiv is silent, staring out of the windscreen. Bob continues - almost as if convincing himself.

                    BOB (CONT'D)
You are dead right mate, running is the worst possible thing that we do, it gives them all the excuses they need.

Stiv is turning it over in his mind, finally he nods, it is the only course of action that made any sense.

VIEW THROUGH THE WINDSCREEN, THEN AERIAL

Out through the windscreen, the mist clears momentarily, the copse covering the Sinkhole coming into sharp focus, they both look at it for an instant, then the mist swirls back, greying out the landscape.

                                        FADE TO BLACK

INT. ULVERSTON POLICE STATION. CONFERENCE ROOM. DAY

The conference room fills with uniforms and suited men and women. There is an air of something big being announced. At one end of the long-polished table sits Chief Constable (CC) Denise Wakefield-Jones (50). The seats around the long table fill quickly, other officers stand along the walls. The CC looks tired and drawn.

Insp. Jean Lafitte, impeccable and guarded sits slightly apart.

> CHIEF CONSTABLE
> (Glancing up from papers)
> OK everyone, can we get started please. We have this room for one hour only, then we need to vacate.
> (A beat, distasteful smirk)
> Apparently, HR need it for some really important reason.
>
> The reason I have called this meeting today is to ensure we are all on the same page regarding a series of executive actions to be taken in the next 24 hrs.
>
> My thanks to colleagues from Scotland who have travelled south to Ulverston for this meeting, also attending today are Officers from SWAT, as well as local officers. We also have Inspector Jean Lafitte from Interpol attending for the French link.

Looking around the room, acknowledging Scots officers and Lafitte.

> CHIEF CONSTABLE (CONT'D)
> This meeting has a total 'Schedule D' news blackout colleague. Do not discuss meeting content with anyone else who is not in this room today.
> (Pause, glancing around)
> Are we clear?

There is a rumble of assent.

                    CHIEF CONSTABLE (CONT'D)
          Right, the backstory.
                    (A beat)
          10 weeks ago a French Diplomat
          was shot dead, assassinated, while
          he was attending an 'invitation only'
          Scottish Game Shoot. It was a pro
          hit, clean and effective - single shot
          though the heart.

          Obviously, we are highly
          embarrassed from a national
          perspective, and questions have
          been raised at Government level
          both in London and Paris.
                    (A beat)
          On a personal level, I am deeply
          concerned by this situation just over
          our borders. Our regional record for
          many years has been exemplary,
          and I want this crime to cleared
          up as fast as possible. The Scotland
          Shoot was attended by several other
          VIPs from Showbiz, Westminster and
          the EU, and ripples from this incident
          have been felt in several countries.

          Investigations are on-going, but to
          progress these, we now need to
          interview at least one, possibly two
          key witnesses. This is the reason for
          this meeting.
                    (Glancing around)
          Everyone OK? This is where it gets
          complicated.

The room is silent, attentive, officers take notes. The CC is weary,
she takes a breath.

CHIEF CONSTABLE (CONT'D)
The Scottish Game Shoot, like many
others this time of year, recruits
itinerant BEATERS to drive game
towards the SHOOTERS. One of these
men, it turns out, signed up using a
false name. Interestingly, this same
man was beating a path directly in
line with the sniper's layup position,
(Looking around)
which seems a remarkable
coincidence, to say the least.

There is a sound of agreement from two Scottish officers.

Our assumption, and this is not yet
ratified, is that these two people
were working together on the
assassination, the Beater, and the
Shooter - in perfect harmony.

The CC paused, her flinty gaze sweeping the rapt faces.

CHIEF CONSTABLE (CONT'D)
I must repeat my earlier condition
colleagues. What is said here today,
stays here.
(A beat)
To continue.

We have now identified the BEATER
who signed onto the Scotland
Game Shoot with a false name. He
is Robert (Bob) Kramer of this town.
He lives with his Mother, Iris Kramer
here in Ulverston. He was in fact,
routinely interviewed in this station
in connection with the killing of 2
Bulgarians locally 12 months ago,
as well as the recovery of a number
of military grade weapons from an

flooded mine working known as a
Sinkhole.
(A beat)

Kramer's lifelong friend,
collaborator, and shooting partner,
was also interviewed back then as
well. His name is Stephen (Stiv) Parry,
also of Ulverston.

(Looking around the room,
pausing)
Colleagues, we believe, as yet
unproven, that Parry could be our
SHOOTER. Both of these men are
known to be expert rifle marksmen,
and both hold current, and legal,
Firearms Certificates.
(A beat)
To summarize, we now have
two suspects for the Scotland
assassination, both are fit and
strong, they are expert shots, they
are armed, we suspect they are
killers, and...
(A beat)
they live less than a mile from this
room.

The Chief Constable sat down abruptly to a silent room, her head
down. Faces continued to look at her until finally she raised her
head to look around.

CHIEF CONSTABLE (CONT'D)
(Weary)
I suggest that we take 5 minutes
colleagues. Then we will reconvene
to look at strategy.

The room erupts with an excited buzz of conversation. Someone
brings a cup and saucer to the Chief Constable, which she

accepts gratefully. Officers go out and return with paper cups of coffee. Five minutes later the Chief Constable reconvenes the meeting with renewed energy.

> CHIEF CONSTABLE (CONT'D)
> Colleagues, please come back to order.
> (Waiting, glowering around)
> I'm sure that even with the breadth of experience in this room colleagues will be surprised and dismayed that a small Lake-land Town like Ulverston could spawn not one, but two international assassins.
>
> Lots of circumstantial evidence, but much of this is yet to be proven of course, the next questions that spring to mind are, WHO initiated the HIT Contract? WHY, and who are the Assassin's HANDLERS? And WHAT might these two do next?

The CC makes eye contact with Lafitte, her eyes questioning. Lafitte shakes his head minutely.

> (A beat)
> I am going to request a HIGH-RISK WARRANT, so at this stage I'm going to ask Major Glen Anders of SWAT to give us his thoughts on the forward arrest strategy.
> (Looking to the left)
> Major...

Major Glen Anders 49, ex-Marine, 24 years of SWAT experience stands confidently in his black uniform.

> GLEN ANDERS
> (Nodding to the CC)
> Thank you Chief.

(Slow look around the room)
The next task is to bring the two
suspects into custody. Under the
circumstances of what we know
and suspect, this should be a 'NO
KNOCK' SWAT operation with local
officer back-up if necessary.

We know for certain these guys
are armed and are expert shots.
We suspect they will not hesitate
to shoot if pushed. It is imperative
that they are taken alive in order
to continue investigations. I expect
to work with designated officers,
with appropriate training and
experience, to come up with an
operational plan.
(A beat)
An enormous number of variables
can affect the outcome of a SWAT
arrest. The best-case scenario is
where the suspects surrender, or are
disoriented enough to be pinned
and cuffed. Worst case is that the
suspects force an exchange of fire
that results in loss of life.
(Looking at Chief C)
That's it. Thank you, Ma'am.

The Chief Constable rises and looked around the room for DI
Wilson, spotting him and nodding.

CHIEF CONSTABLE
(Glancing at Anders)
Thanks Major, DI Wilson, you
interviewed both of these men
last year, you are also a local man
who has some knowledge of their
families. Can you work with Major
Anders please to bring these men

215

into custody? I would also like two
officers from Scotland to be at the
forefront of this operation.
(A beat)
Everyone else on standby please.
This operation has the eyes of British
and French Governments on it and
has some distance to run yet.

Thank you everyone.

The Chief Constable stands, collects her papers and abruptly
leaves the conference room.

FADE OUT

FADE IN:

EXT. INT. BOB'S HOUSE. ULVERSTON. DAY

Stiv pulls up along the street from Bob's house, expertly slotting the
Land Rover into a space. He gets out, walks to Bob's front door.
As he walks, a black Range Rover passes, taking it slow between
the parked vehicles. He glances in but the darkened windows
prevent him seeing anyone inside. He has seen this vehicle
around Ulverston in the past few days. He turns to watch it lazily
take a right, brake lights flaring, then out of sight.

Stiv knocks, and is let in by Iris.

IRIS
(Warm smile)
Hey Stiv. You haven't been round for
ages, you OK?

STIV
I'm good Iris, he in?

Iris stands to one side, lightly brushing against Stiv as he passes. She smiles to herself at his discomfort. He enters the front room. Bob is watching SKY NEWS

                    BOB
          Hi mate, sit.

                    STIV
          Cheers, anything?

                    BOB
          Nothing. Thought they might have
          said something about Scotland, but
          they are hardly going to advertise it
          are they?

                    STIV
          Suppose not.
                    (Nodding back to the
                    kitchen)
          You haven't said anything?

Bob shook his head.

                    STIV (CONT'D)
          Shall we go out somewhere? Not
          comfortable talking here.

Bob nods and stands. Stiv goes to the front door, waving briefly to Iris as he passes the kitchen. Both men exit the house, Iris walks to the kitchen window, distractedly watching them get into the black Land Rover.

                                        CUT TO:

EXT. HEATHROW AIRPORT. DEPARTURES. DAY.

Insp. Jean Lafitte joins the queue at Customs, dutifully surrendering his briefcase, cell phone and pockets contents, glancing enviously across to the fast-moving First-Class departure point.

THE ARREST

EXT. FELL OVERLOOKING A590 AND DISTANT SINKHOLE. DAY

Stiv's Land Rover noses up to the edge of steeply sloping ground that runs down to the busy A590 road out of Ulverston.

CUT TO:

EXT. FELL OVERLOOKING A590. 300M WEST OF LAND ROVER. DAY, CONTINUOUS

In a small stand of trees 300M away, Michael O'Leary sits in cover with his back against a tree, he is watching the Black Land Rover through binoculars. His own Range Rover is parked nearby in cover behind small bracken covered rise.

CUT TO:

EXT. FELL OVERLOOKING A590 AND DISTANT SINKHOLE. DAY

Stiv and Bob are pensive. Its a clear day and they can see waves breaking on the Morecambe Bay shore two miles away. Below them the A590, traffic moving both ways, busy.

>   STIV
> You didn't hear any more from
> Wilson then?

>   BOB
> Nothing didn't expect to. Do you
> think it was a bit of bullshit? Maybe
> trying to scare us a bit?

STIV

Could be, hmm, No. I thought he
was quite upset about it. Maybe
he was genuine, and he's being
fucked over as well. It's hard to tell,
maybe he...

Stiv abruptly stops speaking, he is leaning forward over the
dashboard looking downwards towards the road several hundred
meters below, frowning in concentration.

BOB

I've stopped bloody sleeping again
now, ever since we had that....

Stiv, now alert, twists in his seat, looking around both ways, then
looking back downwards at the A590. The atmosphere in car
shifts, Bob looks at him bemused.

BOB (CONT'D)
What's up, what are you doing?
STIV
(Pointing west towards
Ulverston)

Dunno, something going on down
there. The traffic has stopped on the
590. Look. Its all backing up towards
Ulverston.

CUT TO:

**EXT. FELL OVERLOOKING A590. 300M WEST OF LAND ROVER. DAY,
CONTINUOUS**

Michael O'Leary takes his binocular down from his eyes.
Something else has caught his attention. Over to his left he sees
a movement some 40 meters away. A man in cammo gear steps
out of some brush, carefully laying down prone on a hummock
and opening a rucksack beside him. The man clearly has not
seen O'Leary.

O'Leary raises his binoculars and watches with growing fascination as the man assembles a rifle, fixing a telescopic sight, and loading a magazine. The man is clearly aware of the Land Rover, over to his left, but is facing away from it.

O'Leary non-plussed, sweeps his binoculars back to the black Land Rover. Nothing has changed, two men are inside looking out over the Bay.

O'Leary carefully crouches, working his way through thick brush, to a raised hummock near to where he has parked his vehicle. From his new position, he begins searching the higher ground with his binoculars where the rifleman is facing.

EXT. HIGHER GROUND OVERLOOKING THE LAND ROVER VIEWPOINT. DAY. CONTINUOUS

Major Glen Anders leans against a dry-stone wall and carefully looks through high power binoculars at the black Land Rover, parked at the fell viewpoint 200M away. Next to him leans one of SWAT Team Jim Basford.

>   GLEN ANDERS
> They are just sitting there talking by
> the look of it. By the way, where is DI
> Wilson, he should be here before we
> proceed.

>   JIM BASFORD
> No idea where DI Wilson is Boss,
> he had the all the same arrest
> timetable that we had. I tried his
> phone a few times, but it rings out.
>
> We have stopped traffic on the
> 590 Boss, they will probably spot
> that, but will probably think its an
> accident or a breakdown with any
> luck. That happens fairly regularly
> anyway.

GLEN ANDERS
Try Wilson again, if he doesn't reply
we will proceed without him. We
could take them both down from
here, but that's not the job today
Jim. We need these guys fit and well
for interrogation.

Anders scans the single lane fell road both ways of the parked
Land Rover, then consults a map folded into a small square.

GLEN ANDERS (CONT'D)
They only have one road Jim, they
either come towards us this way, or
back towards Greenodd.

JIM BASFORD
Both ways are blocked Boss. Plus, if
they got past us, which they won't,
the A590 is totally static both ways.
They are bottled up.

Anders is thinking. He scans the fell road both ways again, then
swings his binoculars back to the Land Rover, the two targets are
still sitting there.

GLEN ANDERS
OK, Jim, tell the guys to keep their
sights on these guys. They are
shooters, but this does not look
immediately threatening at this
moment. We have to assume they
have rifles in the rear of the car,
but they are not in a position to use
them sitting in the front seats.
        (A beat)

We are 200M away. That's 30
seconds of travel max. Take away
15 seconds for them to react, they
would need to get to the rear of the

vehicle, deploy their rifles, lock and
load and fire on us in 15 seconds.
Not possible.
            (A beat, nodding)
We have the fuckers Jim.

Jim Basford, his eyes slitted, scanned the escape routes himself,
swinging his gaze back to the Land Rover. He checked the
handgun on his hip.

                    JIM BASFORD
            Wherever you are ready Boss.
                                                    CUT TO:

EXT. FELL OVERLOOKING A590. 300M WEST OF LAND ROVER. DAY, CONTINUOUS

Michael O'Leary spots the SWAT Team on the hillside 300M away
from his position. He carefully raises his binoculars, sweeping them
back and forth, focusing on two heads slightly raised above a
dry-stone wall.

O'Leary's heart rate begins to pick up. He is looking at a SWAT
ambush, happening right in front of his eyes. O'Leary struggles to
understand the significance of the other rifleman nearer to him -
and FACING TOWARDS THE SWAT Team, and NOT facing the two
men in the Land Rover.

O'Leary can only surmise the possibly the two young assassins
have anticipated their ambush, and had positioned another
rifleman to protect them, and maybe effect their escape.

He shakes his head, he would never, in a month of Sundays,
believe the two young men that he had been following for a
couple of weeks now, had that level of military thinking and
capability. Unlikely, but his respect for the two young assassins is
growing.

O'Leary scans back along the fell road, Black Transits were
positioned in trees along both escape routes, the Land Rover

was well boxed in. O'Leary wasn't too worried for his own escape because he has come over several open fields to get his Range Rover in position nearby. he hadn't wanted to be seen on any of the approach roads following the young men.

CUT TO:

EXT. FELL OVERLOOKING A590 AND SINKHOLE. DAY. CONTINUOUS

Stiv is puzzled, and his discomfort is being communicated to Bob. Stiv is looking along the A590 below, where a serious traffic jam seems to be developing.

> STIV
> Something weird here Bob, must be
> an accident. It looks like the '90' is
> backed up both ways. We'll not get
> out either, this fell road exits onto
> the 90.

Bob is unconcerned.

> BOB
> There are always hold-ups on the
> '90' mate. Its normal. It only takes
> a breakdown, or a smash, and the
> fucking road stops. I've sat there for
> hours sometimes.

Stiv leans back, resigned.

> STIV
> Well, we are not in a rush are we.

CUT TO:

EXT. HIGHER GROUND OVERLOOKING THE SINKHOLE VIEWPOINT. DAY. CONTINUOUS

Major Glen Anders is growing in confidence. His targets are truly boxed, and below, the A590 is blocked both ways. His targets are unlikely to be able to deploy an armed response in the time it would take for two SWAT vehicles to converge on them from both of their escape directions. he nods to Jim Basford.

                    GLEN ANDERS
            On my signal Jim.

Jim Basford turned away momentarily to where several other SWAT members were deployed with rifles aimed at the black Land Rover. He spoke into his radio.

                    JIM BASFORD
            Drivers go on my signal. Shooters
            stay on them, but they are NOT,
            repeat NOT a threat at this time.
                    (A beat)
            Only shoot on my command. Clear?

One by one, Driver 1 and Driver 2 responded, then his Shooters Team responded in their numbered order. He nodded to Anders.

                                        CUT TO:

EXT. FELL OVERLOOKING A590. 300M WEST OF LAND ROVER. DAY, CONTINUOUS

O'Leary is in a high state of excitement. He swings his binoculars from the Land Rover, to the SWAT positions, and back to the lone RIFLEMAN, who is now looking though his telescopic sights TOWARDS THE SWAT TEAM.

EXT. HIGHER GROUND OVERLOOKING THE SINKHOLE VIEWPOINT. DAY. CONTINUOUS

Glen Anders glanced back to Jim Basford, nodded.

> GLEN ANDERS
> Go, Go, Go.

As Anders looks towards his deputy, Jim Basford grunts in shock, suddenly doubling over and sitting down awkwardly, then falling onto his back. An milli-second later, the sound of a rifle-shot cracked white-hot across the landscape. Anders, shocked, immediately looks at the Land Rover for the shooter, NO SHOOTER, nothing has changed, both occupants are still sitting in the front seats. Anders looks around the immediate landscape wildly.

Another shot rings out, and one of his SWAT shooters is hurled backwards, sprawling in the brush, his rifle flying out of his grasp.

Anders finally understands that his SWAT Team are under fire. He shouts into his radio as a fusillade of shots came from his team.

> GLEN ANDERS (CONT'D)
> Everyone stand down. Do not fire.
> Drivers stand down.

He swings his binoculars back to the Land Rover. Both doors are now open, but neither of the two targets are in sight.

> GLEN ANDERS (CONT'D)
> Can anyone see another shooter?

CUT TO:

EXT. FELL OVERLOOKING A590 AND SINKHOLE. DAY

Stiv and Bob hear the first shot somewhere behind them, then hear a second shot following within seconds. Neither men are experienced in military techniques, and their first reaction is to exit their vehicle and look at what was going on.

                        STIV
                     (Pointing)
          Fuck, did you hear that? Someone
          is firing a rifle from somewhere over
          there in that brush.

                        BOB
          I can't see anyone, definitely heard
          two shots though.

Stiv, suddenly remembering the conversation with DI Wilson.

                        STIV
                     (In panic)
          Bob, get down, NOW. Is it the
          fucking SWAT? What the fuck?
Both men go flat to the ground as high velocity shots clang into
the side of their Land Rover rocking it violently. Holes are punched
in the immaculate paintwork, glass and dust cascaded on them.

                                              CUT TO:

**EXT. HIGHER GROUND OVERLOOKING THE SINKHOLE VIEWPOINT.
DAY. CONTINUOUS**

Anders screams into his radio.

                   GLEN ANDERS
          Who fired?

Several metallic voices crackle in his radio simultaneously. Anders
rolls towards where Jim Basford was lying, his fingers searching
Basford's throat pulse. He is dead, hit just above his body armor,
exit wound showing blood spray on the ground behind him.

                 GLEN ANDERS (CONT'D)
          Status, Shooter's report in numbers.

                         SHOOTER 1
                  No visible targets boss. Holding on
                  target vehicle.

There is silence.

                         GLEN ANDERS
                  Shooter 2, respond.

Silence.

                    GLEN ANDERS (CONT'D)
                  Shooter 3 respond.

                         SHOOTER 3
                  Shooter 2 is down Boss.

Anders is in serious shock. He is a professional soldier before
SWAT, but this situation has taken him completely by surprise. The
presence of a third unknown shooter had not been anticipated
by anyone.

                         GLEN ANDERS
                          (On radio)
                  All SWAT shooters. We have
                  two known targets by the Land
                  Rover. A further shooter's position
                  unidentified, possibly over the left
                  of the land Rover in cover. This new
                  shooter is now a THIRD high priority
                  identification target.

                  Identify and report three target
                  positions. Eyes on and targets
                  acquired, but DO NOT FIRE.

There is silence on the fell. Ander's binoculars sweep the trees to
the left of the Land Rover. Nothing.

                                              CUT TO:

EXT. FELL OVERLOOKING A590 AND SINKHOLE. LAND ROVER POSITION DAY

Stiv and Bob are flat on the ground covered with broken glass.

> STIV
> Bob, you OK? we need to get away
> from this Land Rover. It must be the
> SWAT bastards. Stay low mate.

They crawl into low lying scrub and bracken. Bob is panicked and white faced.

> BOB
> (Shaky)
> Stiv, what are we going to do? They
> are gonna fucking kill us. I thought
> they would just arrest us.

> STIV
> Stay down flat, let's get into those
> trees over there. I think the shots are
> coming from that higher ground to
> our left.

CUT TO:

EXT. FELL OVERLOOKING A590. 300M WEST OF LAND ROVER. DAY, CONTINUOUS

O'Leary glasses the brush where the unknown riflemen is positioned. The riflemen had moved now, and O'Leary could no longer see him. O'Leary swings his binoculars to the higher ground where the SWAT ambush is positioned, he can see nothing. He smiles grimly, the SWAT TEAM's ambush had backfired on them today, but who was the WILD CARD shooter...

CUT TO:

EXT. FELL OVERLOOKING A590 AND SINKHOLE. LAND ROVER POSITION DAY

Stiv and Bob crawl further into the scrub and bracken. The fell is silent now. Sounds of traffic below on the blocked A590 had faded in their awareness. They keep moving with no specific direction in mind other than to stay low and not present a target.

CUT TO:

EXT. HIGHER GROUND OVERLOOKING THE SINKHOLE VIEWPOINT. DAY. CONTINUOUS

Anders was in trouble and he knew it. Two of his men were KIA and he was on the back foot in terms of response strategy. Basically, he was pinned down.

> GLEN ANDERS
> (On radio)
> Driver 2 respond.

> DRIVER 2
> Here Boss.

> GLEN ANDERS
> Can you spot the shooter from your position?

> DRIVER 2
> Nothing Boss. We are reluctant to shoot anyway because he is directly between our two positions. Your position is in our line of fire.

> GLEN ANDERS
> OK, spread your positions to address line of fire issue. Stay low.

Anders breaks the connection in frustration.

GLEN ANDERS (CONT'D)
(On radio)
All shooters, spread your positions,
move right and left, stay low and
shoot only at verified targets. At
this time we have two targets to
be arrested and one unidentified
target. DO NOT SHOOT AT TEAM
MEMBERS!
(A beat)
The two arrest targets and the
unknown shooter are now ALL re-
classified as 'shoot to kill targets'.
Confirm back in numbers.

There follows a series of confirmations from the SWAT Shooters.

CUT TO:

EXT. FELL OVERLOOKING A590. 300M WEST OF LAND ROVER. DAY, CONTINUOUS

The fell is silent, O'Leary is reluctant to move further away from his vehicle. From the raised hummock he carefully scans the ground between him and the black Land Rover. After several moments he sees movement in the bracken, it is Stiv and Bob, and they are crawling in his direction.

O'Leary knows that the standoff will end very soon. The Swat Team had been effectively pinned, but it was a single RIFLE. By chance, or by clever design, the unknown RIFLE had positioned directly between the main SWAT position and the second SWAT vehicle. They were unable to fire on the rifle shooter's position because the line of fire was compromised.

O'Leary scans his binoculars back to Stiv and Bob's position in the bracken. He estimates they are now within 30M of his own position, and still moving. He stays low, considering his options.

CUT TO:

EXT. STIV AND BOB'S FELL POSITION. DAY

It had been silent for several minutes, Stiv and Bob keep crawling in the same direction. In front of them is a raised hummock.

> STIV
> Bob, can you see that hummock in
> front of us?

> BOB
> I see it.

> STIV
> If we get behind that, we will be out
> of sight of the SWAT shooters. We
> can run like fuck for those woods on
> the far side of that raised ground.

Bob grunts accepting, this modicum of a plan, they go forward. Both are sweating and very frightened.

CUT TO:

EXT. ANDERS POSITION. DAY

Anders knows he is going to have to call for backup. He is extremely reluctant to do that for many complex reasons, not least his own vanity and pride. He wants to bring this situation under control with his own resources. He looks at his watch, it is 14 minutes since the first shot had been fired. His radio crackles.

> GLEN ANDERS
> (On radio)
> Report Team

> SHOOTER 1
> I think we see the rifle-shooter
> Boss. No detail, but his position is 11
> o-clock low from you. Watch below
> a small fir tree.

> GLEN ANDERS
> Did everyone get that? Do not
> engage if your shot has the remotest
> chance of crossfire casualties.
> Confirm back.

Confirmations crackle back through his radio.

CUT TO:

EXT. STIV AND BOB'S POSITION. DAY

Stiv reaches the hummock, parts the bracken and is met with the muzzle of O'Leary's handgun to his forehead. O'Leary doesn't speak, but motions Stiv to continue forward to the lower ground behind the hummock.

Stiv is astonished into total compliance. Immediately behind him, Bob appears. O'Leary's handgun covers them both.

> MICHAEL O'LEARY
> (Quietly)
> Well lads fancy meeting you here.
> It's a better day weather wise, don't
> you think?

O'Leary motions with his handgun, finger to his lips. Both men are in a state of total shock.

> MICHAEL O'LEARY (CONT'D)
> (Quietly)
> Bob, come forward son, your ass
> is going to be shot off if you stay
> where you are.

Bob crawls to the lower ground where Stiv is sitting. O'Leary is sitting casually with his back to a rock, but his handgun is steady, covering them both.

                    MICHAEL O'LEARY (CONT'D)
          Listen up my lovely boys.

                    We have a difficult situation here, I
          am going to put my weapon away,
          but first I need to be sure you are not
          going to get us all shot to fucking
          rags.
                    (A beat)
          We have minutes maybe. And the
          SWAT boys will be all over us like shite
          in a blanket. If you look over behind
          me, my car is there. On my signal,
          both of you run, keep low and get in
          the back seats and get down low.

                    Am I clear?

Both men nod, gulping.

                    MICHAEL O'LEARY (CONT'D)
                    (Checking around)
          OK, Go.

Both men run in a crouching position and scramble into the back
of the black Range Rover. O'Leary follows and gets behind the
wheel. He leans back to Stiv, holding out his handgun to him, butt
forward.

                    MICHAEL O'LEARY (CONT'D)
          Stiv, be a good lad and shoot any
          fucker you see outside of this car,
          particularly if they have a gun
          pointed at us.

Stiv takes the handgun, automatically checking its loaded status.
O'Leary notes this and grins wolfishly.

The Range Rover purrs into violent movement, all four wheels spinning, bursting out of the brush into an open meadow, effortlessly gunning up a slight slope.

                                                    CUT TO:

EXT. ANDERS POSITION. DAY

Anders hears the sound of a powerful engine but can see nothing. The sound is coming from behind raised ground to his left.

                              GLEN ANDERS
                    Report, report. Engine sound at 10
                    o-clock low.

Anders radio crackles with responses, but no-one has a line of sight. The engine sound fades. Anders decides to act decisively.

                         GLEN ANDERS (CONT'D)
                    We are going to take down the
                    shooter. This has gone on long
                    enough now. Shoot to disable if you
                    can. Confirm back.

Confirmation's crackle.

                         GLEN ANDERS (CONT'D)
                    Shooters 1-5 stay low, focus on the
                    target area. Shooters 6-8 move
                    forward NOW.

Anders scans the area where his man has spotted the rifleman. There is a movement, then a single shot rings out.

                         GLEN ANDERS (CONT'D)
                    Report, who fired, anyone hit?

Confirmations come back immediately, no-one had shot or
been hit. There is silence for two minutes, then Ander's headset
crackles.

> SHOOTER 3
> Boss, I think the Rifleman has topped
> himself. I can see his legs, he is still.

> GLEN ANDERS
> Careful, go forward. Everyone, stay
> sharp.

Two minutes pass. The fell is silent.

> SHOOTER 3
> Boss, the Rifleman is down. Repeat
> down. We think the other targets
> have flown.

Anders sits up carefully, thinking it through.

> GLEN ANDERS
> Shooter 3 ensure the rifleman is safe
> and the scene secure.

> SHOOTER 3
> All secure Boss.

> GLEN ANDERS
> OK, everyone else. Stand down. Stay
> clear of the rifleman's position, its a
> crime scene. Whole team collect at
> Driver 1 position.
>   (A beat)
> Unlock.

Anders checks his watch, 18 minutes from first shot to UNLOCK.
He gets wearily to his feet and carrying his weapon, walks down
the wooded slope to where two of his team are standing below
a small fir tree looking downwards. Lying on his side, his hand on

a hunting rifle, with the side of his head blown away, is Detective Inspector Joe Wilson.

FADE TO BLACK

FADE IN:

EXT. M6 MOTORWAY NORTH OF CARLISLE. DAY

The Range Rover sweeps effortlessly north at 75mph in light traffic. There had been silence in the car for more than an hour. The two men in the rear of the vehicle sitting in their own world, endlessly replaying the events of the day. O'Leary does nothing to break the silence, considering his own options as he drives.

CUT TO:

EXT. CRIME SCENE OF DI WILSON'S SUICIDE. LATE AFTERNOON

More than a dozen vehicles are parked along the single lane fell road high above, and parallel to the A590, 5 miles outside Ulverston. Blue lights are flashing on several vehicles and people in white sterile suits are erecting a tent above DI Wilson's body. Other officers are taping off a secure area around the scene. A photographer is working nearby, and a senior CSI is bent on one knee examining the body, speaking quietly into a mini tape recorder. Other officers are taping off the scene around the black Land Rover nearby.

Chief Constable Denise Wakefield-Jones stands disconsolately gazing down at DI Wilson's uncovered body. Three other officers are close by.

> CHIEF CONSTABLE
> I guess it is a suicide then. No
> chance of him being shot from
> another source.

                              CSI
           We'll need to do a lot more work
           back at the lab Ma'am, but at
           this stage we are pretty sure it's
           a self-inflicted shot under the
           chin - classic.

The Chief Constable turns away, walking several paces into the
bracken, impatiently motioning other officers nearby to join her.

                    CHIEF CONSTABLE
           I'm having difficulty believing what
           I am seeing here, where the fuck is
           Major Anders?

         CHIEF SUPERINTENDENT GEORGE HENLEY
           He's over by the SWAT vehicles with
           his team Ma'am, do you want to
           speak to him?

                    CHIEF CONSTABLE
           No I do not. I'll meet him under
           caution back at the station. What
           are your thoughts George?

The Chief Super speaks quietly to the other two officers and they
respectfully withdrew several meters away.

         CHIEF SUPERINTENDENT GEORGE HENLEY
           Ma'am, I have known Joe, sorry, I
           mean DI Wilson, for 20 years. He's
           never been a highflyer, but he's
           always been rock solid. He was a
           local copper, respected, reliable
           and straight talking. Always lived
           in the South Lakes. His wife died a
           few years ago, since then he has
           lived alone. I believe he has either
           relatives or friends in France, he
           goes there regularly, don't know if its
           a woman, not sure.

(A beat)
Quite frankly Ma'am, I am shocked
to my core. Circumstantial evidence
at the moment indicates he fired
on the SWAT Team and killed two of
them just as they were initiating the
arrest of our two suspects. He was
supposed to be with the SWAT Team
for the arrest, but obviously he never
turned up.

                    CHIEF CONSTABLE
Interesting, so he had the SWAT's
arrest schedule then?

        CHIEF SUPERINTENDENT GEORGE HENLEY
Yes Ma'am, he did. He's on the copy
list.

The Chief Constable turns slightly to gaze across the alluvial plain
to the Bay, her misery showing. With an effort she turns back to
Henley.

                    CHIEF CONSTABLE
Oh yes, our two assassins, how can
we forget them. And where the fuck
are, they? Pray tell.

        CHIEF SUPERINTENDENT GEORGE HENLEY
We have no idea Ma'am. Their Land
Rover is here obviously, pretty badly
shot up by more than 30 rounds of
SWAT fire. No evidence of either of
the two suspects being hit. No Blood
trail, nothing.
                    (A beat)
It looks like they had another
accomplice here, as well as DI
Wilson, but to be honest, nothing
much makes any sense right now.

                    CHIEF CONSTABLE
                    (Shaking her head in
                    disbelief)
          Hmm, these two young men are
          not what they seem are they?
          How could we miss this? What an
          unbelievable cluster-fuck George!

          Right, I'm going. Get that idiot
          Anders to my office in an hour from
          now. Tell him to bring an IOPC Rep
          with him.
                    (Independent Office for
                    Police Conduct)
                    (Independent Office for
                    Police Complaints)

The Chief Constable goes to her car and cursing softly to herself,
negotiates carefully in the failing light between other flashing
police vehicles parked hap haphazardly along the fell road.

CUT TO:

INT. CHIEF CONSTABLE'S OUTER OFFICE. ULVERSTON POLICE STATION. EVENING

Major Glen Anders sits, still dressed in his blood stained black
SWAT uniform, at a polished conference table. Next to him
is a suited IOPC Rep. On the other side of the table sits Chief
Superintendent George Henley, a minute taker, and two other
uniforms. The middle seat facing Anders is vacant and everyone
waits in silence.

Through the glass wall, The Chief Constable can be seen, in
her inner office, making what looks like a difficult phone call.
presently, the call ends, and the CC places the receiver down,
then sits with her head lowered for several moments. Eventually
she gets wearily to her feet, walks the several meters into the outer
office, then sits heavily down in the vacant seat.

                   CHIEF CONSTABLE
                   (To minute taker)

          Can you record attendees and
          times, but give me a moment first, I'll
          tell you when to start recording?

The Minute Secretary nods, eyes down to her papers.

                   CHIEF CONSTABLE (CONT'D)
          Anders, right now I have difficulty
          even looking in your direction. I am
          not going to prolong this meeting,
          because I do not want to spend
          a moment longer than absolutely
          necessary in your fucking company.
                   (A beat)
          I fervently hope I feel different
          tomorrow because we all have
          some distance to travel in
          unravelling this cluster-fuck of such
          epic proportions. If I had seen what
          has happened here today in a
          cheap film, I would say it was too
          far-fetched. Unfortunately...
                   (A beat, then to Minute Sec)
Major Glen Anders sits totally still, his eyes on the CC, a pulse
throbbing in his temple.

                   CHIEF CONSTABLE (CONT'D)
          OK, switch on the recorder.

The Minute Sec names the attendees, location and time, case
number, then nods to the CC.

                   CHIEF CONSTABLE (CONT'D)
          Anders, speak...

                   GLEN ANDERS
          Thank you, Ma'am.
                   (Looking down at notes)

240

CHIEF CONSTABLE
(Sharply)
No notes please. Let's keep this first
meeting anecdotal. Give me your
version of events today verbatim.

GLEN ANDERS
Yes Ma'am.
(A beat)

We followed the two suspects to
the fell road overlooking the A590,
5 miles east of Ulverston. They were
on a single lane road looping off the
A590 both ways. We boxed them
and stopped traffic on the A590
both ways, so the suspects had no
escape route.

SWAT were positioned in three
locations at the arrest site, two
vehicles with three men each
blocking both escapes, then nine
men positioned on higher ground.
(A beat)
The two suspects were alone, to our
knowledge. We observed them over
30 minutes or so. They sat in their car
talking.

At the point we initiated the arrest,
two officers were shot from cover
somewhere to the left of the
suspects' vehicle.

The suspects did not appear to have
knowledge of the other shooter.
They exited their vehicle unarmed,
as several SWAT shooters fired on
their vehicle.

CHIEF CONSTABLE
Was DI Wilson involved in the
detailed planning of the arrest of
the two suspects?

GLEN ANDERS
Yes Ma'am. We formulated an
outline plan which would be
triggered by specific activities of
the suspects. He was copied into
the Arrest Schedule on the day. He
should have been in attendance.
Several calls are logged trying to
locate him.

CHIEF CONSTABLE
Expand.

GLEN ANDERS
Yes Ma'am, we were conscious of
the danger a 'High Risk - No Knock'
arrest would pose to the public. So
we were all, including DI Wilson, on
a 24/7 standby to proceed if the
suspects travelled to an appropriate
area.

The fell location fitted that criteria,
so we SCRAMBLED, that is DI Wilson
AND the SWAT Team.

CHIEF CONSTABLE
Hmm, and did you authorize your
shooters to fire at the suspects Major
Anders?

GLEN ANDERS
No Ma'am. They were told NOT to
fire.
                (A beat)

I guess they were shocked when two of their comrades were shot from an unknown location without warning.

CHIEF CONSTABLE
(Faint, but grim smile)

Quite Major Anders, but at that point you, as Commanding Officer, lost control of your Unit.

Pray continue.

GLEN ANDERS
(Stiffly)
There followed a standoff because the unknown shooter was in direct line of fire between our two SWAT positions.

No other shots were fired then, until the single suicide shot.

In that hiatus, we heard a vehicle revving close by, but it was behind higher ground, so no-one had sight of it.

CHIEF CONSTABLE
(Leaning forward)
So, you have no idea of who, what where, how, in other words, you know nothing about this mythical vehicle at all...

GLEN ANDERS
No, nothing Ma'am. At this stage we could only assume that this vehicle was DI Wilson's - the Rifle-shooter's getaway means, and that he wasn't alone.

(A beat)
We then converged on the Rifle-
shooter's position to discover DI
Wilson's body. At that point we
'UNLOCKED' and called the incident
in. It was 18 minutes from the first
shot to the call-in.

Anders falls silent. The CC glances at silent colleagues on either
side, all are white-faced staring at Anders.

                    CHIEF CONSTABLE
          Major Anders, I want you to
          speculate for a moment, you must
          have thought about this over the
          past hour or two. Why would DI
          Wilson bring a firearm to the arrest
          location, then fire on his SWAT
          colleagues? and who was the
          driver of the unknown vehicle, who
          may have been Wilson's getaway
          assistant?

Anders stares at the CC. Showing the strain of the past few hours.

                    GLEN ANDERS
          Wilson fired twice Ma'am, from a
          distance of around 120M. He used a
          223-hunting rifle with a good quality
          scope.

          At that range, and with that
          equipment, almost anyone could hit
          a man-sized target. Both shots were
          effective kills, placed specifically
          above the level of the body Armor.
          Textbook sniping.

The CC leans onto her elbows, her flinty gaze unblinking.

                    CHIEF CONSTABLE
Go on...
                    GLEN ANDERS
I have known DI Wilson for several
years; other colleagues have known
him much longer. None of us had
any knowledge that DI Wilson could
even shoot or had any interest in
shooting.
            (A beat, thinking it through)
It looks like he was trying to protect
the suspects, but killing two
colleagues...

Anders tails off, clearly emotional. The CC keeps silent, waiting.

                GLEN ANDERS (CONT'D)
                (Recovering)
Or maybe, and I haven't thought
this through Ma'am, he was trying
to force SWAT to shoot the suspects
dead.

Neither of the two suspects returned
fire, so...

                    CHIEF CONSTABLE
So, when SWAT came under lethal
fire, it changed the status of the
arrest to 'Shoot on sight'. Yes?

                    GLEN ANDERS
                (Tears in his eyes)
Yes Ma'am.

The CC glances at her colleagues on either side, then back to
Anders, her gaze pitiless.

                    CHIEF CONSTABLE
That's it?

GLEN ANDERS
Yes Ma'am.

The CC indicates that the Minute Sec should close the recording. Then she stands without another word and leaves the table. She pauses at the glass door and turns back to the face the room, her face weary and lined.

CHIEF CONSTABLE
Just so you all know, the phone call
I took before this meeting, was from
the Home Secretary.
(A beat)
Not often he rings Ulverston.

The CC leaves the room. The rest of the occupants sit there in silence.

DISSOLVE TO:

1 hour later.

INT. CHIEF CONSTABLE'S OFFICE. DAY

The CC and Chief Super sit with coffees either side of a large desk.

CHIEF CONSTABLE
So, its an interesting one George.
Years back I would have given
my eye teeth to have a case like
this, now...
(A beat, fist hits desktop)
Fuck, fuck, fuck.

CHIEF SUPERINTENDENT GEORGE HENLEY
Quite Ma'am.

CHIEF CONSTABLE
Either way, it looks like Joe Wilson
had an agenda. An agenda I am at
some pains to explain to the Home
Sec. (1) He protected the suspects
using lethal force, that option would
have almost certainly resulted in his
death. Or (`2) ...
        (A beat)
...he fired on the SWAT Team
to provoke them into killing the
suspects. In which case he would
have pulled back and survived.

Out of the two choices, I prefer 2.
What do you think George?

CHIEF SUPERINTENDENT GEORGE HENLEY
It looks very much like he wanted
the suspects dead Ma'am.
        (A beat)
Under the circumstances, SWAT,
anyone, would have immediately
assumed that the targets were firing
at them. This would have changed
the arrest status immediately.

CHIEF CONSTABLE
Exactly. The implication of this either
way, is pretty awful. Wilson is, was,
up to his fucking eyes in something
I don't even want to speculate on,
and who was Wilson's getaway
driver, if indeed that's what he/
she was?

We must assume this unknown
vehicle took our two suspects away,
and left Wilson behind, pretty shit
getaway driver huh George?

Both Police officers sip luke-warm coffee. The CC puts her coffee down, grimacing at it.

                    CHIEF CONSTABLE (CONT'D)
                         (Resigned)
              I've got to make some phone-calls
              George.

                                        FADE TO BLACK

INT. SALON DES ORDNANCES, ELYSEE PALACE. PARIS

Lafitte waits to be shown into De Freyn's office. The Aide sits at his desk ignoring his presence.

Lafitte had tried to ring DI Wilson prior to being called to this rapidly arranged appointment, but Wilson had not replied. Lafitte is worried. The phone raings on the Aide's desk. The Aide nods to Lafitte as he replaces the handset.

Lafitte stands, the Aide smoothly rises and opens the ornate door, standing to one side. Lafitte enters. De Freyn is writing, he ignoring Lafitte. Lafitte remains standing. Presently De Freyn stops writing and irritably indicates that Lafitte should sit.

                         M.DE FREYN
              I assume you have heard.

                         JEAN LAFITTE
              Heard Sir?

                         M.DE FREYN
              Don't fuck with me Lafitte, it is not in
              your interests, believe me.

Lafitte remains silent, belly churning.

                         M.DE FREYN (CONT'D)
              I have taken several calls in the
              past 2 hours, one of which was

from UK's Home Secretary. They are
investigating links between a British
Detective, a DI Wilson, and yourself
Lafitte.

Lafitte's world rocks, but he doesn't show any emotion.

                    JEAN LAFITTE
The links are clear and proper Sir,
we have been involved in a joint
investigation for over a year now.

De Freyn leans back in his seat, hands flat to the desktop,
regarding Lafitte with hooded eyes. He takes a long breath, then
turns his chair slightly, facing a large hanging tapestry.

M.DE FREYN

                    (Musing)
This room was once a bedroom
Lafitte. Princess Caroline Murat,
brother of Napoleon once slept
here. Later it was a library and
even later a smoking room used by
President Georges Pompidou.

Now it is my office.
                    (A beat)
It could also be the scene of your
total and absolute destruction, not
to say that event would be recorded
in history, or even that anyone would
care to read of it.

De Freyn swivels his chair back to face Lafitte, his eyes slowly rising
to meet Lafitte's.

                    M.DE FREYN (CONT'D)
                    (A beat)
A few hours ago, your DI Wilson
of Cumbria Police shot himself,

after killing two SWAT Officers who
were attempting to arrest your two
protege assassins. They are both on
the run at this moment.

Lafitte is shocked to his core. Despite his normally rigid
composure, he gasped. De Freyn notes his shock.

                    M.DE FREYN (CONT'D)
Metaphorically Lafitte, I suspect that
your fingerprints are all over this.
          (A beat)

You will withdraw from this situation
and leave no trace of anything that
could harm or implicate us from this
point onward.

Assist any formal investigating
officers, but Lafitte, tread very softly.

Are we clear?

                    JEAN LAFITTE
Clear Sir.

De Freyn turns away from Lafitte, leans back into his chair and
closes his eyes. There is a faint sound behind him as the Aide
takes his position to one side of the desk, eyes downcast. Lafitte
rises immediately and leaves the room, his tread soundless on the
carpet.

The Aide waits silently as the Minister turned his chair slightly
and meets his eyes. De Freyn shook his head minutely. The Aide
immediately drops his eyes and leaves the room quietly closing
the door.

                                    FADE OUT

INT. WALNEY DIVE CENTER. OFFICE. DAY.

Dave Geddings and Mike Kramer sit with coffees at their cluttered desk. Kramer is distraught.

> DAVE GEDDINGS
> Do you want something stronger in
> that coffee?

> MIKE KRAMER
> Where do think they are Dave? No
> answers on their phones.

Kramer gets up and paces, Geddings watches, silent.

> MIKE KRAMER (CONT'D)
> I saw their Land Rover on the back
> of a low loader coming down from
> the fell road. It was shot to bits,
> wrecked. They can't have been in it.
> Iris is going round the twist. Laidlow is
> missing as well, she hasn't seen him.

Kramer reacts, spinning to face Geddings.

> MIKE KRAMER (CONT'D)
> Laidlow! They are with fucking
> Laidlow! How the...

> DAVE GEDDINGS
> Sit down mate, carry on like this
> you'll have a bloody coronary.

> MIKE KRAMER
> He's my son Dave. How the fuck
> would you know anything about a
> father-son relationship?

Dave Geddings comes out of his seat, his eyes blazing. Both men stand facing each other for a beat. Abruptly Geddings turns and exits the office.

After a beat, Kramer follows.

EXT. WALNEY DIVE CENTER. YARD. DAY.

Dave Geddings stands in the yard surrounded by diving paraphernalia, tanks, pumps, other rusting equipment. He is quivering with emotion, eyes swimming with tears. He senses a movement behind him.

> MIKE KRAMER
> Dave, I'm sorry mate. My fucking
> head is not on right at the moment.
> I shouldn't have said that. I'm really
> sorry.

Dave stands facing away. Presently Mike takes a step forward and puts his hand on Dave's shoulder. Dave doesn't turn.

> DAVE GEDDINGS
> You need to go and be with Iris.

AERIAL SHOT

Kramer drops his hand away. After a beat he walks away, leaving Dave Geddings standing like a statue amid the detritus and clutter of the yard.

DISSOLVE TO:

EXT. IRIS'S FRONT DOOR. DAY

Mike Kramer's battered van parks in the street and Kramer knocks. After a beat, Iris opens the door. Seeing Dave, she floods with tears and collapses into his arms.

CUT TO:

INT. ULVERSTON POLICE HQ. SWAT'S ALLOCATED TEAM ROOM. DAY

A sparsely furnished room, with several bare tables, metal filing cabinets and one wall covered with heavy metal shelving stacked with equipment. In the corner a sticky coffee/tea station. The other wall has a glass window to Glen Anders small office.

6 SWAT Team members are lounging around in various poses, some reading, others talking quietly. The room gradually becomes silent. All are covertly watching Glen Angers in his office.

Anders sits at his desk. He is reading a document that has just been delivered by a HR Officer. After several beats Anders gets up to lean in the doorway.

> GLEN ANDERS
> OK Team listen up.
> (A beat)
> Tony, you are now in Operational
> Command from now. You are the
> next most senior officer. This will be
> confirmed to you in writing but take
> as read from me now.
> (A beat)
> I'm gone lads, its official.

The shock permeated through the team. In the past few days they have lost two colleagues and now their Commanding Officer.

> TONY CLAY
> Boss, I don't want this, you...

> GLEN ANDERS
> Its not a negotiation, its an order, so
> do it. And get this place cleaned
> up, it looks like a fucking tip.

Anders turns back into his office, throwing a few possessions into a rucksack. He comes back into the main room and stands, his rucksack on one shoulder. Silently his team rise and stand to attention, their eyes on him. Anders holds each man's gaze in turn, then exerting massive control, nods to them, drawing himself into attention for a long moment. After a beat, Anders stands down, then strides from the room, the door swinging shut behind him.

CUT TO:

EXT. ULVERSTON POLICE STATION. FRONT ENTRANCE. DAY

Anders exited the front doors, takes several steps, then turns to look back.

CLOSE UP, THEN ZOOMING UP INTO CIRCLING AERIAL SHOT

Anders hefts his rucksack, looks up at the building for a long moment, turns and walks to his car.

FADE TO BLACK

ESCAPE TO IRELAND

FADE IN:

EXT. A75. DUMFIES + GALLOWAY. NEAR CROCKETFORD. EARLY EVENING

The Range Rover enters the small village of Crocketford, turning right onto a B Road at the medieval, white-washed Galloway Arms, then picking up speed again out of the village.

O'Leary has kept close to the speed limit but has maintained a constant fast pace from Cumbria. The road narrows, with some stretches becoming a single lane. Stiv is asleep, his head lolling. Bob is wide awake, staring out at the wooded countryside.

MICHAEL O'LEARY

> (To Bob in the mirror)
> We will stop soon Bob, you must be
> ready for some tea.
> (A beat)
> You OK?

No reply from Bob. O'Leary shakes his head, flicking on sidelights as the light dropped.

CUT TO:

EXT. SEMI DERELICT FARM. GALLOWAY FOREST. NIGHT

The Range Rover pulls into the yard of an unlit farmhouse. Against the dark sky were the crumbling walls and ghostly silhouette of some previous existence. The abandoned house stands composed, momentarily lit as the headlights swept across it.

> MICHAEL O'LEARY
> Well lads, here we are then. Home
> sweet home eh.

The car becomes immediately dark as the headlights died. A torch flares as O'Leary opens his door.

> MICHAEL O'LEARY (CONT'D)
> Well, come on then. Things to do.

Stiv and Bob stiffly climb out, standing uncertainly in the darkness.

> STIV
> Where the hell are we? Looks like
> Frankenstein's fucking castle.

> MICHAEL O'LEARY
> We are home, for the next couple of
> days at least Stephen. I have some
> organizing to do. There is another
> torch in the boot, and a few bags,
> bring them if you wouldn't mind.

O'Leary disappears into a black doorway, torchlight flickering.

> BOB
> What is this place? I'm not staying
> here.

                    STIV
              (Rummaging in the rear of
               the Range Rover)
        Well, that's no problem is it? I
        imagine there will be a Travel Lodge
        somewhere in this wood. You stay
        there mate. We'll meet up with you
        tomorrow for breakfast.

Bob snorted, turns away. Stiv carries bags into what used to be
someone's front room. A floor of stone slabs, remnants of furniture
and shattered windows, traces of flowered wallpaper and a
broken open fireplace.

                 MICHAEL O'LEARY
        There are some old chairs over
        there, break them up and get a fire
        going, we'll soon liven the place up.

Later

The three men illuminated by the flickering flames, sit around the
fireplace.

              MICHAEL O'LEARY (CONT'D)
        This is all right. People have bonded
        around fires since the dawn of time
        you know.

        My old Dad used to say that it
        lowers blood pressure, and folk
        are generally nicer to each other
        around a fire. I'm sorry that I didn't
        stop for supplies on the way here, I
        thought it better if we didn't.

O'Leary looks at his two companions benignly.

MICHAEL O'LEARY (CONT'D)
It would be good if you talked to me
a bit you know. I've always found
silent people hard to take.

We have traveled a bit of distance
now together, and I think we have
more to go yet. Not to mention me
hauling your asses out of a cauldron
of hell-fire back there.

BOB
What do you want to talk about?
MICHAEL O'LEARY
(Wearily)
Oh shit, I don't know...

'The time has come, the Walrus
said, to talk of many things, of shoes,
and ships, and sealing wax, and
cabbages and Kings...and why the
sea is boiling hot, and whether pigs
have wings...'

O'Leary pauses, thinking.

MICHAEL O'LEARY (CONT'D)
I'll tell you what, let me start. I'll tell
you some stuff about me and what
I think about it all, and then maybe
you might feel like talking back.
(A beat)
What might you think about that?

Both of the other men grunt, but their body language has shifted,
a coolness had gone out of the atmosphere.

MICHAEL O'LEARY (CONT'D)
I'm Michael. I was Daniel's boss
back in the day. You'll remember
Daniel Laidlow I'll wager.

                    (A beat, eye contact)
              The man that you executed, along
              with his two divers. You are chalking
              up quite a reputation quietly.
                    (A beat)
              Was Scotland one of yours as well...?

O'leary waits a beat, then smiles.

                    MICHAEL O'LEARY (CONT'D)
              Amazing! You are becoming
              valuable assets you know.

O'Leary shakes his head ruefully. Both other men are now rapt.
Their eyes on O'Leary.

                    MICHAEL O'LEARY (CONT'D)
              But Daniel was a Jack-the-lad
              wasn't he?

              If you hadn't a done it then
              someone else would have, to be
              sure. He was a good friend of mine
              was Danny, but I don't hold any
              grudges against you's. Sure now, I
              wouldn't have rescued you lads if I
              did. And there was plenty of days
              when I wanted to kill Daniel myself.
                    (A beat)
              Them guns, the ones down in the
              Sinkhole, they are mine. Did you
              walk in on that, then it all went
              haywire?

                    STIV
                    (Slowly)
              That's about the size of it, yes. The
              fucking Bulgarians were gonna kill us.

                    MICHAEL O'LEARY
Ah, the Bulgarians. Them boys are a
bit fiery to be sure. First off, kill a few
folks, then think about it next, that is
their way. The trouble is, you can't
un-kill people, can you? It's all a bit
final.

                    (Grin)
Particularly when you shoot their
fucking ass off. So, you see lads, we
are all tied together in a funny sort
of way.

O'Leary gets up to throw wood on the fire, sits down again. He
stares into the fire.

                MICHAEL O'LEARY (CONT'D)
You do know that you are both
dead men walking now, don't you?

                        BOB
                    (Resentful)
None of this is our fault.

O'Leary regards Bob with look of distaste, considering.

                    MICHAEL O'LEARY
Robert, or Bob is it? Somebody once
wrote 'The moving finger writes,
and having writ, moves on. And all
thy piety not wit can lure it back to
cancel half a line, nor all thy tears
wash out a word of it'.
                    (A beat)
God, do you know how much I'd
love to be the man that wrote that!

So, Bobby boy, fucking live with it!
What's done, is done.

O'Leary pauses, shakes his head and smiled.

>   MICHAEL O'LEARY (CONT'D)
>   When you finally have all the right
>   cards in your hand, everyone wants
>   to play fucking chess.
>
>   Sooner or later, it will be payback
>   time, they will kill you, or put you
>   away. That's your future now boys.
>   So, all you can do is to have the best
>   time you can, until the day comes.

Both men look at O'Leary. He grins broadly, his teeth flashing in the firelight.

>   STIV
>   So, who are you then Michael
>   O'Leary. You are just a name to me -
>   us. You saved us back there, but I
>   have a feeling we have gone from
>   being in the fat to being into the fire.

>   MICHAEL O'LEARY
>   Very poetic Stephen. You could
>   be right, but you are here, and not
>   there.

O'Leary stretches like a cat, gazing into the flames

>   MICHAEL O'LEARY (CONT'D)
>   My folks had some great
>   expectations of me. I was the third
>   son. Two others, both staunch
>   Republicans, in the ground for the
>   cause. Me, they put their soul, and
>   their savings, into my education, but
>   the Universities are a fertile hotbed
>   of political dissatisfaction. Within a
>   year I was itching for the fight. Within
>   two years I was a willing terrorist.

I saw the use of terror tactics as a
perfectly proper political expedient
for people who had used up, or
couldn't afford, other alternatives.
By the third year I had evolved into a
FIXER, my current incarnation.
                    (A beat)
Years back there was a western on
the telly. A man in black. He was an
educated man who made a living
as a gunslinger. He had a business
card with the emblem 'Have Gun,
will Travel'
                    (A beat)
You should have seen that! One of
my heroes.

                                                    CUT TO:

INT. IRIS'S HOUSE KITCHEN. DAY

Iris and Mike are sitting at the kitchen table, a bottle of Irish Whisky
and two shot glasses between them. Iris is tear stained but heart
breathtakingly beautiful in her pain. Mike gazes at the Mother of
his son, his eyes filled with love.

                    IRIS
        You have to drive; you shouldn't
        have any more.

Mike takes both of her hands in his, his head ducking downward
to hide his emotions.

                    MIKE KRAMER
        Iris, you know that I...

Iris leans in towards him, bending her head slightly to see his eyes.

                              IRIS
          Shh, stop now, before you say
          something that will complicate our
          lives even more. We share a son
          Mike, nothing more.
                    (Gently)
          We had our time. It was amazing
          for a while, but it's gone now. We
          messed it up, but you are still my
          best friend you know. That doesn't
          change. And you are our Bobby's
          Dad - whatever he's done.
                    (A beat)
          I choose not to believe that Bobby
          has killed anyone, I don't care what
          they say or what proof they the
          show me. I just...
                         MIKE KRAMER
          Iris, I saw...

Iris gets up, clattering the kettle loudly, opening the tap, water
sluicing into the sink.

                              IRIS
                       (Sharply)

          Stop It! Stop it NOW! I won't hear it!
          Do you want tea?

She turns to face him tears streaming. Then more gently, voice
breaking...

                         IRIS (CONT'D)
          Do you want some tea?

Mike comes up from the table, taking her into his arms and
holding her tightly. Iris pushes her head down hard into his chest,
while the kettle boils blowing steam.

                                                   CUT TO:

EXT. PORTPATRICK HARBOUR. SCOTTISH WEST COAST. DAY

O'Leary's Range Rover noses onto a promontory overlooking
Portpatrick harbour. It is raining and banks of mist swirl, obscuring
the grey seascape. O'Leary kills the engine and leans back,
gazing through the rain-streaked windscreen.

> MICHAEL O'LEARY
> Ireland is 22 miles directly in front
> of us. On a clear night you can see
> lights along the coastline. It looks a
> bit grim today though.

> BOB
> (Sullen)
> Ferry is it?

> MICHAEL O'LEARY
> Aye, a ferry of sorts Bobby. I've
> arranged a boat for you's a bit
> further up the coast. Best you stay
> off the grid don't you think. I'll be
> doing the ferry with the car.
> (A beat, musing)
> You know, I had a niece, lovely
> lass. She ran away over here to
> Portpatrick to get married. Happens
> quite a bit, even now. A bit like the
> other Scottish border place Gretna
> Green.

> Broke our hearts she did.

> BOB
> Up the duff was she?

O'Leary turns fully to face Bob, his usually good natured face like
stone.

> MICHAEL O'LEARY
> (Quietly)

Do not mistake my natural good
humour for weakness. It would take
me less than one second to put you
down Robert. You would be here,
and then you would be gone.
            (A beat)
If any of my family or friends had
heard you say what you just did,
you would be a dead man within 24
hours.

Both young men stare at O'Leary, colour draining from their faces.

                         BOB
            I, I didn't mean...
                   MICHAEL O'LEARY
            The difference between you and
            me Bobby is this, I know how my
            story ends. I have no doubts you
            see, I know, so I don't care much.

O'Leary shudders briefly, winked at Stiv.

                   MICHAEL O'LEARY (CONT'D)
            Phew, someone walked over my
            grave just then Stephen.
                   (Glancing at his watch)
            We better be going.

                                              FADE OUT

EXT. RIB. THE RED FOX. EN-ROUTE SCOTTISH COAST TO LARNE. DAY

The Rigid Inflatable Boat (RIB) named RED FOX is 30ft long,
powerful and rides the breakers effortlessly. The crew of 3 are not
communicative, one of whom was a black haired, blue eyed
beauty of 28. Even in her heavy waterproofs, she has a feline
grace with strong sure movements, and is confident and familiar
operating the RIB.

Stiv and Bob are strapped into seats with flotation vests over borrowed outer waterproof clothing. They watch the feminine graceful movements of the brunette and exchange glances.

                    STIV
Nice eh?

                    BOB
Not my type mate.

                    STIV
Oh yeah, right!

What you really mean is, she's out
of your class, out of your reach and
wouldn't touch you with a fucking
barge pole.

Bob retreats into his shell, looking out over the bow into the mist.

                    STIV (CONT'D)
                (To the female crew
                member)
What's your name?

                    GEORGIE
I'm Georgie
                (Smirk)
You can call me 'Captain'.

                    STIV
Hmm, Captain Georgie. I like it.

                    GEORGIE
                (Firmly)
By the time we get to Larne and
you've thrown up a few times, you
might not be liking me very much.
So don't be wasting any energy on
trying it on with me Mister, wrong time,
wrong place, and wrong people.

Stiv withdraws into his private hell as the RIB charges head on into the grey waves.

CUT TO:

EXT. CAIRNRYAN FERRY POINT. SCOTTISH WEST COAST. DAY

O'Leary nosed the black Range Rover onto the Ferry for 3.5hr crossing to Belfast. He had dropped Stiv and Bob off at a small inlet 20 miles north of Portpatrick. His daughter Georgie would take them over the water to Larne on her RIB. O'Leary would drive north to Larne from Belfast after docking later in the day.

O'Leary lowers the back of his seat, closes his eyes, and settles down.

CUT TO:

EXT. LARNE HARBOUR. NORTHERN IRELAND. DAY

The heavy sky hangs like a thick gray blanket over the chimneys and black slate rooftops with a reddish flush over the horizon where the sun is doing its best to break through. Bob and Stiv, the other 2 crew members and Georgie stand shivering by the harbor wall and strip off three layers of wet seagoing clothing.

A battered white Transit reverses down the ramp with a long boat trailer and hooks up the RIB, hauling it out of the black water where it stands dripping onto the concrete. The van driver (Benny) is at least 70, but grizzled and strong with a seafaring hat pushed to the back of his head.

> BENNY
> (To Bob and Stiv)
> Well, my lovely boys, welcome to
> Ireland. You'll be wanting a cuppa
> tea, I guess.
> > (Indicating the rear of
> > the van)

Chuck all your stuff in there and
climb in and we'll get going.
(To Georgie)
You are late Podge; I've been
waiting here you know. Was getting
a bit worried.

GEORGIE
No need Ben, all shipshape and
fancy free. Is my Daddy here yet.

BENNY
Rang earlier, he's just docked at
Belfast, says we should head on up
to the farm, he'll be there presently.

CUT TO:

AERIAL. LARNE HARBOR. DAY

With everyone crammed in, the white transit hauls the RIB up the
slope from the harbour. It threads along the high street, uphill
though the town as a watery sun breaks through, shedding yellow
orange along the wet rooftops.

DISSOLVE TO:

**EXT. YEWTREE FARM. 6 MILES WEST OF LARNE. DEEP
COUNTRYSIDE. DAY**

Benny pulls the Transit into the farmyard, then effortlessly reverses
the long RIB trailer into a corner. The Farm is no longer a working
farm but looks cared for. It is nestled in the lee of a hill in a
stand of firs looking towards the sunset. Benny emerges, wiping
his hands, from behind the transit to where Stiv and Bob were
standing - both looking disoriented and vaguely lost.

BENNY
(Indicating a doorway)
Tea in there lads, wipe your feet.

They enter the farmhouse through an outer boot-room hung
with harnesses, coats, stacks of boots and a gun rack with three
shotguns. Along one wall is long workbench with a vice and racks
of tools. Several diving tanks with a stack of paraphernalia are in
the corner.

A doorway leads to a huge kitchen dominated by a massive AGA
COOKER festooned with pans and cooking tools. It feels warm
and welcoming, clearly someone's home. Battered cornices are
peeling but still decorative, a big open fireplace with a border
of tiles with hunting scenes design. Three huge leather settees,
the covers torn, padding spilling out like intestines surrounded
the hearth. The wall is covered with paintings, lots of cornflower
blue etched onto creamy white - representations of a romance.
Another showing a man beneath a tree playing a lute. A third
showing a couple, the same man, standing amid grasses locked
in an embrace, behind them tethered a grazing horse.

Bob and Stiv gaze around them, their spirits lifting, despite their
desperate plight. Georgie is busy with a kettle at the AGA, she
smiles at them briefly.

                    GEORGIE
            Sit yourselves down lads, be at
            home. You'll be here a day or two
            I'm thinking.

They sit on benches up to a huge, long farmhouse table. Benny
and the two RIB crewmen, Liam and Robbo, sit hunched. Georgie
slammed down pint mugs of tea and hand-carved hunks of toast.

A vehicle sound from outside, the door pushes back. O'Leary
enters with a wide grin.

                    MICHAEL O'LEARY
            Well now, what a party. Top of the
            day to all here.

Georgie goes to her Father, kisses him hard on the mouth, taking
his hands in both hers, his arms go around her.

MICHAEL O'LEARY (CONT'D)
(Concern)

Are you all right Podge my darlin'?

GEORGIE
Rough crossing, but the Red Fox
brought us home Father.

O'Leary disengages, his hand briefly tangling her hair, sits at the
table, pulling one of the enormous cups of tea towards him. He
grins across at the two young men, raising his mug in a toast.

MICHAEL O'LEARY
Well now, here we all are then. A
new chapter begins...

Everyone looks at the two new arrivals. Stiv and Bob look
uncertainly back.

FADE TO BLACK

FADE IN:

**EXT. YEWTREE FARM. 6 MILES WEST OF LARNE. DEEP COUNTRYSIDE.
MORNING**

The farmhouse table is laden with breakfast debris. Around the
table are Georgie, Benny, Stiv and Bob. O'Leary sits with a vast
mug of coffee; he is in reflective mood.

MICHAEL O'LEARY
Our family had this farm for more
than 400 years. It was vast once,
created like a small empire, feeding
off its communities, and feeding
them back in return. I carry that
history with me every minute, mixed
up with all the joy and pain of
Ireland.

Georgie gazed at her Father, rapt, her hand seeking his. Stiv gazed at Georgie, also rapt.

> MICHAEL O'LEARY (CONT'D)
> They had great hopes for me you
> know, my folks, a classical education
> and here I am with a gun in my
> hand, instead of a textbook.
> (A beat, to Stiv and Bob)
> I'm like many here, created in the
> wealth of empire, then alienated by
> circumstances. But you know lads,
> I don't think of us as failures, words
> like that are grand ideas, but don't
> apply in any useful sort of way.
>
> We have to make the best of our
> situation and take our joy and
> satisfaction from it for as long as
> we can. Then when the day of
> confrontation comes, we will be
> content to live with the accident of
> our history, and the things that we
> did, that brought us all together,
> and may, in the end, force us apart.

O'Leary sinks into silence, gazing into his coffee. No-one else speaks. Georgie carefully disentangles her hand from his and leaves the room momentarily. She returns almost immediately with a package, sliding it in front of Stiv and Bob.

> GEORGIE
> Satellite phone. It will work
> anywhere on the planet.
> (A beat)
> It's not to be used unless its a matter
> of life or death. It doesn't leave a
> footprint on the cellular network,
> BUT its signature, both sending and
> receiving, can be traced by people

who have the inclination and
technology to look for it.
(A beat, eyes on theirs)
NOT to be used unless life or death,
you lads got that? Keep it charged.

They both nod. Georgie paused while Stiv opens the package.

GEORGIE (CONT'D)
In return for this bad boy, and to
show that we trust each other,
can you please pass me your cell
phones. Even ONE call back home
from a mobile will blow yours,
and our gaff. Do not, under any
circumstances, and however bad
you may miss your folks, ring home
on a mobile or a landline.

Keep this SAT-PHONE with you at all
times. If it rings, it will be us ringing
you, no-one else. If and when it
rings, do not reply, stay silent and
listen hard.

FADE TO:

EXT. 2 MILES WEST OF LARNE. URBAN COUNTRYSIDE. DAY

Stiv and Bob are walking through copses and thinly populated
urban countryside.

A watery sun is falsely bright with white puffy clouds and yawning
patches of blue. The two men follow a dim path towards a
perfect VEE in the hills where a grey sea sits, slab-like, immovable.

To the left and downward is Larne. A town of machinery and
tall cranes and chimneys, mainly slate grey with odd splashes of
colour. Intermediate serpents of smoke trail here and there and a
black river estuary merges into piles of infirmary-like buildings full

271

of windows reflecting the sun. The town emits a monotonous hum of engines faintly rattling and trembling all day long.

There is nothing in Larne that isn't to do with work in all its forms. All the public inscriptions are alike in severe characters of black and white. There are several large streets all very like one another, and many similar smaller streets, and people who looked like each other and share the same vaguely melancholy appearance. There is a timeless aspect where every day is like yesterday and tomorrow would be the same, and every year is the same as the last.

Stiv paused, looking out towards the harbour.

                    STIV
          Picturesque eh?

                    BOB
          Quite good to get out of that
          fucking farmhouse for a bit. Any
          ideas of what we might do next?

                    STIV
          All sorts of ideas, but we haven't got
          any 'gelt' have we Bobby? There
          wasn't the time to draw down any
          cash while we were dodging SWAT
          bullets mate. We are bloody skint -
          and then some.

                    BOB
          I know it. Have you had any
          conversations with O'Leary, you
          seem to get on with him better than
          I do?

                    STIV
          Nothing really. He sort of hints that
          he might have some work for us at
          some stage, but I've no idea what
          he has in mind. He says not to worry.

He says batten on down and enjoy
Larne.
(A beat)
He's right, I guess. Our descriptions
will be 'out there' everywhere, and
I can only assume that our previous
arrangements with Wilson and the
Frog have all gone to rat-shit...
(Thoughtful)
Interesting that O'Leary knows
everything about everything
isn't it...?

Bob thrusts his hands into his pockets gloomily, gazing down to the
distant harbour, he yawns.

                    BOB
Any joy with the beautiful Georgie?

                    STIV
I wish.
(A beat)
Can't imagine O'Leary wants me for
a fucking son-in-law though? Or to
be the father to his grandson?

Or even worse, spending Sundays
sitting in some miserable park
watching kids on a swing for two
hours, then delivering them back to
their Mother.

                    BOB
Hmm, I know what you mean Stiv, I
guess I wouldn't either.
(A beat)

Not much fun being an international
hit man is it...

To their right a rounded hill thrusts up into low cloud. Halfway up the slope nestles a whitewashed cottage in a stand of evergreens. The cottage is small and square, standing in a tiny garden. The windows of hand-made glass are shuttered, paint faded to a delicate creamy green, cracked and bubbled. Here and there are scattered whitewashed stones, smooth as saucers, a cobbled path winds impossibly down the hill towards the town.

An ancient woman dressed head to foot in black climbs laboriously up the steep path towards the cottage. She is carrying a bright red canvas bag with the legend 'K Jones+Daughter. Butchers'. The old lady doesn't stop to rest or draw breath as she climbs. Her progress upwards towards the cottage relentless and certain.

The two men stop walking and stare at her.

                    BOB (CONT'D)
                (A beat, murmuring)
            We need to get the fuck out of here
            Stiv.
                                        FADE TO BLACK

EXT. PUB: THE SQUEALING PIG. LARNE. NIGHT

The pub, just outside the town, is a cluster of long low building on the banks of a river of clear water that runs along a bed of polished stones, white and enormous like prehistoric eggs.

Stiv, Bob, Georgie, Benny, Liam and Robbo pile out of a white transit van and cross the carpark towards the garishly lit doorway.

                                        CUT TO:

INT. PUB: THE SQUEALING PIG. LARNE. NIGHT

The air inside is a warm wind laden with hot greasy scents of cooking meat, beer, cigarettes smoke, humanity and noise. The large room, unpretentious and homely, is a heady mix of drinking den, grocery shop, funeral home, job centre, restaurant, brothel and meeting place. A neutral ground for poets and revolutionaries alike.

The senses are battered by worn wood, bric-a-brac, flat caps, banjos, bodhrans and the honey and hops aroma of Guinness everywhere, rocking to the sound of The Clancy Brothers look-a-likes in a heaving group by the huge open fireplace.

Georgie, jostled by the crowd, her laughing face flushed with pleasure, holds up a leather purse up high.

> GEORGIE
> (Loud, above the noise)
> I have the kitty here my fine
> gentlemen, I shall deposit this with
> the trusty barman. He will tell us when
> and if this runs out. So tonight boys,
> the drinks are on Mr. Michael O'Leary.

Benny, knows everyone in the place, laughing, greeting, glad handing in all directions, he clears a space around a huge, battered table and they sit. Stiv manoeuvres himself near Georgie. Pints of Guinness are smashed down on the tabletop, automatically assuming everyone's drink preferences. All around are noisy conversations, laughter and music.

> STIV
> (To Georgie, grinning widely)
> I love this! Your local?

> GEORGIE
> (Voice raised above the
> noise)
> Aye, it is to be sure, for at least six
> generations of our family.
> > (Raising her pint, eyes
> > meeting his)
> Cheers Stiv.

Stiv already intoxicated by her impossible blue eyes and her mane of jet-black hair, gulps his own Guinness and glances

around him. No-one is looking at him or Bob, the place is rocking.
He begins to relax for the first time in days. He catches Bob's eyes
across the table, raises his glass again and toasts. Bob grins back,
his own glass already a third of the way down. Georgie sees the
exchange, smiling at both men.

                    BENNY
              (Leaning close to Bob)

      Are you all right son?
                    BOB
      I'm good Benny, thanks.
              (Indicating round)
      This is great!
                    BENNY
      Get some Guinness down ye lad,
      forget your cares for an hour or two.
      We didn't say it before, but you lads
      have had a tough old time of it over
      the past week or two. Michael has
      told us a bit.

Bob, embarrassed in spite of himself, feels a stab of emotion
at Benny's kindness. Benny puts his hand on Bob's shoulder,
squeezing briefly.

                    BENNY (CONT'D)
      Do you sing?
              (Chin thrusting towards the
              cluster of musicians)
      Or play?

                    BOB
              (Grinning)

      I shoot.

                    BENNY
              (Winking)
      Oh yes, I heard that.

Across the table, Liam and Robbo hear the exchange, both break into infectious grins, thumbs upwards towards Bob. He grins back, feeling his inhibitions relaxing.

Opposite, Stiv and Georgie are deep in conversation, their heads together.

CUT TO:

INT. THE SQUEALING PIG PUB. BAR AREA

A door opens behind the bar. Michael O'Leary appears. He nods briefly at the barman to his left and helps himself to a pint of Guinness. O'Leary's eyes sweep the room, searching the maelstrom of faces for strangers, anything unusual. His eyes finally rest on Stiv and Georgie. He watches them thoughtfully across the crowded pub as his glass slowly fills.

FADE TO BLACK
FADE IN:

EXT. BELFAST INTERNATIONAL AIRPORT. OYSTER BAR IN CENTRAL SHOPPING AREA. DAY.

Michael O'Leary, suited and booted, walks into the main area of duty-free shops and spins on his heel slowly scanning the crowded shops and seating.
(A beat)

He makes his way to the circular oyster and seafood bar, easing himself onto a tall stool. He orders a sparkling water and six tempura oysters with champagne aoli.

There are 15 other people at seats around the circular bar, his eye sweeps over them, an urbane pin-striped businessman momentarily makes eye contact.

O'Leary dips an oyster into the aioli and swallows it, as the businessman from the other side of the bar slides onto a stool next to him.

                    MICHAEL O'LEARY
                    (Continuing eating)
            Enrique, I hope you are well. The
            oysters are good. Can I get you
            some?

Enrique Dada (49) is Puerto Rican American, black hair with silver streaks above his ears. He represents a company called Clearwater Inc. that among other interests, runs covert missions for Governments around the globe.

                    ENRIQUE DADA
            I am well Michael, thank you. I will
            pass on the oysters.
                    (Glancing at his watch)
            I have maybe an hour, then on to
            Paris. Are you OK to speak here,
            or do you need somewhere more
            private?

O'Leary grunts, slides off his stool and indicates with his chin towards a corridor. They pass through two more doors, then into a small room with a table and chairs. They sit.

                    ENRIQUE DADA (CONT'D)
                    (Business-like)
            Michael, as an outcome of this
            meeting I need three things. If you
            say NO to (1), then 2 and 3 are
            irrelevant.
                    (A beat)
            (1) An indication from you that
            you are interested in an executive
            mission for Clearwater?
            (2) Can you plan and equip for 4
            weeks hence?

And (3), Are you OK using 'Clean Skin Disposables'? My information is that you have two available right now.

O'Leary is immobile for 20 seconds, then...

> MICHAEL O'LEARY
> Yes, to all 3. Can you elaborate Enrique?

Enrique Dada smiles, his teeth dazzling white.

> ENRIQUE DADA
> Thank you Michael.
> (A beat)
> Clearwater is working almost exclusively with the CIA, but we have been asked to assist the French Govt with a small matter. Two French Diplomat double agents have been blown, one has been removed already, the other is identified, and will be in a HIT location 8 weeks from today.
>
> The first HIT in Scotland was impeccably executed by two 'Clean Skin Disposables' contracted by the French.
> (A beat, grimace)
> But as you well know, they were NOT DISPOSED, and they are now with you. It has left a few 'TIDYING UP' problems in UK, but nothing that can't be resolved.
> (A beat)
> To some extent, WE ARE NOT TOO UNHAPPY WITH THE RESULT, because the two Clean Skins are EXCEPTIONALLY TALENTED

SHOOTERS, and now with your help,
we propose to use them again for
the second HIT.
(A beat)
However, Michael, THIS TIME, THEIR
DISPOSAL MUST HAPPEN.

Dada goes silent, regarding O'Leary through hooded eyes.
O'Leary, comfortable with the silence, allows it to draw out.

                    ENRIQUE DADA (CONT'D)
I and my colleagues fully realize
that exceptionally talented, and
amoral, non-politicized shooters are
very hard to find. But Michael, these
two individuals cannot be allowed,
by whatever circumstance, to be
exposed to an aggressive QC on a
witness stand. You know this!
(A beat)

O'Leary remains silent and watchful, waiting for the inevitable
question. It comes...

A question Michael, Why did you
intervene in the Clean Skin's disposal
by Cumbria SWAT?
(A BEAT)

This had been carefully planned.

O'Leary eyes crinkles with humour, a slow lazy grin creasing his
even features.

                    MICHAEL O'LEARY
Hmm, my answer Enrique, is this,
(Smiling)
A cat can have kittens in the oven
Enrique, but that doesn't make them
biscuits.

Enrique Dada holds O'Leary's gaze for several beats, then shaking his head in exasperation...

> ENRIQUE DADA
> For fuck's sake Michael. One of
> these days...

> MICHAEL O'LEARY
> I still have an agenda in Cumbria
> my friend, the two Clean Skins are
> inextricably involved in that desired
> outcome. I do not want then dead -
> not yet - my decision.

Dada nods, a faint smile, his fingers unconsciously adjusting sleeves and revealing diamond cufflinks.

> ENRIQUE DADA
> I see.
> (A beat, eyes straying away
> from O'Leary)
> Will it be a problem disposing of
> them next time?

> MICHAEL O'LEARY
> It will not.

Dada smiles into O'Leary's eyes, nods, his hands moving flat to his thighs, feet planted flat to the floor, consulting his watch.

> ENRIQUE DADA
> I have to go Michael, my flight...
> (A beat, eyes rising to
> O'Leary)
> Thank you, my friend.

> MICHAEL O'LEARY
> You are most welcome Enrique,
> enjoy Paris.

Enrique Dada makes a face, shaking his head minutely. The two men embrace briefly, then walk calmly away in different directions from the door.

FADE TO BLACK

FADE IN:

EXT. REMOTE FELL COUNTRY. NEAR LARNE. DAY.

A battered white Ford Transit is parked in a hollow, in a small stand of trees on a deserted fell.

Liam and Robbo are ZEROING gun sights by shooting at paper targets on a variety of firearms. Benny had told them patiently to set up targets at 20M; 50M; 100M and 150M. They have done this but are having difficulties zeroing the weapons at the longer ranges. They take a break, sitting in the white Transit's rear doors out of the wind, drinking tea from a flask.

LIAM
(Grimace, looking into
his cup)

This your idea of tea?

ROBBO
What's up with it?
(Drinking)

Sure, it's like nectar. Ambrosium

LIAM
I think you mean Ambrosia, you
twat!

Right, come-on, let's get back to it. I'm a bit lost with this; we got the scopes setup to hit the 20M target OK but can't seem to hit at the

longer range. What's the matter with
the fucking things?

They go back to the lay-up position where several rifles are laid
on some sacking. Liam flops down and sights on the target 150M
down range in the heather. Robbo picks up binoculars. Liam fires.

> ROBBO (CONT'D)
> Crap can't see it, you missed.
>> LIAM
>> It must be there; I'm aiming
>> dead on.

Liam shoots another 4 shots.

> ROBBO
> Nothing. Not a single shot showing
> on the target. Can't even spot
> where they are going.

Liam snorts in frustration. Ejecting a spent shell and rolling away
from the rifle.

> LIAM
> Fuck it. Benny is gonna go mad, not
> to say Michael. These guns are shite.

An Engine sounds. A moment later a Land Rover appears several
hundred meters away, it stops, a single vehicle in the heather on
the vast rolling fell. Robbo focuses his binoculars.

> ROBBO
> It's the two brits. Probably looking
> for us.

Robbo waves, nothing. The Land Rover is immobile. Liam watches.

> LIAM
> They haven't seen us. Wait a mo.

Liam shoots two shots in the air, waves. The Land Rover moves forward and bumps its way over to them, parking next to the Transit. Stiv and Bob exit, coming over to Liam and Robbo.

                         STIV
              How's it going lads?

                         ROBBO
              Fuckin' awful, how about you's?
              These guns are total shite. Michael
              paid bloody good money for these.
              Maybe its the scopes? I'm buggered
              if I know.

Bob is squinting down-range at the paper targets that have been setup.

                         BOB
              What's the longer-range setup down
              there?

                         LIAM
              150M. We paced it out. We got them
              hitting at 20M, but they won't hit on
              any of the longer-range targets.

Bob kneels, looking closely at the rifles and boxes of ammo without actually touching them. He indicates towards the guns.

                         BOB
              Do you mind if I take a look?
                         LIAM
              (Shrug)

              Be our guest...
              (Smirking at Robbo)

Bob picks up each of the weapons lying on the sacking and ejects magazines and breech shells to make them safe. He then picks up a Sako 225 Bolt Action and looks down range at the 150M target through the rifle scope.

                              BOB
                            (to Stiv)
                 What do you reckon? 40mm drop?

Stiv takes the binoculars and looks at the 150M target for several
beats. Bob waits.

                             STIV
                 About that, yeh. Bit of a crosswind as
                 well. Maybe 10mm right to left. Try a
                 sighting shot on the 20M target.

Bob snaps 5 rounds into a magazine, slots it into the rifle and
rapidly shoots all five at the 20M target.

                        STIV (CONT'D)
                    (Looking through binoculars)
                 Yep, all there. Go to centre on the
                 150M target, then give it five clicks
                 up and three left across.

Bob rolls to his side, clears the weapon, then makes Stiv's
adjustments to the scope. Liam and Robbo exchange smirks.

                             LIAM
                 We can hit the near target all right,
                 you pair of dipsticks. That's not the
                 problem. We could hit that with a
                 fucking catapult.

Bob doesn't reply, snaps a new loaded magazine into the rifle.
Stiv raises his binoculars. Bob sights, then fires five rapid shots at
the 150M target.

Stiv grunts, exchanges a glance with Bob, nods. Liam looks
questioningly at Stiv. Stiv grins at him and nods.

                             STIV
                       All in the black.
                             LIAM
                       (Rounding on Stiv)

Fuck off, you're kidding me! He
didn't hit that. Gimme those fucking
glasses.

Stiv grins, passes over the binoculars. Liam focuses. Looks at
Robbo, focuses again.

> LIAM (CONT'D)
> All five in the BULL - shit!
> (To Bob)
> Do that bugger again!

Bob reloads, sights and shoots ten shots in a continuous fluid
stream. Ejects, reloads, flicks on the Safety, passes the gun up
to Stiv. Stiv eases off the Safety, then fires ten shots at the target,
freehand - standing up.

> LIAM (CONT'D)
> (Looking through binoculars)
> Well, I can see it, but I don't fucking
> believe it!
> (Wonder in his voice)

Liam hands the binoculars to Robbo, who looks at the target a
long time.

> ROBBO
> What about we move that target
> down-range a bit? Say, to 200M?

Bob glances at Stiv, who shrugs. Non-committal

> BOB
> Why don't we say 500M? This gun
> will do it.

Liam snorts, goes to the Land Rover and jumps in, spinning it
around, slewing to a stop next to them, glaring at them a second,
then accelerates away into the distance.

They watch as he gets out of the land Rover, small with distance, places three black 5 gallon drums an impossible distance away on a far hillock. He fiddles with the drums for a few moments, then goes back and forth a few times to his vehicle. Finally he gets into the Land Rover and returns. He parks, then wanders over to them with a nonchalant grin.

> LIAM
> Have a look at them 3 bad boys
> then. They have a bit of petrol in
> them. I've shook them up and lit a
> rag on top of each of them. If you's
> can hit them fuckers, we should
> have a nice little firework or two.
> (He winks)
> Old Republican Army trick.

Bob is still lying on the ground. He squints up at Stiv. They exchange a glance, then Stiv hands him the rifle. Bob loads, looks though the scope a long moment. There is total silence, everyone's eyes on the three indistinct black dots in the distance.

> BOB
> Zero at 100, so what? 400m
> holdover. Wind left to right, so 300m
> left.

Stiv grunts.

Bob fires, the sound dies away for a moment as the slug flies down range towards the target. Then the black dot on the right silently flares, blooming into bright red flame, changing to a plume of black smoke, then the sound of the distant detonation rolls back across the moor to the group of men watching.

Bob fires twice more, two more violent detonations, the smoke drifting to the right in the cross wind. He clears the weapon, squints up at Stiv, nods, clears the weapon and rolls away from it.

(Several beats)

LIAM
Fuck me...

Liam and Robbo stand respectfully looking from Bob to Stiv.
Robbo steps over to Bob, palm outwards to pull him to his feet. He
embraces him, holding him close. When he lets go, there are tears
in his eyes.

FADE TO BLACK

FADE IN:

EXT. DE FREYN'S APARTMENT. ISLE SAINT LUIS. PARIS. DAY

A taxi pulls up next to the footbridge on Rue Jean Du Bellay.
Lafitte steps into the watery sunshine, glances up at the 3rd floor of
the classical building frontage above the Optique St Luis. He can
see that De Freyn's French window door onto the balcony is open,
but he is early for the meeting. He crosses the cobbled street,
sitting at a pavement table of the Le Lutetia Brasserie. From there
he can see De Freyn's apartment, and any taxis that might drop a
client outside.

The Brasserie chalkboard lists several delicacies that under other
circumstances might have piqued his interest, instead he orders a
black coffee from the disinterested waiter.

Five minutes later a black BMW 7 Series glides to a stop 20M away
on the cobbles, moments later, pulling away silently, brake lights
flaring briefly, turning right.

Enrique Dada is standing with his back to Lafitte. He is looking at
street numbers. Lafitte stares hard at the back of his head. Dada
stiffens, slowly turns, his eyes searching.

Lafitte lifts a finger. Dada walks over, dropping into a seat
opposite.

JEAN LAFITTE
Bon Jour Enrique.

ENRIQUE DADA
Bon Jour Jean, you are well?

JEAN LAFITTE
Black?

ENRIQUE DADA
Indeed.

Lafitte lifts a finger, then pointing downward at his cup. The waiter nods, disappears, then a moment later places a cup, saucer and shortbread biscuit in front of Dada. Dada sips, glances at his watch.

ENRIQUE DADA (CONT'D)
We are summoned to the inner
sanctum Jean. I have never been
here before.

JEAN LAFITTE
Only once before for me Enrique.
(A beat)
You met with Michael?

ENRIQUE DADA
(Faint smile)
In Belfast, yes. He is provisionally
contracted. He will be using your
two ex-proteges in his team - briefly.

JEAN LAFITTE
Yes. Very talented young men. Its
a shame we cannot extend their
careers more but needs must.

Lafitte glances upwards at De Freyn's apartment frontage, checks his watch.

JEAN LAFITTE (CONT'D)
We must go up Enrique.

CUT TO:

INT. M. DE FREY'S APARTMENT. DAY

De Freyn meets both men at the door, nods briefly and
turns away, stalking along an ornate hallway into his lounge
overlooking the footbridge over the Seine. He indicates two seats
at a small round table next to the French window, disappears
briefly, returning with a pot of coffee and three cups.

De Freyn is barefoot, wearing faded Levis and a white silk shirt,
casually unbuttoned down to his muscled stomach. Lafitte and
Dada exchange glances, neither had seen him out of his normal
'power dress'. Both men reflected privately that De Freyn seemed
somehow younger.

De Freyn sits opposite them, pours black coffees, he places two
envelopes on the table.

                    M.DE FREYN
          Gentlemen, thank you for honouring
          my small home. Under the
          circumstances I thought it best keep
          our discussion private.
                    (A beat)
          Our man has been clearly identified,
          and the necessary clearances
          have been sought and have been
          confirmed. So as of this moment,
          the project is LIVE. I trust your
          preparations have been successful.

Both men nod.

                    M.DE FREYN (CONT'D)
          Lafitte, notwithstanding
          the excellence of your two
          DISPOSABLES, we do not have
          any appropriate missions for them
          right now.
                    (To Enrique Dada)
          Mr. Dada, is this the same for you?

                    ENRIQUE DADA
Indeed, M De Freyn. It will be best
if we tidy up the outstanding loose
ends within this mission.

                    M.DE FREYN
                (Glancing at Lafitte)
Good.
                (A beat)
I want to turn to the mission itself.

Both men react with a sharp glance.

                M.DE FREYN (CONT'D)
                (Faint smile, palm upwards)
Non, I do not want to talk about
operational details. It is important
that as the event unfolds, that I am
surprised, shocked even. No, I want
to make an important point that we
all understand.
                (A beat)
There will be perhaps 35 - 40 people
in this TRADE MISSION to the Oil Rig.
I will be one of them in my new role
as Foreign Minister.

De Freyn rises fluidly out of his seat, stepping silently to the French
window, looking down towards the St Luis Brasserie opposite, his
hands deeply thrust into his jeans pockets. He stares downwards
for several beats, his eyes following a small boat out of sight.
Finally, he turns, his eyes burning into each of theirs.

                M.DE FREYN (CONT'D)
I want at least an 80% casualty rate
on this HIT. But gentlemen, I do not
wish to one of them.
                (A beat)
And there is something else
gentlemen, something very
important.

> (A beat)
> To enhance my new position
> and standing with French and
> International colleagues, and also
> may I say, the Public, I WANT TO
> TAKE DOWN AT LEAST TWO OF THE
> ATTACKERS MYSELF - personally.
> (A beat)
> But this aspect of our project is
> between the three of us here
> today. This part must not be
> communicated to Mr O'Leary,
> or any of his team, under any
> circumstances whatsoever.

> ENRIQUE DADA
> But M Minister, how can this be
> planned for and achieved, we...

> M.DE FREYN
> (Firmly)
> I will undertake the mechanics of
> this aspect myself.

> Are we clear?
> (A beat)

De Freyn leans forward, his cold blue eyes fixing both of his companions fiercely.

> M.DE FREYN (CONT'D)
> Are we clear on what we have
> discussed here today gentlemen?
> It is very important that we have a
> very clear agreement on this.

The implications of De Freyn's words sink into both men's consciousness over several seconds. The silence draws out, De Freyn maintains his aggressive stance, staring in turn at them both, until both men nod and confirm.

De Freyn nods in turn.

                    M.DE FREYN (CONT'D)
                Thank you, Gentlemen.
                    (A beat)
                That is all.

De Freyn rises smoothly from his chair, padding silently on his
bare feet onto his balcony. Both hands on the rail, his face turned
upwards to the watery sun, eyes closed.

Lafitte and Dada sit there for a beat. Then both get up and leave
the apartment.

                                                    FADE TO BLACK

INT. COSTA COFFEE BAR. BIG CITY CENTRE. DAY.

Glen Anders enters, orders coffee at the counter. He is dressed
in jeans, baseball cap and casual jacket. He takes his coffee
to a table in the corner and sits, his back to a wall, takes a sip.
Sweeping the other occupants, he sees nothing of interest. He
logs into Costa's internet and opens BLACKWATER SECURITIES's
website, scrolling to OPPORTUNITIES.

                                                    FADE TO BLACK

                                                        FADE IN:

EXT. LARNE HARBOUR. NORTHERN IRELAND

Michael O'Leary leans on the handrail and watches the P+O
European Causeway Ferry from Cairnyan docking at the busy
ferry-point below him. Over to his right, partly lost in mist, the
Ballylumford Power Station looms like a grey monolith. The grey
seas below the mist are choppy and O'Leary reflects that poor
old Larne was not exactly gifted in charm. The street-scapes has
a number of once attractive Georgian buildings, but there is
general feeling of dreariness, run-down buildings, gap sites and

wasteland, here and there boarded up windows and overflowing bins.

(A beat)

An altercation below and to his left catches his attention. Several men are unloading a cattle truck and O'Leary watches fascinated as two donkeys attack several sheep, scattering them among the cars and trucks. The men eventually round up the sheep, their angry Gaelic herding shouts drifting upwards to O'Leary on the icy wind. The owner of the donkeys resentful, patting the animals as if they were his children.

CUT TO:

EXT. LARNE HARBOUR. NORTHERN IRELAND

O'Leary straightens, He has spotted his man. The unmistakable military bearing, the obligatory BERGEN rucksack, Ray-Bans impassively surveying the Harbour, then sweeping along the skyline, passing O'Leary, then sweeping back to him.

O'Leary and Glen Anders stand stock still, their gaze across the 50M of ancient harbour locked, curious, professional, and without fear. Both men warriors of earlier battlegrounds.

CUT TO:

INT. LARNE HARBOUR. NORTHERN IRELAND SMALL COFFEE SHOP RESTAURANT

Glen Anders sits, back to a wall, by a misted window looking out a street clogged with slow moving freight trucks and mud-spattered tractors mixed with cars, their windscreen wipers swishing. The street sloped up from the harbour, rows of boarded up shops, closed shutters and grilled windows, some still showing the dog-eared posters for events that happened months ago, giving a sad diminished impression to the grey town.

His eyes slide around the interior of the cafe. A few genteels mixed with the mainly down at heel, everyone jostling for space.

294

He watches the tall self-assured figure of Michael O'Leary carry a tray of coffee mugs and bacon rolls though the melee back to their table. O'Leary is completely at ease in his surroundings, acknowledging several people here and there, an easy grin on his battered handsome face.

In another life O'Leary would have been his target, now most likely his new boss - if things went well.

O'Leary slides into his seat, his grey eyes appraising and measured. He pushes a mug and bacon roll towards Anders.

> MICHAEL O'LEARY
> Well, Glen, welcome to the
> salubrious town of Larne, Northern
> Ireland. Some say that Larne is the
> healing place of the soul.
> > (He glanced around the
> > cafe, grimaced)
> Me, I'm not so sure, but the bacon is
> good to be sure.

Anders tastes his coffee, unrolls paper from the bacon roll and sniffs.

> GLEN ANDERS
> Thank you, Mr O'Leary.
> MICHAEL O'LEARY
> Michael please.
> > (Easy grin)

The two men appraise each other, then both attacking the bacon rolls with relish. Anders, his mouth full of food, looks around, indicates an unintelligible sentence chalked across the bottom of the menu blackboard screwed to the wall opposite.

> GLEN ANDERS
> What the fuck does that say?
> MICHAEL O'LEARY
> > (Glancing at the chalkboard,
> > concentrating, then gravely)

It says 'And our spirits rushed
together at the touching of our lips'

Anders pauses, stops chewing, he looks again at the chalkboard, then at O'Leary, questioning. Slowly he grins, nodding, then swallowing, he laughs, wiping his mouth on a napkin, he laughs again, louder.

O'Leary meets his gaze, initially serious, then a slow grin. He looks around the crowded cafe, then back at Anders, his grey eyes crinkled with merriment as he laughs as well.

CUT TO:

EXT. LARNE HARBOUR. NORTHERN IRELAND. RAINY STREET

Establishing shot across a rainy street, two men framed in a cafe window, sitting at a high table facing each other. Next to the cafe an incongruously posh interiors shop selling Farrow and Ball paint and wallpapers. On the other side, a garish Pound Shop, its sign hanging at an angle from one chain.

The camera pulls back as the rain stops. On the opposite corner, the Charlemont Arms Hotel advertised 'Steak Night' every night between 6 - 8.30. A watery sun appears, the granite paving stones twinkling, the bleak industrial landscape softening.

CUT TO:

AERIAL. EXT. LARNE HARBOUR. NORTHERN IRELAND. RAINY STREET

The camera rises higher, a derelict petrol station, a muddy roundabout and giant KFC outlet stood on its own in front of a rubbish strewn wasteland.

A huge billboard showing 'Welcome to Larne, Northern Ireland'.

FADE TO BLACK

FADE IN:

INT. IRIS'S HOUSE KITCHEN. DAY

Iris sits forlorn with a teapot and mug. Her cell phone trills, Mike Kramer's name on the screen, she grabs the handset.

PHONE CONVERSATION

> IRIS
> Mike, did you hear...
> MIKE KRAMER
> Iris, you sitting?
> IRIS
> Oh God Mike...
> MIKE KRAMER
> No baby, it's not that. He's safe. Both
> of them are safe. He's...
> IRIS
> (Emotional)
>
> Thank God. Where...?
> MIKE KRAMER
> He's out of England Iris. I had a
> call. Can't tell you any more right
> now. They are both safe, but not
> contactable, do you understand?

Iris is in floods of tears, her relief overcoming her curiosity for the moment. Both her and Mike are silent for a beat, she can hear Mike breathing, then the phone hangs, dead in her hand.

CUT TO:

EXT. BELFAST INTERNATIONAL AIRPORT. CARPARK. DAY

AERIAL

O'Leary's Range Rover and Benny's Transit enter the short stay carpark and park side by side. Six men exit the two vehicles carrying single sports bags. The two vehicles drive off as the men walk towards the Departures terminal.

CUT TO:

EXT. OUJDA AIRPORT. MOROCCO. DAY

The Royal Air Maroc Flight RAM462 from Belfast to Oujda, Morocco lands at Angad Airport Runway 1 at 1540pm. The 7hr flight from Belfast is on time.

Michael O'Leary, Stiv, Bob, Glen Anders and two others (Liam and Robbo) pass through customs without incident. The arrivals section is quiet as they queued separately through passport control and then pick up their luggage from the sparsely populated carousels. The six casually dressed men stretch their legs after the flight, then head to...

CUT TO:

INT. OUJDA AIRPORT. SMALL AIRPORT COFFEE BAR. DAY

The 6-man team are seated on high stools against the coffee bar. O'Leary sips his coffee, grimaces, and looks around the newly tiled concourse.

> MICHAEL O'LEARY
> Welcome to Morocco lads, decrepit
> and seething, barren yet frenetic.
> Oujda is a bit less busy than most
> other Moroccan airports these
> days. The Algerian border has been

closed for 20yrs now and this city
has lost its 'mojo' a bit.

                    BOB
            (Pushing his coffee away)
Coffee is shite.

                MICHAEL O'LEARY
                (Grinning)
Not the best Bobby lad, I know. This
used to be a party town back in the
90s. You could even get alcohol -
under the counter mind you, but
even so, it was a swinging place.
Mainly students come here now,
there's a big university here. Most
of the rest of the population are
involved in smuggling stuff back and
forth across the Algerian border, 10
miles in that direction.

                    (Indicating vaguely west,
                    then rubbing his hands
                    together, a business-like
                    tone)
Right, taxi to the hotel lads. We are
about 7 miles out of downtown. A
couple of days of sightseeing for
you's while I make a few calls eh.

                    (a beat, crooked grin)
Remember lads, everything you see
here is merely a metaphor for all the
things that you do not see.

Stiv and Bob look at O'Leary in puzzlement. Glen Anders is used to
O'Leary's homespun philosophy by now, he winks at them.

                    GLEN ANDERS
                    (standing)
Come on lads, enough poetry
already. I'll treat you to a goat curry
later, it'll blow your bollocks off.

                    (a beat)

Look after your passports, no
passport at one of the random stop
and searches, and you are fucked -
big-time. You say you are both from
Cumbria? That wouldn't be around
the Ulverston area would it by any
chance?
                    BOB
You know Ulverston then Glen?
                GLEN ANDERS
Oh, I passed through there once
you know. I don't know it well. Nice
place I recall.

Stiv hears the exchange, picking up a vague nuance of tension
from Anders.

                    BOB
We both born and bred in the South
Lakes. We...
                    STIV
            (Hard look at Bob)
Let's get moving lads, shall we. We
are getting left behind.

Anders lets it ride; he has put it together. He knows, and he thinks
that maybe Stiv knew as well. They hurry to catch up with the
others.

                                                CUT TO:

EXT. OUJDA AIRPORT. MORROCO. CARPARK. DAY

The 6-man team emerge from the air-conditioning into the
Moroccan afternoon 39c heat. Several multi-coloured Mercedes
190s, at least 25 yrs old are parked along the shaded side of the
concourse, the drivers in a cluster, smoking.

                MICHAEL O'LEARY
                (Good humoured grin)

Salaam Alaikum men, I hope
you are well my friends. Would it
be possible that you transport us
forthwith to the Atlas Orient Hotel?

The drivers look non-plussed.

> MICHAEL O'LEARY (CONT'D)
> (Looking from one to the
> other)
> Oh, come on fellers, you know the
> one, it's in the plaza where old train
> station used to be. It's very classy,
> and I'm told you can get a beer and
> have a swim there.
> (Grin widening)
> I'm also told it serves PORK these
> days. Now that's a big change from
> the old days eh.

A couple of drivers hustle to load luggage into the trunks of the
190s. O'Leary, clearly enjoying himself gently harangues them.

> MICHAEL O'LEARY (CONT'D)
> Now don't you guys be charging
> us too much for the trip, its only 15
> minutes away to be sure, and you
> know, we might be needing you
> again later.
> (A beat)
> And another thing, we won't
> wanting any nice ladies for
> company thank you very much. We
> are working men don't you know.

CUT TO:

Later:

EXT. ATLAS ORIENT HOTEL BAR. NIGHT

The bar is a brightly illuminated circle in the midst of a vast dimly lit salon populated by smaller pools of low light from ornate lanterns on tables. Punters are scattered here and there. A fake waterfall gurgles in the distance, and a jazz guitarist plays lift music as he wanders around the tables somewhere in the semi darkness. A card on the table tells readers that personal music is $30.US and advises that the Concierge will to happy to discuss any other personal needs and requirements in private.

The Hit Team sit apart from other guests, freshly showered and fed, sprawling around a circular table with beers and cocktails.

Michael O'Leary sits upright, looking around before addressing them in a low voice.

> MICHAEL O'LEARY
> Right, now listen up lads.
> (Eye contact all around)
> The French delegation will arrive in
> Algeria 7 days from now, so we have
> 6 days to do a number of things.
> (A beat)
> 1) We cross into Algeria and set
> up a base. 2) We stake out our
> hit location. 3) We plan and fine
> tune the hit and getaway. It goes
> without saying, we need to pick up
> our guns - they are all sorted and
> waiting for us. I have a local fixer
> who has arranged the crossing and
> the base, so we need to focus on
> the hit proper now.
> (Looking around)
> Are you with me boys?
>
> OK now, this is the pitch. The French
> Trade delegation, including our
> target, will fly in from Paris to Sidi
> Bel Abbes. They will have a few

meetings in the day, then take a
small jet south to a lovely Oasis
called Mecheria, less than an hour's
flight from Sidi. It's a beautiful spot
in the desert, very nice hotel, lake
etc. They are going to meet senior
Oil Rig staff there and some Algerian
politicians, usual dinner, overnight
etc. French - Algerian political shite,
it's gone on for generations. The
French fund a lot of the oil rigs, the
Ain Sefra Rig is a big payday for
France.

Next day, its a convoy of 4*4s to Ain
Sefra Oil Rig. 43 miles of dust roads.
No military escort, just CPOs, its been
fairly quiet in the desert for the past
couple of years.

                    STIV

CPOs...?

                    MICHAEL O'LEARY
Close Protection Officers. These are
usually ex-military mercenaries. A
bit like us really. Don't sell them short
though, some handy lads, might
even know some of them.

We have a few days to set up the hit
in that 43 miles dust-road section.
Glen has spotted three or four
possibles sites on Google Earth, but
we need to walk the ground.

The 5 team members are focused and alert. O'Leary pauses,
head tipped to one side, appraising his team. He turns to Glen
Anders.

                    MICHAEL O'LEARY (CONT'D)
Glen, you have a lot of experience
on both sides of a hit. I know

you haven't walked the ground,
but you've done a lot of outline
planning to get us going.

Anders sits upright, glancing around the vast salon, then satisfied
no-one is in earshot...

> GLEN ANDERS
> (Low voice, military style)
> First thoughts are these Michael.
> Our team has a particular skill-base,
> snipers and close-up shooters.
> (A beat)
> Right, our team, there are 3 Levels
> of Command. 1) Overall is Michael.
> He calls it. 2) Next command level
> down, me. If Michael goes down, its
> then me. If both of us go down, then
> its Survival Mode. 3) Take care of
> your brothers, kill anyone/everyone
> else and get the fuck out of there.

O'Leary leans back, a faint grin on his face. A small gesture
indicated that Anders should continue.

> GLEN ANDERS (CONT'D)
> Skill-base.
> (A beat)
> Two sniper rifles working from
> two corners of a front triangle -
> firing back to oncoming targets.
> Specifically, their targets are first,
> stop the convoy. Then hit the Close
> Protection Officers - The CPOs. Either
> take them down or render them
> ineffectual with suppressing fire.
> (Looking at Stiv and Bob)
> That's you guys. Your job is NOT
> to search for and fire on our
> target - you got that? Unless of

course it presents itself, which is
unlikely.

Do not WASTE your firepower. Talk to
each other through your headsets,
do not shoot the same targets. Do
not look away from the action. Do
not relax, even if things go quiet.
        (Leaning forward, hands flat
        to the tabletop, eyes on the
        two young men)
And do not shoot your brothers on
the ground.

Stiv and Bob are rapt with attention. Both nod, mute.

        GLEN ANDERS (CONT'D)
        (Addressing the two
        remaining team members)
My own self, Liam and Robbo are on
the ground. We take out the target
at close quarter with assault rifles
and handguns.

Grenades are for clean-up once
we know for certain the target is
acquired - not before.
        (A beat)
Got that lads? Once we have
him, only then a grenade in each
vehicle - not before.
        (Glancing at O'Leary)
We are looking for an 80% kill of
personnel - Michael will say more
about that in a minute.

Liam and Robbo nod. O'Leary is silent, sipping his beer.

        GLEN ANDERS (CONT'D)
OK, location.
        (A beat)

We haven't walked the walk yet as Michael said, but we are looking at four possible 'PINCH POINTS' that will slow the convoy and inhibit vehicle movement down to a single file.

This is likely to be a natural feature that is out there waiting for us. Most likely it will be a bridge, or a creek, or a corner, or a dip in the road. We will know it when we see it. If we can't find it, then we create it - maybe a fake vehicle breakdown, not sure yet.

Anders pause, looking at O'Leary.

> GLEN ANDERS (CONT'D)
> Michael, you have overall command, and a roving commission. You fill any and all gaps that might emerge during the HIT. That includes any casual travellers who might stray into the action. If things go well, you will have little to do.

O'Leary nods, gesturing for Anders to continue.

> GLEN ANDERS (CONT'D)
> Right, The 5 stages of the HIT. They overlap.
> (A beat)
> Stage 1, Snipers. Take out drivers, vehicle engines, tires. The objective is to STOP the convoy. Sustained accurate fire with heavy calibre amour piercing slugs.
> (A beat)

Stage 2, Snipers. Disable/render
ineffectual the CPOs. Sustained
accurate fire.
          (A beat)
Stage 3, Ground Shooters go in.
Clean up any CPOs that are still
active. Snipers select any targets
that present themselves. Close
shooters take down our TARGET.
O'Leary to check acquisition of our
target.
          (A beat)
Stage 4: Ground Shooters. Clean-up.
Grenade to each vehicle. O'Leary
to identify 'Specific Hit Survivors'.
              (A beat, looking around the
              table)
Stage 5. Everyone. Getaway plan.
Fast drive across border to city limits,
merge with normal traffic. Dump
guns - except handguns. Get to
Oujda, then dump handguns. Flights
out ASAP.

Anders leans back, picks up his drink. There is silence around the
table for several minutes. Michael O'Leary drinks from his glass,
ice clinking.

              MICHAEL O'LEARY
              (Quietly)
Thank you, Glen. Tomorrow we cross
in Algeria and pick up weapons.
It's no big deal. That's what this city
is for.

One thing Glen mentioned, a
couple of French Govt big shots are
with our target, we don't want to
kill them, maybe shake them up a
bit... one of them is our PAYMASTER.

I'll deal with selectivity of that
particular issue on the ground - OK?
              (Several beats, musing)

Abraham Lincoln, Gandhi, The
Kennedys, Martin Luther King,
Malcolm X, John Lennon. They
all said, 'Let's try to live together
peacefully'.
              (A beat)
Then, BAM...!
              (Smacking a fist into his
              palm)
...a SLUG, right in the fucking head.
              (A beat, crooked grin)
We join illustrious company boys.

                                        FADE TO BLACK

EXT. N17 ROAD SOUTH FROM OUJDA TO TENRARA. EARLY MORNING

The team check out of the hotel before 7.00am. Three black
VOLVO XC90 4*4s are waiting for them along the hotel frontage.
They board the vehicles, two men to each. O'Leary gets into the
passenger seat of the lead vehicle, indicating Stiv to drive.

              MICHAEL O'LEARY
You don't mind Stephen, do you?
I'm a better passenger than a driver
you know.

Stiv grunted and slid into the driver's seat.

              MICHAEL O'LEARY (CONT'D)
There's a Satnav, but it won't work
here. We are looking for the N17
south to Tendrara. Its a nice road,
smooth and not much traffic these
days. 120 miles or so, should be
there before lunchtime.

The three identical vehicles convoy south out of the city on the smooth black bitumen. The centre of Oujda and the ancient Medina with its labyrinthine walls is enclosed in centuries old fortifications, with black holes and gaps housing small workshops and businesses. Tourists are non-existent. People, bikes, trucks, market carts, animals, flow around each other like shoals of fish. Along the main road, people are selling wares, plastic buckets, oranges, mint, saffron, livestock, goats, pots and pans, guns and ammunition. Stiv is excited and fascinated with a vague feeling of pride swelling his chest.

They pass a weaver sitting at his loom, a jeweller stringing beads, a butcher's shop where a goat's head sits on a spike, its skinned carcass hanging beside it, testicles bloated in the sun.

O'Leary, one foot up on the dash, leans back into his seat, at ease and self-assured. They pass a young woman, incongruous in jeans, tee shirt and hijab, walking south towards the desert with two wolf-like creatures circling her. O'Leary watches her through RAY BANS, then grinning across at Stiv...

>   MICHAEL O'LEARY (CONT'D)
>   Direct descendants in line from the
>   Queen of Sheba Stephen.
>   (A beat, grin widening)
>   The dogs, I mean. She had creatures
>   like that.

O'Leary slides down his window, hot dry air flooding in, gesturing and calling something at a group of girls as they pass. They giggle, wave and yell right back. He waves, smiling, sliding his window back up, the air-con regaining its coolness again.

>   MICHAEL O'LEARY (CONT'D)
>   If we had the time, I would take you
>   to the Riad Omar Mixed Hammam
>   Stephen. It's a bit un-nerving, but an
>   interesting experience, particularly
>   in a Muslim country. Out there they
>   cover up every inch of themselves.

Then you go through a doorway,
and BANG, they take off everything.
          (A grave look sideways at
          Stiv)
Acres of flesh, all pinkly
scrubbed - fabulous!

Great pendulous watermelon
breasts and monolithic thighs. You'd
love it Stephen!

It's a cross between a municipal
shower room and a Women's
Institute Meeting. White tiles, noise,
screeching.

Stiv listens idly to O'Leary, and settles into the journey, glancing in the mirror at the two identical VOLVOs following. He is aware the road is steadily rising out of the green city valley into high desert, the temp gauge in the dash showing 42c. They pass stepped terraces of green, layered with dry stone walls covered with the dust of ancient storms. Almond trees with pale pink blossom that wafts a honey smell through the air con. Goats are everywhere, arrogantly eating everything in sight, sometimes climbing high into trees for nuts.

Even early morning, the sun's heat is intense. As the city limits fall away, the light orange sand landscape stretches in all directions. Oncoming trucks materialize as indistinct images, mirages in the heat haze rising silently up from the swirling tarmac. Out of the city, the road is curiously empty, suggesting that the three vehicles were traveling nowhere important.

          MICHAEL O'LEARY (CONT'D)
We'll have a spot of lunch at
Tendrara, then we are off-road. Off
the tarmac at any rate.
          STIV
Where then?

> MICHAEL O'LEARY
> Oh, about another 40 miles or so
> Stephen, towards the Algerian
> border. My fixer has got a secure
> little base a couple of miles this side
> of the border. It's a deserted farm.
> Some water.
>> (Glancing at Stiv)
> No phone, no internet, no electricity.

Stiv grunted.

> MICHAEL O'LEARY (CONT'D)
> You are a long way from Ulverston
> Stephen my son. Are you OK?
>> STIV
> I'm good, yes.
>> (A beat, glancing at
>> O'Leary)
> I like it.

O'Leary is silent for a long moment. He regards Stiv's profile with narrowed eyes as he drove.

> MICHAEL O'LEARY
> Yes, I think you do Stephen. I think
> you do.
>> (A beat)
> What about your mate Bob, do you
> think he likes it as well?

They exchange glances.

DISSOLVE TO:

EXT. MOROCCAN DESERT 2 MILES EAST OF ALGERIAN BORDER. LATE AFTERNOON

The 3 VOLVOs pull up in a cloud of orange dust by a cluster of sand-blasted mud buildings in remote desert. An ancient Toyota Land Cruiser is parked nearby. In the dark waist high doorway sits an old lady dressed in black hijab and abaya. She must be at least 80 years old, sitting next to mounds of nuts and flour, making flatbread on an open fire. Around the fire lay an array of ancient cooking tools, a pestle+mortar, a large pot tagine and several sacks. Leaning against the wall next to her was a battered Kalashnikov AK47, its wooden stock splintered and worn.

O'Leary exits the car in the settling dust, stretches and walks over to the old lady.

> MICHAEL O'LEARY
> (Gravely)
> Salaam Aleikum My Mother. I hope
> you are well.

The old lady adjusts her HIJAB and continues cooking, totally ignoring his greeting, then turning her head, calls a stream of rapid Arabic through the dark doorway. Presently a large round-faced Arab appears. O'Leary smiles.

> MICHAEL O'LEARY (CONT'D)
> Salaam Aleikum Zami, it's good to
> see you again my friend.
> (Turning to Stiv)
> Stephen, this is my friend
> Mohammad Al-Zamil, Zami to his
> friends, of which I am honoured to
> be one.

Zami steps forward immediately into O'Leary's personal space and embraces him warmly.

ZAMI

> Mister Michael, Salaam Aleikum to
> you. Welcome to our humble, but
> temporary, house.
> (Indicating the old lady)
> This is Hakira, my Mother. She is
> preparing food for us later.

O'Leary bows with great ceremony and respect to Hakira

                    MICHAEL O'LEARY
            Hakira, I am very happy to meet
            you. Thank you for your hospitality
            and kindness.

Zami translates in rapid Arabic. Hakira gives zero
acknowledgment, ignores everyone and continues cooking.

                    ZAMI
            (To O'Leary, then turning to
            address the rest of the team)
            Hakira is very pleased and
            honoured to meet you and your
            friends and cook for you today, and
            she wishes you well in your travels
            and your work and hopes that all
            your families are in good health.

Bob and Stiv looked from Zami to Hakira in jaw dropped
astonishment.

                    BOB
            She didn't say anything.
                    MICHAEL O'LEARY
            (Severely)
            Lads, her love and care for you
            is enshrined in the food that she
            cooks. She speaks to you through
            her beloved son Mohammad.
            (A beat)
            Plus, the fact that she didn't shoot
            your fucking ass off 2 seconds after
            you got out of the car.

Zami smiles at everyone indulgently, sweeping his hand in a wide
circular motion.

                    ZAMI
         Please sit everyone. Rest yourselves
         after your long journey.

The Team sit around the fire in a circle with Zami and Hakira. Zami
handed out handfuls of dates from a sack, then passes around
flat-breads and small tin cups of sweet mint tea.

Hakira quietly continues cooking, her face dark in the shadow of
her hijab.

                                        DISSOLVE TO:

**EXT. MOROCCAN DESERT 2 MILES EAST OF ALGERIAN BORDER.
EARLY MORNING**

Bob, Stiv and Liam emerge from the low doorway bent double,
straightening with effort in the dazzling sunlight. Hakira is in
exactly the same position as the previous day, making flatbread,
surrounded by her bits and pieces. She ignores them as usual.
The Kalashnikov AK47 leans next to her. Zami appears from
somewhere. He engages Hakira in an unintelligible stream of
guttural vowels, glottal stops and poor dental hygiene for several
minutes. At no point does Hakira acknowledge his existence or
stop what she is doing.

                    ZAMI
              (Turning to the 3 team
              members)
         Hakira hopes that you have had a
         pleasant night, and that you are all
         well today. She also passes on her
         best wishes to your families.

Stiv and Bob exchange glances, then bob their heads towards
Hakira.

                 STIV AND BOB
         Salaam Aleikum Hakira, thank you.

Zami smiles profusely, Hakira ignores everyone. They eat flat-bread and olives and drink mint tea. Presently the whole team are there.

                    MICHAEL O'LEARY
                       (To Zami)
                 Now Zami, the weapons?

Zami turns to Hakira with his usual stream of guttural vowels. Hakira laboriously gets to her feet and lumbers painfully across to the Land Cruiser, unlocking and opening the tailgate. She stands beside the vehicle, looking arrogantly back at the group. Zami stands, his arm sweeping in a circular motion.

                         ZIM
                 Gentlemen please...

The 6 men converge on the rear of the land Cruiser. Hakira sweeps aside several layers of sacking to reveal well-oiled modern guns, ammunition and equipment.

                    MICHAEL O'LEARY
              Zami, my man. You never disappoint.

Zami beams, Hakira lumbers back to her fire, flopping down.

                MICHAEL O'LEARY (CONT'D)
                    (Stepping back)
                 Glen, your guns.
                     GLEN ANDERS
                (Stepping up to the Land
                    Cruiser tailgate)
                 Stiv, Bob, step up. Two Barret M82
                 50cal Rifles. 10 round Mag, semi-
                 auto floating barrel fitted with
                 Vortex scopes. These beauties will
                 stop an armoured vehicle and
                 penetrate steel-clad vehicle engine
                 bays like a hot knife through butter.
                 2 hundred rounds of amour piercing

shells each, plus a hundred rounds
of practice ammo for zeroing.
(Glancing at Bob and Stiv)
OK for you?

The two young men step up, Stiv beaming, Bob white-faced,
each hefting a rifle in its gun-slip, and several metal boxes of
ammunition.

GLEN ANDERS (CONT'D)
Also, two Glock 17 handguns in
speed holsters.

Loaded with firepower, the two assassins step away from the
Land Cruiser. Both are engrossed with the weapons, silent and
thoughtful.

GLEN ANDERS (CONT'D)
OK, everyone else. Glock 17s all
round. Plus, Kalashnikov AK47s.
(Catching looks from Liam
and Robbo)
Aw, come-on lads, AKs are standard
fare here in North Africa. Difficult
to get anything else, plus ammo
is everywhere, they even sell it in
roadside fuel stations here. Dead
reliable, you could dunk an AK in
sand, shake it, and it would fire.
You've all used them.
(A beat)
Finally, the 'clean-up' box. Frag
Grenades. These only to be used
after target kill confirmation. They
are CLEAN-UP only. In the open,
these bad boy's kill radius is 5M.
Casualty radius 15M. Inside a
vehicle, everything is mincemeat.
(To everyone)
Lads check your firearms and
ammo, then get setup to shoot

some Zeroing rounds - to make sure
we are not firing wide on the day.

    (To Stiv and Bob)

Guys, zero your guns for 100M. You'll
be familiar with Vortex scopes, I
guess.

    (Glancing at O'Leary)

That's it.

    MICHAEL O'LEARY

OK lads get stuck in, the rest of
today is about the weapons. Make
sure everything is a 'GO'. Let me
know immediately if anything
doesn't work in the way you want
it to. By tonight I want everything
zeroed and ready.

    (A beat)

Tomorrow, its handguns only, we
cross into Algeria and find that
pinch point.

               DISSOLVE TO:

LATER

EXT. MOROCCAN DESERT. DAY

Zami and Hakira are at prayer, their black clad figures bent
double in the shade of the building, foreheads to the ground.
Stiv and Bob have paced out 100M and set up paper targets
to zero the scopes. Stiv has just grouped 5 shots into the black
and is screwing down the scope's mounts. Bob is dis-interestingly
watching.

        BOB

That's good mate, spot on. Do you
want to do the next one?

                    STIV
               (Looking up at Bob,
               surprised)
          What the fuck Bob! You need to zero
          your own rifle for yourself. You'll be
          the one shooting it.
                    (A beat, frowning up at Bob)
          Are you OK mate?
                    BOB
          I'm fine, I just thought...
                    STIV
               (Annoyed)
          Don't think you useless twat! Zero
          your fucking rifle like I just did. You
          are making me really nervous mate.
          This shit is scary enough without
          you wanting suck on your fucking
          Mum's tit.

Bob goes white with sudden rage, breathless, his vision blurring.

Stiv, working on his scope, looks up just in time to throw himself to
one side as Bob launches himself at him, fists flailing. The two men
roll in the blazing hot sand. Stiv is at a disadvantage, sweat and
sand in his eyes as he defends several heavy blows from Bob. Bob
is enraged, he throws battering punches, then picks up a steel
tripod, raising it high to beat Stiv with it.

Over by the building, Zami casually picks up his AK47, pulling back
the slide.

Suddenly Bob's weight lifts magically from Stiv and he blinked to
clear his sight, sitting up.

Michael O'Leary sits astride Bob, riding him, easily oblivious to his
struggles. The rest of the team, curious, come to watch. O'Leary
pulls a Glock17 from a holster and holds it to Bob's forehead in a
two-handed hold. He flicks off the safety catch, knuckles white
with tension. Bob, wide eyed, stares up at him, becoming very still.
O'Leary holds the position for several beats.

                    MICHAEL O'LEARY
                    (Evenly to Bob)
          Do not speak or move you fucker,
          you can breathe, but do it lightly. It
          is entirely possible that you are living
          your last few moments upon this
          earth my friend.
                    (A beat)
          I am considering my options
          right now.

No-one speaks, O'Leary is still as a rock. Anders holds his Glock17
behind his back - safety off, watching everyone. The whole
mission could fragment at any moment. Anders is sure that Stiv
will defend his friend, even though Bob had attacked him. Liam
and Robbo were O'Leary's men. Anders was acutely aware that
Zami was behind him to his right. Anders had his own agenda,
and he also wanted to be paid - but first he had to survive. Finally,
O'Leary speaks quietly and distinctly.

                    MICHAEL O'LEARY (CONT'D)
          Bob, I'm going to get up now. You
          will move only when I tell you. Do
          you understand your instruction?

O'Leary waits, Bob is still, gulping, he nods. He then takes his
weight from Bob's chest, rising easily to his feet, spread eagled
above Bob. He continues to hold the Glock in a two-handed
hold, aimed at Bob's head.

                    MICHAEL O'LEARY (CONT'D)
          Stand, now, very slowly, then face
          away from me.

Bob, white faced and shaking, does exactly as he is told.

                    MICHAEL O'LEARY (CONT'D)
                    (Clear, uncompromising)
          Now, slowly, kneel down. Do not
          look at me.

Bob kneels down facing away from O'Leary. O'Leary moves behind Bob, the Glock forward, touching the muzzle to the back of Bob's head. Feeling the touch, Bob jumps, making a choking sound, slightly raising his arms.

> MICHAEL O'LEARY (CONT'D)
> Do not fucking move. Drop your
> arms. Face away.

O'Leary touches the Glock to the back of Bob's head. Anders holds his breath, his own Glock hot in his hand.

No-one else moves. Anders becomes aware that Zami has moved forward and is standing slightly behind them all, an AK47 held loosely across his chest, his face inscrutable.

> MICHAEL O'LEARY (CONT'D)
> (Calmly, evenly)
> The last time I was here in this desert,
> I was in a small town. A celebratory
> feast was being prepared. I had
> dozed off in the shade you know, I
> awoke to see four men stood over
> a sacrificial cow. I had missed an
> earlier struggle you see; the cow
> was pretty battered. I was in time
> to see the cow's head hacked
> completely from its body with knives
> that were far too short for such a
> task. It was very spectacular in a
> technicolour sort of way.
> (A beat)
> The mess of its great neck, red,
> white and oozing, its hide peeled
> away like the skin of ripe fruit. I never
> forgot that you know.
>
> Tradition endures here you see,
> death is expected, and welcomed.
> (A beat)

There are villages here in this desert
where a floating bowl in a bucket
of water has a tiny hole in it. When
it fills and sinks, an hour has gone
by. The clock-keeper ties a knot in a
piece of string. That man, the Clock-
Keeper, does this from morning
to night, never stops. To him its an
important job, it describes infinity.

They have mobile cell phones you
know, but no clock. They prefer their
own ancient method of keeping
time.

Anders feels himself relaxing slightly but stays alert. He is aware
that O'Leary is talking himself down from his peak of tension.
Abruptly O'Leary stands away from Bob, his Glock down, safety
clicking ON. A long outward breath...

        MICHAEL O'LEARY (CONT'D)
You have gazed into abyss today
Bobby boy. Not many men do and
see the light of day on the other
side. You survive here today only
because of your mate here, Stiv. He
doesn't know it, but he saved your
life today.

He has my trust you see. You do not.
        (A beat)
You have to rebuild that trust Bob.
For me, for Stephen, and for your
brothers here. Do it or die like that
fucking sacrificial cow.

And the Clock-Timer will tie another
knot in his string to mark your
passing.

Looking at no-one to seek approval, O'Leary walks away to the shade of the building. Anders slid his Glock fully down into his holster, the tension flooding from him. When he looks round, Zami was no longer stood behind him with the AK47.

DISSOLVE TO:

EXT. MOROCCAN DESERT 2 MILES EAST OF ALGERIAN BORDER... NIGHT

The desert sky is a vast vibrant midnight blue merging to black where it meets the horizon. Hakira's fire is burning creating a bright circle, merging into black shadow. Some of the team lounge around the fire area on mattresses, necks beaded with sweat. The events of the day have affected everyone except Hakira, who has reacted in her usual way by ignoring it. The fire flares briefly as Hakira dumps the remnants of leftover food, and there is a metallic sound as Anders fiddles with a handgun.

O'Leary sits alone on the bonnet of a Volvo, his feet dangling down, staring into the darkness. Zami is nowhere to be seen. Anders snaps the slide of a Glock17 handgun, the sudden sound drawing everyone's glance, except Hakira who doesn't react. Anders gets to his feet, walks over and drops down next to Bob. He is silent for several beats, then...

> GLEN ANDERS
> (Low voice)
> A question. Do you want to save this mission? Or fuck it up the arse and possibly kill some of us?
> BOB
> (Resentful)
> What do you mean?
> GLEN ANDERS
> Its a simple question Answer it. What do you want?
> BOB
> I'm not trying to...

GLEN ANDERS
You are not trying anything, you
are a fucking stupid useless lump
of gob-shite. You shouldn't be
within a hundred miles of a military
operation; you are a petulant child
who is putting every other member
of this operation at risk - including
the man who you say is your mate.
>   (A beat, looking around the
>   campfire)
Let me tell you what is going to
happen. In the next few days,
we will hit the French convoy. We
won't go home you know; we are
committed to this mission. Walking
away from here without finishing
the job will kill everyone here within
months. None of us will survive
walking away. Do you hear what I
am saying Bob?
>   (Leaning forward)
You have entered an ordered and
disciplined world Mister. It may not
seem like that to you, but it has more
rigid rules than you have ever seen
in your short and infantile fucking
life. We are Guns for Hire. We get
paid vast amounts of money and we
travel the world. We live an exciting
and fascinating existence where we
perpetuate the old western myth of
roving gunslingers. Free spirits, and
no man is our master.
>   (Bitter laugh)
It's all bollocks.

We are not free. Once we sign up
for a HIT, we complete, or we die.
The people who take the decision
to unleash the Dogs of War, that is

US - do so with great reluctance. But
once done, there is no going back.
It cannot be undone.

You my friend are a bad omen.
You have split your brothers into
fragments and divisions, and you
have taken away the sharp edge
that we all need to get through this.

There are men here around this fire,
that will kill you in the next few days.
Not because they hate you or want
to harm you, but because they want
to survive, and make it through, and
get back to someone back there
in the world that they are doing it
all for.

You have fucked up my friend. You
will be a casualty of this HIT; you will
not make it back to Cumbria.

Bob reels back with horror, tears springing into his eyes, blurring
the campfire scene. He tried to digest and understand what
Anders was saying. He stares at Anders, utterly devastated.

                    BOB
        I didn't know.
            (A beat)
        What can I do? Is there anything?
                GLEN ANDERS
        You have fucked everyone here
        Bob. Made us all into fools, not
        professionals working as a focused
        team.
            (A beat)

        I don't know for sure if you are man
        enough, it may all be buggered
        already. But you can try to put this

right. Get off your fucking arse and
make it right with O'Leary. Then with
Stiv.
            (A beat, getting up)
Your choice.

Anders walks away into the darkness. Bob sits there staring around
the campfire. No-one meets his eyes. He knows in his heart that
Anders is right but has no clue how to repair the subtle warrior
bond that had existed between them all before his meltdown.
Bob gazes into his private abyss, sensing his fragile mortality.

There is a movement in the darkness to his right, a shifting change
in the blackness of the desert night. There is a rustle of robes and
the slight smell of cooking. Hakira materializes from the shadows
like a black wraith, lumbering, but with a grace he had never
noticed before. She hunkers down beside him, her old body
touching him along his leg and hip. She didn't look at him, didn't
speak. Her face beneath the hijab is in deep shadow. Minutes
go by, then her hand slides from her robe to cover Bob's hand,
initially still, then her fingers enclosing his, gripping, holding him
tightly.

Bob takes a long shuddering breath, his heart thumping, tears
springing into his eyes. Hakira is still as rock.

20M away, O'Leary raises his head, suddenly aware of a vague
thrumming in the darkness, a vibration. He looks towards Bob and
Hakira humped together. They were lit to one side by the glow
of the fire. As he looks, Hakira slides her hijab from her head and
turned her face towards O'Leary. She stares at him unblinking, her
eyes black as coal with pinpoints of flickering red reflecting the
firelight.

O'Leary is country Irish; he had been raised through his childhood
and formative years with the extraordinary wizardry and
witchcraft of the supernatural. It was embedded in his soul but
suppressed and blunted by the life that he had chosen and had
lived. Hakira grips Bob's hand and stares at O'Leary, her old face
inscrutable, but somehow softened with an ethereal beauty he
had never noticed before.

O'Leary feels a pressure in his chest, a tightness. Hakira holds his gaze and he slowly nods, then his eyes shifting to meet Bob's eyes, he nods again. Bob's eyes glitter, swimming with silent tears.

Around the fire, Stiv, Liam and Robbo stare from Hakira to O'Leary, aware of something, but not knowing what. By the corner of the mud building, Glen Anders pauses, something catching his attention, he stops, turns and looks across at Bob, suddenly thinking maybe he had been too hard on him. After a beat, he pushes the thought away, stoops and goes into the low doorway.

Zami appears out the darkness next to O'Leary. He leans against the side of the Volvo, silent and dangerous, the firelight gleaming dully along the barrel of his AK47.

FADE TO BLACK

INT. TURKISH AIRLINES FLIGHT 186A PARIS TO SIDI BEL ABBES, ALGERIA. FIRST CLASS. MORNING

M. De Freyn emerges from a daydream as the intercom announced that that they are due to land at Sidi Bel Abbes in 35 minutes. Across the aisle his beautiful Aide gives him a few moments, then slides smoothly into the vacant seat next to him.

> AIDE
> Monsieur Minister, Good Morning,
> I hope you have had a restful
> flight. We will be landing at Sidi in
> approximately 30 minutes. Can I get
> you anything?

> DE FREYN
> Thank you, Adele. Some orange
> juice please.

The Aide disappeared briefly, re-appearing with a crystal glass of pure orange juice. De Freyn sips minutely, then hands the glass back. Leaning back into his seat.

                              AIDE
                Monsieur Minister, if you are
                disposed, may I quickly review our
                itinerary with you.

De Freyn makes a small gesture, closing his eyes.

                         AIDE (CONT'D)
                      (Consulting a file)
                We will be met by a small
                delegation of Algerian Ministers
                plus our own Ambassador. There
                will be a short reception for some
                local dignitaries, then yourself, our
                Ambassador and Algeria's Minister
                for Trade will withdraw to a private
                suite.
                      (Passing over a single typed
                      page)
                The agenda has been agreed.

De Freyn scans the agenda, then passes it back without
comment.

                         AIDE (CONT'D)
                At 1530 we will take a short flight,
                less than 1 hour, to Mecheria. This
                is a beautifully developed oasis in
                the desert, very nice hotel, lake etc.
                Here you will meet senior Oil Rig
                staff and more Algerian politicians.
                Dinner, overnight etc.

                Next morning after breakfast,
                we drive to Ain Sefra Oil Rig,
                approximately 2 hours.

De Freyn digested this without comment. His eyes slide across
the aisle to rest on the back of the head of a perfectly groomed
man in his 40s. De Freyn, his lip curling, reflects with distaste that
the hair was dyed an impossible jet black. The man, sensing De

Freyn's gaze, turns, and their eyes meet. Both men nod minutely, and the link is immediately broken as De Freyn looks away.

                    DE FREYN
                  (To the Aide)
          Thank you, Adele. I wish to make a
          private call now.

Adele slides away immediately. De Freyn takes a sleek handset from his inside pocket and speed dials while gazing at the orange dunes sliding beneath the wings.

                    DE FREYN (CONT'D)
          Lafitte, report please.

De Freyn listens. The plane is passing through haze, bumping slightly, the engine note deepening. Then suddenly a clear unobstructed view of rolling orange dunes, an arrow straight black strip of dual carriageway and then a vast square of greenery with a large house and what looked like stables along one side, immediately lost beneath the wing.

                    DE FREYN (CONT'D)
          Thank you. We are on time and
          proceeding.

De Freyn breaks the connection. The Intercom bongs.

                    INTERCOM
          Ladies and Gentlemen, as we start
          our descent, please make sure
          seat backs and tray tables are in
          their full upright position. Make sure
          your seat belt is securely fastened
          and all carry-on luggage is stowed
          underneath the seat in front of you
          or in overhead bins. Thank you.

Several Hostesses walk the aisles, dipping, adjusting, flirting, closing overhead lockers, smiling dazzlingly at the First-Class passengers. The plane trembles as last-minute line up adjustments

were made and glaring strips of bright sunshine danced across
the cabin.

FLIGHT CAPTAIN

> Flight attendants prepare for
> landing please. Cabin Crew, please
> take your seats.

CUT TO:

INT. INTERPOL BUILDING CENTRAL PARIS. MORNING

Lafitte is at his desk. He stares at his cell phone screen as it clears
back to its home screen display. He immediately dials again.

> JEAN LAFITTE
> Michael, Lafitte. Proceeding. timings
> unchanged.
> > (Listening)
> Good.

Lafitte breaks the connection, then clears the phone's memory
and taking out the sim card, places the handset on his empty
desk in front of him. With precision, he lines up the handset
perfectly beside three other handsets, then leans back, spinning
his chair on its axis to watch workers crawling like ants on the
facade of Notre Dame Cathedral several hundred meters away..

EXT. AERIAL. ALGERIAN DESERT. TWO LANE DUST ROAD. DAY.

Three VOLVO XC90s follow a dim track across the rolling dunes
and hard-pan desert floor. The international border is no existent
and completely featureless.

CUT TO:

INT. VOLVO.

Eventually their track joins a more established two-lane track. Anders and O'Leary are in the leading vehicle.

> MICHAEL O'LEARY
> (Consulting his map, then
> gesturing to his right)
> This must be the road. Head in that
> direction until we see the rig.

Presently they spot the tips of several structures on the horizon. A massive flame billows upwards from the tip of a black pipe.

> MICHAEL O'LEARY (CONT'D)
> That's it. Turn the other way now and
> we will drive back along the road.
> How far do you reckon to your first
> pinch point?
> GLEN ANDERS
> 2 miles or so I guess.

The road winds through rolling dunes, sometimes disappearing under blown sand. Rose coloured rocky outcrops become more prevalent with sometimes steep drop offs along the side of the track. They pass through a small canyon. O'Leary is looking up at rocks above them.

> GLEN ANDERS (CONT'D)
> What are you thinking?
> MICHAEL O'LEARY
> Pull up Glen.

Anders pulls into the side of the track. The other two vehicles pull up behind. O'Leary is looking upwards, then goes to the tailgate, rummaging in the rear of the vehicle. he emerges with a pinch bar.

> MICHAEL O'LEARY (CONT'D)
> (to Liam and Robbo)

On me lads. Grab a couple of bars.

The three men scramble up the steep loose shale to the rocks above. O'Leary, older than the others, is still agile and strong. He shouts down from high above.

                    MICHAEL O'LEARY (CONT'D)
               Pull those vehicles along a bit.
Within a few minutes, the three men cascade several tons of loose rocks down the hillside. The rocks rolling out onto the track, a pall of orange dust gradually settling. O'Leary grins down at Anders wolfishly.

                    MICHAEL O'LEARY (CONT'D)
               Our pinch point boys. Let's step it out.

Back down on the road, the team assemble around Glen Anders.

                    GLEN ANDERS
                    (Briskly)
               Stiv, Bob, pace 100M along in that
               direction. One rifle each side of the
               road. Set up a station for yourselves.
               Use your phones - take plenty of pics
               for later.
                    (Looking around, then to the
                    others - gesturing)
               Layups here and here, both sides,
               plenty of rocks for cover.

Anders pace around the area looking at angles, taking photographs with his phone handset. Squinting upwards, finally walking completely out of sight in the direction their target would be coming from. He returns, nodding.

                    GLEN ANDERS (CONT'D)
               Its good. Looks like a natural rockfall.
               Someone else might be along this
               road in the next day or two. If they
               clear it, its ok.
                    (Looking upwards)
               Plenty more up there.
                    (Looking around everyone)

Happy? Any questions? None? Right
lads let's get the fuck out of here.

They get back into their vehicles and clear the area, soon back
onto the smaller track back and across the invisible border into
Morocco.

DISSOLVE TO:

EXT. MERCERIA OASIS HOTEL. ALGERIA DESERT. DAY

The convoy of 6 Mercedes G Wagons pulls up semi-circled in the
deep shade of the Hotel frontage. Elaborately dressed hotel staff
transport luggage on carts along the tiled reception area. De
Freyn and his entourage are smoothly checked in and taken to
air-conditioned rooms.

The hotel is palatial European/Atlantic, rather than Arabic in style.
Marble columns, vast high ceilings, statement plants and flowers.
Huge dramatic sculptures flooded with natural and ornamental
light, the scale and opulence designed to inspire hushed awe.

Opposite the entrance, floor to ceiling windows overlook multiple
lagoon-like swimming pools with islands of trees, grass and
loungers.

De Freyn walks around his elegant suite of rooms. He is tired and
irritated, the rose coloured bath, luxurious chairs and fittings are
of scant interest to him. He waves the obsequious hotel manager
away and walks out onto a balcony overlooking a vast Zen-like
Eden of water, greenery and cascading fountains. There is a
knock on his door, he turned, annoyed.

DE FREYN

Not now.

The door stays closed. De Freyn considers, relents.

DE FREYN (CONT'D)

OK, what is it?

The door opens.

> AIDE
> Monsieur Minister. Please excuse me,
> may I have a moment.

> DE FREYN
> Adele, yes, come in. My apologies.
> I know you would not disturb me
> unless it was important.

Adele smiles, relieved.

> AIDE
> Thank you Minister. Is it possible
> that you spare a few moments for
> Monsieur Gerard Dupont-Moret?
> He has requested a short discussion
> several times now. I thought maybe
> 10 minutes...?
> > (A beat)
> There is some time before dinner
> tonight perhaps?

De Freyn, his face set, turns away, considering. He does not want
to spend even one minute with this person. As far as De Freyn
is concerned his death warrant is signed and sealed, and he is
living out his last days upon the earth - if of course things went as
De Freyn hoped. Finally, De Freyn speaks irritably.

> DE FREYN
> OK Yes, send him in Adele. Can you
> please 'interrupt' us after 5 minutes.
> AIDE
> Of course, Monsieur Minister.

De Freyn walks to the balcony, gazing out, his hands on the
marble atrium rail and lights an over-sized cigar. Behind him, the
door clicks, and he was aware of a malevolent presence in the
room. For several beats he does not speak, forcing himself not
to turn to face the man who has proved himself to be a traitor to

France, and was personally responsible for a number of deaths of Frenchmen around the World.

The room is still, silent. Finally, De Freyn turns.

> DE FREYN
> Ah, good evening Monsieur Dupont-
> Moret. You asked to see me.
>> (De Freyn lifted his cuff and
>> consulted his watch)
> I am expecting a call from the
> Elysée Palace, you may have to
> excuse me.

Gerard Dupont-Moret is a senior diplomat of long standing to the French Court. As a younger man, he had held roles with two previous Presidents, now continuing with the current incumbent. He is handsome, sleekly elegant and self-assured. Jet black hair with a widow's Peak, with a cruel mouth. De Freyn hates him from the depths of his soul.

GERARD DUPONT-MORET

>> (Bowing slightly)
> Monsieur Minister, thank you for
> seeing me.
>> (A beat)
> It is a small matter. I have a family
> issue, the details of which I will not
> trouble you with, but it entails me
> traveling immediately back to
> France tonight. I am deeply sorry
> that my personal life has intruded
> on matters of state, but I fear on this
> occasion, it is the case.
>> (warming to his theme)
> Of course, I have looked closely
> at the itinerary of our next few
> days and I feel that my presence
> is not essential, indeed, it is entirely
> superfluous for the next week or so.

De Freyn is shocked, but his shock lies under a mask of the impeccable inscrutability that has carried him through a lifetime of international politics. Had Dupont-Moret been alerted...?

His thoughts whirling, De Freyn regards Gerard Dupont-Moret calmly through a spiralling cloud of blue cigar smoke. He opens his mouth to speak, but at that moment, there is a discreet tap on his room door, Adele appears.

> AIDE
> Excuse me Monsieur Minister, my
> apologies for the interruption, I have
> the Elysée Palace on the phone.
> DE FREYN
> Thank you, Adele.
> (Turning to address
> Dupont-Moret)
> I am sorry to cut our conversation
> short Monsieur, I must go
> immediately.
> (A beat, pausing)
> I must say however, it is not for you
> to decide whether or not your
> presence is essential in matters of
> French State. That Monsieur is for
> others to decide, in this case, me, on
> behalf of France.

Gerard Dupont-Moret opens his mouth to speak. De Freyn silences him with an imperious hand, palm outwards like a policeman halting traffic.

> DE FREYN (CONT'D)
> (Sharply)
> Do NOT interrupt me Monsieur. Your
> request is denied.

Adele stands respectfully to one side, and De Freyn stalks from the room without another word. Gerard Dupont-Moret is furious but holds his temper in check without any outward sign.

Down the corridor in Adele's room/Admin Centre, De Freyn, white-faced with rage, picks up a Waterford Lismore Diamond cut vase from a side table, and throws it violently across the room. It shatters on the tiled floor, glittering pieces radiating perfectly outwards from the impact point, sliding to a stop in geometric symmetry.

De Freyn fights for control, taking deep breaths. In the doorway, Adele stands immobile.

FADE TO BLACK

EXT. MERCERIA OASIS HOTEL. ALGERIA DESERT. DAY

The 4 Mercedes G Wagons stand in a semi-circle at the front to f the hotel. Each vehicle holds 2 diplomats, a Driver and a Close Protection Officer (CPO). Another Toyota Land Cruiser with a further 2 CPOs accompanies the convoy on its 43-mile trip to the Oil Rig. All drivers and CPOs are armed with handguns and a Heckler+Koch sub-machine guns.

De Freyn and Adele consult with the CPO Officer, a 40-year-old tough looking ex Legionnaire named Bruno Le May.

> AIDE
> I have the Travel Plan here Monsieur
> Minister. Bruno will be in the Lead
> Vehicle with 1 more CPO. You will be
> in the second vehicle with Monsieur
> Dupont-Moret.
> DE FREYN
> Let me see that.
> (Irritably snatching the list)
> I will not be traveling with DuPont-
> Moret Adele. I would like to be in the
> last but one car, the 4th vehicle.

> BRUNO LE MAY
> Sir, if I may say so, we are traveling
> dust roads. The further back in the
> convoy, the more dust in the air. You
> will see nothing in the last vehicle.

De Freyn ignore the CPO, addressing his full attention to Adele.

> DE FREYN
> This is a business trip, not sight-
> seeing. I do not wish to see the sight
> of sand dunes and rocks thank you. I
> will travel in the 4ᵗʰ vehicle, Monsieur
> Dupont-Moret will travel in the
> second vehicle. Can we get started
> now please?

De Freyn slides into the spacious rear of the G Wagon. Leaning back, then with a frown of annoyance, reaching behind him to adjust the belt holster of the Makarov 9mm Automatic that he had carried throughout his diplomatic career.

CUT TO:

WIDE AND AERIAL. EXT. MERCERIA OASIS HOTEL. ALGERIA DESERT. DAY

Adele, chastened, adjusts her lists, and the party noisily board the vehicles. Bruno Le May shrugs and goes to check the travel plan with his men in each vehicle, synchronizing satellite phones. Satisfied, he then boards the lead G Wagon, and the convoy streams from the hotel, passing through the small oasis, turning off the black bitumen onto the dust and gravel road to the Ain Sefra Oil Rig.

CUT TO:

EXT. AERIAL. ALGERIAN DESERT. TWO LANE DUST ROAD. DAY.

The HIT Team are in position. The dust track is littered with rubble and boulders, ostensibly from a rock-fall. The convoy will have no option, the lead vehicle must stop, and the following vehicles will be forced to pull up behind it.

Bob is positioned 60M directly in front of the convoy's position. Stiv is positioned at a 90-degree angle to create a triangular cross-fire. Ground close shooters are positioned each side of the convoy. O'Leary is in an elevated position in the rocks where he can see all of the action.

All 6 of the HIT Team have satellite phones linked together by a dedicated APP conference call software.

> MICHAEL O'LEARY
> (Satellite phone)
> OK lads, everyone online. I can see
> all of you on my screen, now raise
> your hands please, give me a wave.

O'Leary quickly scans the positions as hands are raised.

> MICHAEL O'LEARY (CONT'D)
> Good, it's a GO. They have left the
> hotel, ETA in around an hour or so.
> There are 18 persons in 5 vehicles. 4
> Mercedes and a Toyota Land Cruiser
> leading.
> (a beat)
> Bobby, your target is the lead
> vehicle, the Toyota. Windscreen,
> engine bay, tires. Sustained fire.
> (a beat)
>
> Stiv, same for you at rear vehicle.
> Front and rear vehicles disabled,
> and no fucker is going anywhere.
> (A beat)
> Everyone, once the convoy is
> stopped, the CPOs must be taken
> down. Don't let them get out of the
> vehicles. Sustained fire at visible
> targets, do not shoot at the fucking
> landscape.
> (A beat)
> Finally - CAR TWO, our target is a
> French dandy with jet black hair
> who looks like Count Dracula. His
> name is Gerard Dupont-Moret.

338

The next to last car has a couple of
folks I'd quite like to save, so get the
two CPOs.
          (A beat)
Good luck my boys, once the
action starts, do not look away for
a millisecond. Welcome the Great
Sandy Desert Turkey Shoot.

DISSOLVE TO:

EXT. ALGERIAN DESERT. TWO LANE DUST ROAD. DAY.

Stiv lays in relentless sun, hot sand under his belly. The M82 sitting
on a bipod, totally comfortable and balanced. 20 fully loaded
magazines are placed where he can change them over in 1.5
seconds.

From his position he can see Bob, around 50M away. They hadn't
spoken since the altercation, but his feeling towards his old friend
had softened, mainly by Hakira's intervention. She had become
Bob's 'stand-in' Mother since the incident, and Zim had watched
over both of them as if they were his wayward family.

The rest of the team had stayed clear of Bob for many reasons,
mostly wanting to get the job efficiently and get the fuck out of
there, but they had a strange respect for Hakira, and her taking
Bob's side had affected everyone, including O'Leary.

In the last few days Bob had hunkered down and done everything
that was expected of him. The rest of the TEAM had no reason to
believe that Bob would not stand up to the OCHE on the day. On
his phone screen he can see Bob's icon. He touches it.

                    STIV
               (On phone)
          OK Bobby.

He sees Bob move in the distance, then...

                            BOB
              I'm good Stiv, you.

Stiv raises his hand in the air. He sees Bob's hand come up. In
the next few minutes, all of the team check in with Bob in the
same way.

Minutes to go, they go silent.

By some miracle known only to Hakira, the TEAM has regained
their warrior spirit and their MOJO.

                                              CUT TO:

**INT LEAD G WAGON, FRENCH CONVOY. ALGERIAN DESERT. TWO
LANE DUST ROAD. DAY.**

The driver of Car 1 reacts to the rockfall, sitting forward in his seat,
braking.

                            CPO1
                      (Into his radio)
              Rock fall guys, I'm going to have to
              stop.

Bruno Le May's hair raises on the back of his head as their car
slowed, then stopped as they nosed up the rockfall. Something
wasn't right. All 5 vehicles came to a stop a few feet between
them. His eyes sweeps the skyline at each side of the road.

                      BRUNO LE MAY
              No-one moves. Stay in your vehicles.
              Everyone alert. Wait.

Le May scans the area, he reaches to the dash to switch down
the air-con fan. The convoy and its surroundings were totally still,
the travel dust slowly settling around them.

                                              CUT TO:

AGERIAN DESERT. BOB'S POSITION

The lead vehicle stops, crystal sharp in Bob's telescopic sight. His heart rate soars in the silence. He sees a flicker of movement behind the darkened windscreen, then his nerves fall away as his first shot stars the windscreen in the centre of his cross hairs. He shifts aim, taking the same shot at where the passenger would be sitting.

> BOB
> (Satellite phone)
> Driver 1 down, passenger miss.

Bob shifts aim again placing two precise rounds into the car engine bay. He waits for his next target, adrenaline surging.

CUT TO:

ALGERIAN DESERT. STIV'S POSITION

Stiv centres cross-hairs on the driver's profile in the last car. His first shot passed through the target's body and also takes down the passenger seated next to him. Stiv's next shot smashed the engine. The convoy is trapped in position

> STIV
> Car 6 disabled. Driver and CPO
> down.

Stiv sweeps his telescopic sight to Car 4. The driver's door is opening as his shot takes down the driver. Stiv places several shots into the vehicle, killing the CPO.

> STIV (CONT'D)
> Car 4 disabled. Driver and CPO
> down.

CUT TO:

ALGERIAN DESERT. BOB'S POSITION

Two CPOs appear at the edge of the convoy, they are disoriented, not knowing where the shots are coming from. Bob's next two shots take them both down efficiently. He waits for his next target, feeling invincible.

                    MICHAEL O'LEARY
            Close shooters move forward.
            Snipers do not shoot your brothers.

On both sides of the convoy, Anders, Liam and Robbo begin their deadly work.

                                        CUT TO:

ALGERIAN DESERT. STIV'S POSITION

Stiv is now shooting continuously, changing over magazines, picking his targets as they present themselves. The CPOs are in disarray, half their number down in less than 5 minutes of engagement. They are unable to return fire against such withering accuracy and firepower. Their vehicles are deadly traps but getting out of the vehicles is almost impossible.

Several CPOs throw their weapons out of the car windows, hands raised skywards. Shots become sporadic, then stop. O'Leary scrambles down from the rocks. He has not fired a shot.

                    MICHAEL O'LEARY
                    (To TEAM handsets)
            Stand down boys, stop shooting.
            But keep your sights on these guys.
            Shoot anything that looks strange.
            Stay in cover.
                    (A beat)

            Glen, on me.

Liam and Robbo stay in cover, Stiv and Bob watch through their telescopic sights. O'Leary and Anders walk warily along the side of the convoy.

                    MICHAEL O'LEARY (CONT'D)
                    (Shouting to the convoy)
                Listen up everyone. This battle is over
                for you, but you can still die here
                today. Listen to me, do not take any
                action that I do not sanction. Stay
                in your vehicles. If you do not do
                exactly as I say, my snipers will take
                you down.

                We are going to take each car from
                the front. Car 1, I want you to exit
                the vehicle and lay down flat with
                your face in the sand. Show me any
                weapons and phones.

                No fast actions, that will get you
                killed. OK, Car 1 NOW!

Several moments pass, then a single CPO from Car 1 Toyota) clambers out and lays down flat. Anders kneels and slips plastic tie cuffs into place. Checking for weapons. A Diplomat and the driver are dead in the vehicle.

                    MICHAEL O'LEARY (CONT'D)
                Car 2 NOW please.

A Diplomat and a CPO emerge from Car 2. They are laid down as instructed. Anders cuffs them, again checking for weapons and checking inside the vehicle. O'Leary and Anders work their way along the convoy. Finally, 10 survivors are laid along the side of the convoy, all cuffed and searched.

                    GLEN ANDERS
                Check please. I have 7 CPOs and 1
                diplomat KIA. That should leave 10
                survivors, 3 CPOs and 7 Diplomats.

O'Leary, highly alert, walk the convoy, coming back to stand next to Anders.

>   MICHAEL O'LEARY
>   Confirmed. Check everyone for
>   weapons.

Liam and Robbo emerge from the rocks and the ten survivors are helped up and moved away from the track into the shade of a huge rose coloured rock 40M away. They huddle together looking at the carnage of their convoy, bloody and frightened.

>   MICHAEL O'LEARY (CONT'D)
>   (Handset to Stiv and Bob)
>   Snipers, stay where you are, put
>   your scopes on these guys. Do NOT
>   look away, shoot if you see anything
>   threatening.
>   (To Anders, Liam and Robbo)
>   Close shooters do not get between
>   the snipers and targets.

O'Leary and the rest of the team move efficiently along the convoy tossing Frag Grenades into each vehicle. One by one the vehicles are destroyed in 5 flat detonations. A pall of dust hangs in the air, blowing away from the survivors across the desert.

>   GLEN ANDERS
>   (To O'Leary, consulting his
>   watch)
>   12 minutes from the first shot.
>   Someone will have made calls, a
>   chopper will scramble over the site
>   in approx. 45 minutes. We need to
>   clear 15 mins before that to get over
>   the border and cover.
>
>   I reckon we have 8 minutes left here,
>   then we are gone.

O'Leary nods. He walks over to the cuffed survivors, scans them. Picks out Gerard Dupont-Moret.

> MICHAEL O'LEARY
> Monsieur Dupont-Moret, please
> come with me Sir.

The Frenchman is pale and blooded, but defiant. He steps out from the group, facing his colleagues.

> GERARD DUPONT-MORET
> Be strong friends. Please tell my
> family that I have not let them down.
> (Turning to O'Leary)
>
> Lead on Sir.

O'Leary nods. He scans the group again, picking out De Freyn. A look passed between them, but no words are spoken. Adele, standing to one side, sees something, she doesn't know what. She doesn't care at that moment; she is too frightened.

O'Leary turns away, then turns back. He looked at Bruno Le May for a moment, puzzled. Le May shifts to face him and returns his look without fear, two battle scarred warriors sharing a moment of empathy. O'Leary nods, and turns away. Le May watches him.

EXT. SHADED AREA AWAY FROM CONVOY. DAY

O'Leary leads Gerard Dupont-Moret 50m away into a shaded area in the rocks out of sight of the group of survivors. He faces Gerard Dupont-Moret 3m away.

> MICHAEL O'LEARY
> How do you want to do this?

> GERARD DUPONT-MORET
> Quickly, I guess.
> (A beat)

Is there any way we...?

                    MICHAEL O'LEARY
          No.

O'Leary shoots him twice in the chest with the Glock.

EXT. LARGE ROCKS CLUSTER NEAR CONVOY. DAY

Back at the group, Anders watches Bruno Le May closely as the
sound of O'Leary's shots rang out. The survivors jump at the sound
of the shots, exchanging frightened looks. Anders orders the
group to sit with their backs against the rock. As they scramble
awkwardly with their cuffs behind their backs, Anders stepped up
close to Bruno Le May.

                    GLEN ANDERS
                     (Quietly)
          It's been a long time Bruno.

Le May doesn't speak or look at Anders.

                GLEN ANDERS (CONT'D)
          Are you going to come after us? If
          you are, we'll finish it here, right now.

Le May looks briefly at Anders. He shakes his head minutely,
dropping his eyes away from Anders. Ander looks at him for
another second, nods, and walks away towards their vehicles
parked 40M away, ready to go.

O'Leary walks back towards their vehicles, waving Bob and
Stiv inwards. Liam and Robbo linger, picking up weapons and
equipment, stuffing them into holdalls.

As O'Leary pushes weapons and equipment into the rear of a
Volvo, an unexplained feeling passed over him. He stops what he
was doing and turns to look back at the group.

                                                    CUT TO:

346

ALGERIAN DESERT. SLO-MO SEQUENCE

In crystal clarity, O'Leary sees Liam and Robbo walking towards him carrying hold-alls. Liam is calling something to Stiv as he approaches the Volvos from a different direction. O'Leary desperately wants to say something, stepping forward, his hand raising, feeling like he is wading through treacle.

De Freyn has got to his feet and has stepped away from the group, his pin-stripe suit bloodstained and dusty but still somehow urbane and elegant. He stands with his body twisted to one side, right side leaning downwards, hands still cuffed behind. O'Leary recognizes the twisted shooting stance, and claws for his handgun holstered to his right leg.

De Freyn shoots several times, the shots fast, almost merging together. Slugs impacted on Liam and Robbo and the sand around them, dust flying from their clothing, they both pitched forward into the dust. There was a another shot within a second. De Freyn is hurled backwards, his shoulders hitting the ground, legs spreadeagled.

O'Leary's pistol clears his holster, weapon thrusting forward, wide legged, covering the group. Everyone is still. O'Leary looks to his right, Stiv is still holding his Glock in the classic two-handed hold, smoke curling from the muzzle, eye along the sights to De Freyn's prone body.

To his left, handgun extended, Glen Anders runs into frame, towards Liam and Robbo.

END SLO-MO SEQUENCE

O'Leary runs forward to Liam and Robbo, Anders is there first. O'Leary runs past his two downed men, onward to De Freyn, kicking away a Makarov Auto. De Freyn looks up at him, a savage pain-filled smile creasing his handsome features, blood on his upper shoulder and in the sand behind him. O'Leary raises his handgun, cantering on De Frey's face, the smile does not waver. O'Leary holds the position for several beats, then keeping the gun centred on De Freyn, he backs up to where Liam and Robbo lie prone.

                    MICHAEL O'LEARY
                    (To Anders, still aiming at De
                    Freyn)
          Tell me...
                    GLEN ANDERS
                    (Head down, emotional)

          Robbo is dead. Liam hit bad. I'm
          sorry Michael, this is down to me. I
          should have found that fucking gun.

O'Leary brings his gun up a fraction, still centred on De Freyn. De Freyn painfully rolls slightly raising himself onto his elbow, his smile fading.

O'Leary holds the stance for several moments, his knuckles white, he suddenly spins and shot downwards twice into Liam's chest. Liam convulsed; Anders sprawled backwards in shock.

O'Leary, his eyes streaming with tears, walks over to Stiv, who was still locked into his shooting position, one knee down. He held his hand out to Stiv, pulling him up to his feet. O'Leary walked quickly back to the lead Volvo.

                    MICHAEL O'LEARY
          Saddle up boys, let's get the fuck
          out of here.
                                                    CUT TO:

ALGERIAN DESERT. AERIAL

Three VOLVO 4*4s spin in the dust, kicking out streams of orange dust. They accelerate away at speed. Camera circles upward showing the devastation of the battleground.

                                                    CUT TO:

348

EXT. TEAM BASE. DESERT. MOROCCO. DAY

The three Volvo's skid hap-haphazardly to a halt outside the mud building of their base. The four remaining assassins exit, rapidly unloading weapons and equipment.

Hakira and Zami, sit by the fire. Zami eating and Hakira cooking flat bread on a steel plate. Hakira doesn't acknowledge their presence in the slightest. Zami gets to his feet, his gaze seeking out O'Leary's eyes, questioning.

> MICHAEL O'LEARY
> (to Zami)
> It was a shit-show, two men lost.

Zami continues to hold his gaze.

> MICHAEL O'LEARY (CONT'D)
> Target was eliminated.
> (To team)
> I am gone. I'll fly out of Oujda
> tonight. I suggest you guys split and
> take another airport, or even cross
> from Tangier to Spain - Its around
> 350 miles to Tangier from here. Stay
> out of cities.

O'Leary pauses, his head down. When he raises his head, his cheeks are streaming with tears.

> MICHAEL O'LEARY (CONT'D)
> (Emotional, to Stiv and Bob)
> I'm proud of you guys. No-one could
> ask for better brothers, you did your
> jobs brilliantly, and we will work
> together again.
> (A beat. To Glen)
> You fucked up Glen. I expected
> better. Losing your men once is an
> accident, twice isn't.

Glen Anders stand respectfully, his eyes downcast. He doesn't speak. O'Leary turns away, quickly embraced Zami, thanks Hakira and left the Base in a cloud of orange dust.

The sound of O'Leary's Volvo dies away, dust gradually settling, no one moves for long moments.

                              BOB
              Glen, I...
                         GLEN ANDERS
                         (Bitter - angry)
              Shut the fuck up Bob. Just shut
              it. I do not need your opinion on
              anything. You two are children,
              fucking kids. You don't know shite
              about anything. Stay the fuck away
              from me, and do not speak, you
              hear me?
                              STIV
              Glen, there's no need to...
Anders rounds on Stiv, eyes blazing.

                         GLEN ANDERS
              You fucking button it as well. You
              think, just because you got a quick
              shot into that French twat, that's it?
              Makes you sort of fucking James
              Bond? Bollocks, you are nothing,
              a couple of chancers playing in a
              game for pros. No hopers.
                         (A beat)
              You came out of this OK personally,
              but you were fucking lucky Stiv.
                         (A beat)
              Lucky...
                         (A beat, slower, emotional)
              Lucky, like you were before - on that
              fell, Ulverston, Cumbria, remember
              that do you? You fuckers?

Got me kicked out the SWAT Team,
finished me. No pension, all those
years. Now this, you have fucked me
with O'Leary as well.

Bob is silent, looking with shock at Anders. Stiv is transfixed...

                    STIV
        That was you, back then...
                GLEN ANDERS
        Yes, you fuck-wit, that was me. I was
        running the SWAT Team in Cumbria.
        Pure chance that we ended up in
        the same hit team for O'Leary, but
        this a small world, so I'm not really
        surprised. O'Leary knew.
                (A beat)
        I was going to leave it you know.
        First of all I was gonna do you both.
        Probably during the firefight back
        there.

        But that didn't work out, besides, I
        have to say, you were both fucking
        top class today.

Stiv, for the first time, sees the Glock in Ander's hand, muzzle
down. His own gun is in its holster on his right hip. Bob isn't wearing
his and is unarmed.

            GLEN ANDERS (CONT'D)
        You did good, and I have to say,
        I got to quite like you Stiv, but
        you guys are done here now, its
        payback time for you.

Anders squints at Stiv knowingly, gesturing down at Stiv's holstered
Glock.

            GLEN ANDERS (CONT'D)
            (Savage grin)

You won't make it Stiv, you'll never
haul that shooter out before I take
you down, you were lucky with the
Frenchman earlier, but I'm on this
now, and I will not hesitate.

Ander's gun is now covering them steadily from 3 meters away.
Stiv knows they have no chance. He glances at Bob, who is mute.
As he looks back towards Glen Anders, Ander's chest explodes.
A volley of heavy slugs literally shredded him, spouts of dust from
the rest of the volley erupted in the sand behind Anders, and he
crumples, collapsing in on himself. Anders's body lays broken,
twitching, a pall of dust hanging in the super-heated air.

Over by the flickering fire, Hakira ejects the empty magazine from
her battered AK47. Zami hands her a full one, and she expertly
slammed it into position, sliding back the cocking mechanism
in one continuous movement. She looks at Anders's eviscerated
body without a shred of pity or remorse, then handed her AK47
back to Zami without looking at him.

Zami checks the weapon, switches it to 'safe', then leans it against
the door jamb in its usual position. Hakira sits down again by the
fire and picks up her cooking tools.

Bob drops to his knees, the dust from the bullet impacts slowly
settling. Stiv looked at Anders's body, then towards the fire,
Neither Hakira nor Zami are looking at them.

STIV
Bob
(Hand to Bob's shoulder)

We should go. Come on mate.

Bob stumbles to his feet, standing with a look of total
bewilderment on his face. Hakira looks across at him, paused,
then lumbered to her feet, crossing the courtyard to stand in front
of him. She pulled back her hijab and reached for both of Bob's
hands, placing them each side of her face. her eyes softened

in grief, she gazed at him, tears beginning to course down her cheeks. She looked across at Zim, holding his eyes.

                    ZAMI
              (To Bob, gently)
          My Mother says that you should
          leave now. The morning will dawn
          again in this place, but your time
          here is over, and you must never
          return.

          Mister Bob, you are now Hakira's
          son, and you carry her love with you
          wherever you go.
                    (A beat)
          Go in peace.

Hakira stands back a pace holding Bob's eyes, then reaching up to her hijab, pulls it back across her face. She returns to her fire and the pile of flat breads. Zami looks towards Stiv briefly

                    ZAMI (CONT'D)
              (To Stiv)
          Mr Michael is a good man, he has
          honour, sometimes he hides this, but
          a clever man can find it.

          Ma'a as-salaama al-hamdu lillah.
          This means Goodbye Mr Stephen,
          until we next meet. Go in peace.

Zami turns away. Stiv gently pulls Bob to the passenger door of the Volvo and pushes him inside. He crosses to the driver's side and looks out of the windscreen. Zami and Hakira are sitting by their fire, their backs to him.

Stiv guns the Volvo savagely, it spins, dust kicking backwards from the wheels.

                              FADE TO BLACK

PART THREE

NEWS HEADLINES. AL JAZEERA TV

VOICE OVER NEWSREEL FOOTAGE

In an incident that has caused a ripple effect across the Middle East, France and United Kingdom, a French Diplomat was assassinated along with Close Protection Officers and other members of a diplomatic trade mission from France to the Algerian Ain Sefra Oil Rig.

This incident follows another assassination of a French Diplomat in Scotland 4 months ago.

Members of the French Trade Mission were traveling from Algeria's Merceria Oasis Hotel along unpaved roads when they were forced to stop at a rock-fall. At this point they came under heavy fire from what seems to have been a meticulously planned ambush. In dramatic scenes later described by survivors, M Gerard Dupont-Moret was summarily executed by the leader of the terrorists.

A later exchange of fire resulted in two of the terrorists being killed by France's new Foreign Minister, M. De Freyn, who was wounded, had concealed a handgun during the fray. Former Legionnaire M. De Freyn has received world-wide accolades for his bravery during this brutal incident and is likely to awarded France's highest honour The Croix de Guerre.

The two terrorists shot by M. De Freyn are believed to British assassins who were on the run from the earlier killing of the French Diplomat in Scotland. The British Government Foreign Office is in disarray as UK-French relations teeter on the brink of the worst political breakdown in 30 years.

EXT. BELFAST INTERNATIONAL AIRPORT. OYSTER BAR IN CENTRAL SHOPPING AREA. DAY.

O'Leary watches the Arrivals screen as he waits for his tempura oysters. The flight from Schiphol has landed 35 minutes ago.

Enrique Dada drops onto the next stool as his oysters are served.

> ENRIQUE DADA
> Hello Michael.

> MICHAEL O'LEARY
> Enrique, good flight? Oysters?

> ENRIQUE DADA
> Today, I will Michael.

O'Leary raises a finger to the bartender, then points down at his oysters. The barman nods. O'Leary looks around at the sparsely occupied bar.

> MICHAEL O'LEARY
> I think today we can stay at the bar
> Enrique. Feedback?

> ENRIQUE DADA
> Well Michael, what can I say. You
> do not disappoint my friend. Your
> payment has been approved and
> transferred.

> MICHAEL O'LEARY
> We aim to please Enrique.
> (Grimacing at pun)
> You will also note the 'disposal' of
> the Clean Skins.

> ENRIQUE DADA
> Perfect! In fact, our benefactor is
> likely to become an international
> superstar as a result. May I ask, how

the fuck did you pull off that one
Michael?

                    MICHAEL O'LEARY
            As the NEWS articles said Enrique,
            meticulous planning, what else?

Dada holds O'Leary's gaze for several seconds, a faint smile
curving his lips. O'Leary looks back at him, weariness showing
behind his usual good humoured eyes.
                    (A beat)
Dada places his hand on O'Leary's shoulder, gripping it tightly, his
smile fading. O'Leary holds the gaze, glittering tears forming in his
blue eyes. After a beat, O'Leary looks away, when he looks back
at Dada, his eyes were dry. Dada's oysters arrive, he glances
down at them.

                    ENRIQUE DADA
            Don't really want these.

Dada glance up at the DEPARTURES screen, then at his watch. He
slides from his stool, doing a slow spin around the vast shopping
area, turning back to O'Leary.

                    ENRIQUE DADA (CONT'D)
            Goodbye Michael. I'll be in touch.

O'Leary nods minutely and Dada walks quickly away. O'Leary
pays the tab, ignoring the barman's questioning look at the
two untouched plates of oysters, and walks towards the huge
'Welcome to Northern Ireland' sign, passing beneath it.

                                        FADE TO BLACK

**EXT. YEWTREE FARM. 6 MILES WEST OF LARNE. DEEP
COUNTRYSIDE. DAY**

Georgie watched O'Leary park in the farmyard. She goes to the
AGA and pours boiling water into a mug, absently stirring it as
O'Leary entered.

MICHAEL O'LEARY
Hello my Darlin' is that a cup of tea
you have there?

GEORGIE
Do you want food Dad?

MICHAEL O'LEARY
A hug is what I need baby.

Georgie holds both hands to her Father's face and kissed him
hard on the mouth. Her arms go around his waist, feeling his hard
muscled body tense and unyielding. O'Leary holds her for a long
moment, releasing her to sit at the long table, pulling his mug
towards him.

GEORGIE
Any word from them?

MICHAEL O'LEARY
Nothing.

Georgie sits with her own tea; she wants to lift the mood but no
words come. She reaches out and places her hand over her
Father's scarred knuckles.

MICHAEL O'LEARY (CONT'D)
They'll be fine my love. Don't fret. Stiv
is my man, he'll get them home.

GEORGIE
Dad, the news reports them both
dead. Will their fake passports hold,
do you think?

MICHAEL O'LEARY
Their passports will hold OK.
They will ring Darlin', give them time.
Once we know where they are, we
can fix anything. Stiv has a list of
numbers to call. He knows the drill;

we went over it until they were all
sick of it.
(A beat)
You like him don't you, Stiv I mean...

GEORGIE
I like him fine Dad. Just fine.

Georgie gets up from the table abruptly. She gathers cups and
noisily clatters pots in the sink. O'Leary watches her bemused.

FADE OUT

EXT. A7 ROAD INTO AGADIR. MOROCCO. DAY

Stiv slows the Volvo as they approach the city. Early afternoon
traffic is light in contrast to the gridlock mayhem that happens
later in the day.

BOB
Keep to the speed limit mate,
last thing we need is a traffic cop
right now.

STIV
OK, don't worry. There's nothing in
the car or on us that might cause
suspicion, we are clean. I'm going
to ring O'Leary, it's been three days
now, I guess he'll be back at Larne.

Stiv pulls the Volvo into a service area, leans back in the seat as
hot air flooded in through the open window. He rummages and
brings out a satellite handset.

EXT. YEWTREE FARM. 6 MILES WEST OF LARNE. DEEP COUNTRYSIDE. LATE AFTERNOON

O'Leary is unloading groceries from the back of the Range Rover. His handset trills. He circles the 4*4, leaning against the side facing the waning sun.

On Phone:

> MICHAEL O'LEARY
> Michael.

> STIV
> Its me.

> MICHAEL O'LEARY
> (Relief in his voice)
> Well now. I trust the weather is good
> where you are?

> STIV
> I'm thinking Agadir to Las Palmas.
> I've been on holiday there once.

> MICHAEL O'LEARY
> That's good thinking, but I'm
> thinking, don't use those passports.
> Have you seen any news?

> STIV
> Nothing.

> MICHAEL O'LEARY
> To be safe we need to get you new
> ID, book in somewhere quiet and I'll
> get back to you.

O'Leary rings off, smiling briefly at Georgie's questioning look. He immediately dials again.

                    MICHAEL O'LEARY (CONT'D)
          Enrique, Michael. I need two
          passports - fast. To Agadir, yes.
                    (Listening)
          Yes, I have copies and photos, I'll
          email them. Have you rung anyone
          else?
                    (Listening)
          Don't, OK.

O'Leary rings off. He sits at the kitchen table and smiles a crooked
grin at Georgie.

                    MICHAEL O'LEARY (CONT'D)
          I think you need a small holiday
          my Darlin, a bit of Canary Island
          sunshine.

Five Days Later

INT. LAS PALMS GANDO AIRPORT. GRAN CANARIA. DAY

Stiv and Bob join the back of the queue marked 'EU Passports
Only'. The 90min MAROC flight from Agadir is uneventful.
Incoming flight traffic is light, but the airport's shopping areas are
well populated.

                    STIV
                    (Low voice)
          You got it?

                    BOB
          Yep, I'm Robert Kristensen, English
          with a Danish Father. At least my first
          name is the same.

                              STIV
                     And I'm Stephen Penfold.
                        (A beat, shaking his head)
                     Fucking Penfold...?

                                                            CUT TO:

EXT. LAS PALMS GANDO AIRPORT. CONCOURSE. AFTERNOON.

The two men emerge into the concourse area of the airport and
into holiday mayhem. Noisy families, fussy exhausted children,
bickering relatives, luggage, unintelligible announcements
echoing, and the smells of food mixed with diesel fumes.

The day is still warm in the ebbing light of the magic hour. The taxi
rank is divided off by concrete posts with white lights set into the
tops. Across the main drag is a coach collection point with tourists
milling around amid piles of luggage. Some are celebrating like its
New Year's Eve.

                              STIV
                        (Looking around)
                     Well, this is the way I remember it at
                     least. Lets find a taxi into Palmas.

Stiv scan the various overhead signs, finding 'Taxis'.

                           STIV (CONT'D)
                     Over here.

They push through crowds towards the queuing taxi ranks along
the side of the outer concourse. A taxi Concierge approaches
them.

                           CONCIERGE
                     Buenas Dias Gentlemen, do you
                     have a hotel?

They were interrupted by a stunningly beautiful brunette in a large sombrero and over-sized sunglasses. She smiles dazzlingly at the men and sweeps off her hat and glasses.

> GEORGIE
> Well, hello my lovely boys, welcome
> to Las Palmas.

> FADE TO BLACK

EXT. SANTA CATALINA HOTEL. POOLSIDE. DAY

The hotel is set in a stand of palm trees by the beach. Exclusive and targeting an expensive clientele, the hotel is not crowded. The pool area is sparsely populated. Georgie, in kaftan and sunglasses, Stiv and Bob, in tee shirts and shorts, are sitting with drinks at a parasol table.

> STIV
> So, how did you know our flight?

> GEORGIE
> Didn't.
>
> I just checked all flights in from
> Agadir. I've come to several flights
> over the past couple of days. I knew
> you'd be on one of them. I didn't
> want to make any unnecessary
> phone-calls. Its bloody good to see
> you two.
> (A beat, more serious)
> I spoke to Michael; he says chill for a
> day or two. Enjoy the sunshine.

> BOB
> I read the newspaper earlier, they
> are saying that we were both shot
> dead at the ambush - by the French

Minister. I guess that means we are
now forced into our new identities.
        (A beat)
I want to ring my Mother and Father,
let them know I'm OK. They will be
relieved.

Georgie reacts immediately, eyes blazing, hand smacking down
on the table top..

                    GEORGIE
        You will NOT! You absolutely fucking
        WILL NOT!

Both men are shocked and dismayed at her forceful reaction,
and also that they are not permitted to make contact with
Cumbria.

                    BOB
        What the fuck do you mean I can't
        talk to my family?

        I'll do what I want to do lady. My
        Mother will be distraught at what's
        on the news, I need to let her know...

                    GEORGIE
        Stop right there Bobby boy, you
        pathetic little schoolchild arsehole.
        You are an international terrorist
        on the run with two high level
        assassinations under your belt.
                (Leaning forward, eye
                contact)

        If I think for a millisecond that you
        are going to compromise my Father
        and our friends, I will kill you right
        here in this hotel.

You are not and can never again
be the person that you were back in
Cumbria. Your family will mourn you
and be suitably shocked that their
little boy has hit the headlines.

Their genuine shock and dismay
will save them...you think carefully
about that. In time we can let them
know, but their reaction to this news
must be plausible and natural. They
are not professional actors are they.
The news media will hound them if
they think they are faking.
　　　(A beat)
People have died so that you can sit
here and drink that fucking cocktail.
I know absolutely that their deaths
were not down to you --- you didn't
directly cause them, but they died
anyway, and now you live.
　　　(A beat, then more softly)
Tread lightly Bobby. Think many
times before you do anything - take
any action.
　　　(Gentle smile)
You need to stick a lot more feathers
up your arse before you become a
peacock.

Stiv is silent as he watches Bob process the shock. He is equally
shocked, but more by Georgie's steely reaction than what she
had said. The things she said made total sense to him. He realizes
now that Georgie is equally as dangerous as her Father, and
Benny, and Daniel Laidlow and the Bulgarians.

Georgie leans back in her seat, her eyes rising and tracking along
the classical hotel facade, perfect lips touching the edge of her
cocktail glass.

GEORGIE (CONT'D)
(Gently, with humour)
Sorry about the speech lads, please,
let's not re-visit that ever again.
(Dazzling smile)
Eh... I don't know about you's, but
I'm gonna get totally fucking pissed
tonight.

FADE OUT

EXT. DIVE CENTER. WALNEY. DAY

AERIAL

Camera circles the Dive Centre compound, the dock area and
container storage in the background. Dave and Mike's vehicle is
parked outside, plus a Police Car.

INT. DIVE CENTER. WALNEY. OFFICE. DAY

Dave, Mike and Chief Superintendent George Henley are seated
around the cluttered desk with mugs of tea. CS Henley, in plain
clothes, regards Mike Kramer thoughtfully over the rim of his mug.

CS HENLEY
(To Mike)
The boys that you and your Ex knew,
local lads that hunted rabbits for
the pot and played on their Play-
stations, are not the men we are
talking about here. The two men we
know were mercenaries. Let me lay
this out for you briefly.
(A beat)
They were part of a highly trained
team of men, we think maybe six
or seven, that ambushed a French
Trade Mission in the Algerian Desert.
They very efficiently killed seven

armed professional Close Protection Officers (CPOs), ex-soldiers, and two French Government Diplomats. One of the Diplomats, M. Dupont-Moret was summarily executed on his own after the firefight.

These are facts, not guesswork. There are ten survivors who lived to tell the tale. These survivors witnessed the aftermath of the firefight where these two men were shot by the French Minister, who had managed to conceal a handgun. He was handcuffed at the time, amazing bravery, not to mention shooting skill. The Minister was shot by another mercenary in that exchange, but he survives.

We have reams of witness statements detailing the ambush and aftermath minute by minute.

CS Henley leans forward, placing his mug carefully back onto the wet ring on the dusty desk.

> CS HENLEY (CONT'D)
> The Chief CPO, man called Bruno Le May is an ex French Foreign Legionnaire for fuck's sake... sorry to swear.
> (A beat)
> So please Mr Kramer, Mike, I know that you and your Ex-wife must be devastated at your loss, but are you really telling me that you knew nothing of this over the past year or two...? Really...?

Mike Kramer is exhausted, and grief stricken. He shakes his head mutely. Every line in his face, every movement, reflects his total devastation and disbelief. CS Henley glances across at Dave Geddings who is also visibly shocked. He shakes his head.

> CS HENLEY (CONT'D)
> Well gentlemen, the French side of
> this investigation is being handled
> by Interpol, and we are contributing
> our part from here. The British
> Government's Home Office is trying
> to repair Anglo-French relations
> as much as possible. These have
> already been strained by BREXIT, so
> it's all a fucking mess. You are not
> in any trouble that I know of, but it
> seems so incredible that your son
> and his mate have had this secret
> life, and no one knew.

CS Henley sits for several beats looking across the clutter at Mike Kramer's total anguish. Finally, shaking his head and checking his watch, he gathers his bits together and stands uncertainly, feeling that there is more to say and do, but looking at Mike's broken demeanour, decides to leave it for the moment.

> CS HENLEY (CONT'D)
> I imagine the press will be after you
> and your ex-wife, so be prepared.
> They can be relentless.

Henley nods to Dave Geddings and leaves the office. Dave stands and watches as Henley gets into his car and pulls away. After a moment Dave goes to the kettle and noisily clatters together another brew.

INT. ULVERSTON POLICE STATION. PRIVATE OFFICE. DAY

Chief Constable Denise Wakefield Jones replaces her telephone handset and regards CS Henley thoughtfully across her tidy desk.

CHIEF CONSTABLE
Resignation may be an option
for me George. The Home
Sec mentioned it twice in that
call, maybe she is trying to tell
me something. Anyway, I'm
considering it.

Aah My Maison in the Dordogne
looks more attractive as each
day's revelations unfold. To say
the Home Sec is angry about all
this is an understatement. She is
incandescent. Now you sit here
telling me that these two local
homesteaders, two fucking hill-
billys, have assassinated two French
Diplomats, one is Scotland and one
in fucking Algeria, and no-one had
a fucking clue...

The CC puts her hands to each side of her face and places both
elbows on her desk, her contorted features gazing at Henley.

CHIEF CONSTABLE (CONT'D)
You believe Michael Kramer then?
And his ex-wife?

CS HENLEY
I do Ma'am. I really do, or, they
are best actors I ever met. I've also
interviewed more that 20 locals
who knew both of these lads since
they were nippers. Not a chink of
uncertainty anywhere.

The CC gets up and walks to the window, watching traffic rolling
relentlessly along the A590 through the town. Silent, on the other
side of triple glazing, trucks thunder past. In the distance the
sentinel of the HOAD Lighthouse stands over the town, silhouetted
against rolling clouds.

368

                    CHIEF CONSTABLE
            And nothing more on Joe Wilson?

                    CS HENLEY
            Nothing Ma'am. Jean Lafitte is
            checking any connections Joe
            might have had in France. He
            used to go there a couple of times
            each year, but as yet nothing has
            emerged.

There is silence in the room. The CC continues to look out of the
window, her back to Henley. After several minutes, Henley gets up
and silently leaves the room.

EXT. LAS PALMAS. SANTA CATALINA HOTEL. POOLSIDE. DAY

Stiv, Bob and Georgie lay on lilos by the pool. They are all in
swimsuits and shades. Bob, with a half-empty Jack Daniels beside
him, is slightly apart from the other two. He has dozed off.

                    GEORGIE
            Stiv, you awake?

                    STIV
            Yep, just enjoying the day. I
            dreamed about you a few times you
            know.

                    GEORGIE
            Oh, go on with you.

                    STIV
            I did, it's true.

Georgie raised herself onto an elbow, looking at him over her
sunglasses.

                                                369

                          GEORGIE
            Michael likes you Stiv, did you know
            that. He sees something in you.
            Something special. he told me what
            you did when the Frenchman shot
            Liam and Robbo.

Bob lays very still. He has awakened but keeps his sleeping
position.

                     GEORGIE (CONT'D)
            I like you too.

Stiv glances at Bob asleep several feet away. He reaches across
and pulls Georgie's lilo towards his. It slides easily on the wet tiles.
Both sit up facing each other, noses almost touching.

Georgie smiles, her open lips brushing Stiv's, the tip of her tongue
wet, electric. Her breath in his face, sweet, intoxicating. They kiss
slowly for a long time.

                          STIV
            I wanted this you know. From the first
            moment.

Georgie breaks the moment. She stands, her finger to her lips to
silence him as she glances down at Bob. She takes his hand.

                          GEORGIE
            Come on...
                                                        CUT TO:

INT. HOTEL BEDROOM CONTINUOUS

It is dark, we don't see clearly, curtains are pulled closed, blowing
in the warm breeze. A man and a woman make love on a bed.
There are mirrors on the walls, and a side table, two drinks with
melting ice. A tape deck plays the Stones 'Sympathy for the Devil'.

Atop him Georgie straddles his chest... her breasts in his face. He cups them, she leans down, kisses him deeply, her black hair falling all over them both, hiding their faces. The camera circles their writhing bodies as their tempo and passion increases.

CUT TO:

EXT. LAS PALMAS. SANTA CATALINA HOTEL. POOLSIDE. DAY

By the pool Bob watches their hotel window as the breeze blows the curtains. The faint sound of the Rolling Stones drifts on the breeze.

DISSOLVE TO:

EXT. LAS PALMAS. SANTA CATALINA HOTEL. POOLSIDE. DAY

Bob is lying on a lilo by the pool staring aimlessly, morose. Stiv appears from the direction of the hotel reception carrying several cold beers. He flops down, placing one of them beside Bob, who ignores it.

STIV

Beer there mate.

BOB

Stick it.

STIV

Please yourself.

Stiv, taken aback, looks at Bob for several beats, then gets up and walks off without further comment. Bob turns slightly, watches him go with narrowed eyes.

CUT TO:

INT. GEORGIE'S ROOM.

Stiv walks in, drops onto the bed where Georgie is reading. She glances up.

> GEORGIE
> You OK Stiv?

> STIV
> Do you know, I sometimes think if I had met him now, we would never have been friends at all.

> GEORGIE
> Bob?

> STIV
> (Nodding)
> I just took him a beer, he told me to stick it.
> (Glancing up)
> What are you reading?

Georgie puts her book down. Pulls herself up with her back to the headboard, knees raised, lustrous blue eyes on Stiv.

> GEORGIE
> My Father doesn't want him on the next job. You know that don't you?

Stiv meets her eyes, shock showing in his eyes.

> STIV
> What, I thought...

> GEORGIE
> He did well, yes, you both did. But Bob has used up his slack. To use an old Irish farming expression, he has sucked the tit dry.

Stiv grins in spite of the seriousness of the implication, nodding at Georgie's loose top.

STIV
Chance would be a fine thing.

Georgie glanced down at her partially exposed breasts, laughs and launches herself on top of Stiv. They grapple playfully, rolling off the bed onto the floor. They land, Georgie beneath, they kiss deeply, the kiss extending...

There is a loud rap on the room door. Stiv breaks away, getting up, opening the door. It is Bob. He is angry and confrontational.

BOB
This is how it's going to be is it? Me
sat around like a fucking spare part,
and you and this Irish tart shagging
yourselves stupid.

Stiv is shocked and momentarily non-plussed. Georgie, her hair dishevelled, wearing one of Stiv's shirts, comes to stand behind him, her hand on his shoulder.

GEORGIE
(Sharply)

Well, the bit about being IRISH is
correct Bob, that I cannot deny, but
tart...

STIV
Bob, what the fuck...

GEORGIE
(Eyes on Bob)
So, Bobby you think that because
I'm a woman, its OK to insult me is it?

Georgie steps out of the doorway into the corridor. She looks both ways. Takes a stance.

GEORGIE (CONT'D)
Right, come on mister, give me your
best shot. My daddy taught me to
mix it with the best of them. Why
don't you show me what you've got.

Bob is slightly shocked and taken off guard. He looked at
Georgie's aggressive stance, then looks questionally at Stiv. In
that millisecond Georgie danced forward and his him hard in
the mouth with a clenched fist. Bob stumbled backwards and sits
down hard, blood bursting from his mouth and nose.

Stiv jumps towards Georgie to stop her follow-through roundhouse
kick.

STIV
(To Georgie)
Bloody hell, enough Podge. Come
on, we don't want to draw attention
to ourselves here do we.
(Pointing down at Bob)

Fuck off Bob. You keep doing this
stuff, like everyone else is to blame,
never you. We are both in this, we
can't fucking undo it and go back
to being local Ulverston lads any
more. We are not kids now.

Georgie shakes herself free from Stiv, pulling her shirt together,
brushing tears of anger from her eyes and blowing on a sore
knuckle.

GEORGIE
Best thing, when we get back to
Larne is to get around a table with
Michael and Benny and decide
what we are going to do about you
Mister. You obviously don't want to
work with us anymore, and to be
honest, we don't want you. You are

a liability that will get somebody,
maybe even yourself, killed before
long.
                (Glancing ruefully at her
                knuckle)

I'm sorry I hit you, I shouldn't have
done that.

Georgie steps forward, reached down to Bob to pull him to his
feet. Bob angrily waves her hand away. He climbs to feet, looking
at his hand covered in blood from his bust lips. He leaned forward,
wiping his blood down the white shirt covering Georgie's breasts.
They all look at the bright blood stain.

                          BOB
          Fuck you Georgie and fuck your
          Father as well. I won't be in Larne
          long enough to discuss my future
          with you thick bastards. I'll be going
          back home to Ulverston, I'm done
          with you fuckers.
                (To Stiv)

          And I'm done with you as well mate.
          You have thrown in your lot now with
          these murdering bastards, and now
          you are shagging this bitch, you and
          me are done.

The tension is high, Stiv controls himself as Georgie reaches for his
hand. There is movement at the end of the corridor as a family of
hotel guest's approach. Bob, quivering with rage, points a bloody
finger at Georgie.

                    BOB (CONT'D)
          You and me Lady, we have
          unfinished business...

Bob turns and stumbles away in the opposite direction. Georgie and Stiv retreat back into their room, closing the door.

CUT TO:

INT. THE FARMHOUSE. LARNE, NORTHERN IRELAND. LATE AFTERNOON

Elongated shadows from the fleeting amber daylight fills the kitchen. Michael O'Leary pours a mug of tea for himself and Benny and sits at the long kitchen table, both hands gripping the mug. Benny sips from his, grimaces and reaches for sugar.

> BENNY
> How's the Frenchie?

> MICHAEL O'LEARY
> He took one high in the right shoulder, it went on through, breaking his collar bone. He'll be OK, it will sting a bit though Ben.

> BENNY
> Young Stiv eh?

> MICHAEL O'LEARY
> Indeed, he cleared his holster and hit your man from 20M. Then kept his gun on him until I kicked away the Makarov. He's a natural, that boy!

> BENNY
> I thought so my own self, he has a look about him you know. Not like his mate. Bobby is a lost soul, as well as being a fuckwit, and not to mention a danger to us all.
> (Squinting at O'Leary)

Sooner or later, we are going to
have to confront that little issue are
we not?

                    MICHAEL O'LEARY
          I know it Ben.

O'Leary's eyes stray to the empty chairs across the table. Benny follows his gaze and clears his throat noisily.

                    BENNY
          What's done is done Michael. We
          can't bring them two boys back.

O'Leary stares at the empty chairs nodding slightly. His expression doesn't change but his eyes fill with tears.

                                                    CUT TO:

EXT. DIVE CENTER. WALNEY. DAY

In the harbour a massive freighter steams silently seawards, wheeling gulls circling. Dave and Mike are bleeding air from tanks, the spurting oxygen showing white in the cold air.

                    DAVE GEDDINGS
          This one needs new rubber seals.

Mike Kramer nods and walks off to a work bench to rummage among equipment. He returns.

                    MIKE KRAMER
          None left Dave, leave it to one side,
          we'll sort it tomorrow.

Dave screws down the knurled top of the tank, carefully standing it to one side. He glanced at Mike.

                    DAVE GEDDINGS
          How's Iris coping?

Mike straightens, watching the massive ship receding to the skyline.

> MIKE KRAMER
> Fucking awful mate. Like me I guess.
> Still can't believe any of this. If I'd
> seen it on a movie, I'd have turned
> off by now, too far-fetched.

He turns back to Dave, his face older and infinitely wearier.

> MIKE KRAMER (CONT'D)
> Maybe its time to pull up stakes and
> get the fuck out of here.
> (A beat)
> Maybe she will come with me...
> we have a dead son in common
> these days, and Mr. Danny fucking
> Laidlow ain't coming back.

> DAVE GEDDINGS
> You'll need a chunk of money for
> that old mate. We have used up the
> last lot now, particularly if you want
> to pull your money out this business.
> I don't have enough to buy out your
> share.

Dave pauses, wondering. He speaks carefully.

> DAVE GEDDINGS (CONT'D)
> Them guns are still down there.

Mike looks sharply at him, then goes back to work, clanking tanks and equipment onto metal storage shelves. Dave watches his partner working for several beats, then walks off towards the office.

CUT TO:

EXT. ELYSEE PALACE. PARIS. FRANCE. DAY.

AERIAL and Ground Shots

An entourage of three limousines turns majestically into the fabulous monumental arched gateway off the Rue du Faubourg Sainte Honore, slowing slightly at the heavily guarded checkpoint, then accelerating along the 2 hundred meters of light orange gravel.

The front and rear vehicles disgorge six CPOs who range into classic defensive positions around the vehicles, all facing outwards. An Aide steps forward from his waiting position on the marble steps and opens the rear door of the middle car. M. De Freyn steps carefully onto the gravel, waving away an outstretched hand. De Freyn straightens with an effort, then nods to the Aide, and follows him up the steps.

The CPOs relax, leaning against vehicles. Some light cigarettes.

INT. ELYSEE PALACE. RECEPTION. PARIS. DAY.

De Freyn enters a silence so extraordinary, so far away from the riotous cacophony of Paris, that it feels like being shut away from life. Now and then he can hear the chime of a golden clock, a faint footstep on deep carpet, or a bird chirping in the perfect gardens outside the floor to ceiling windows. He stands in a world supremely muffled and cocooned as if wrapped in many layers of metaphorical cotton-wool and removed from reality. The Aide disappears through a doorway.

De Freyn stands erect, ignoring his discomfort. Presently the Aide returns and motions him for follow.

INT. ELYSEE PALACE. PRESIDENT'S OFFICE. DAY.

The President's office is smaller than he had envisaged. It faces a quadrangle of manicured garden with a small carefully designed maze of yew tree and shaded seating area.

The Aide flattens his back to the door, eyes cast downwards, and De Freyn walks forward to the extended double handshake of the 25th. President of France, Emmanuel Macron.

PRESIDENT
De Freyn, so good to see you my
dear friend.

The President pauses, concern showing in his boyish features.

PRESIDENT (CONT'D)
My apologies Sir, your wounds.
Please sit.

De Freyn sits, holding himself rigidly upright. The President retreats behind his desk, leaning forward, his eyes to the Aide by the door. He nods, the Aide disappears.

PRESIDENT (CONT'D)
I have many duties, but today my
duties bring me pleasure and pride
in equal measure. This is not always
the case.
(A beat, smiles)

Today I honour a hero of France.
You have shown France and rest
of the World, that we can never,
and must never, be treated lightly
or with derision. You have shown
that behind the suit and inscrutable
face of political ceremony beats the
savage heart of a soldier, a warrior.
(A beat)
You are an extraordinary man, and
today you hold the gratitude and
admiration of France, of the World,
and more particularly of myself.

The President rises to his feet, circles the desk and takes De Freyn's hand like a lover.

PRESIDENT (CONT'D)
Come...

In silence De Freyn rises and side by side the two men enter a corridor, their footsteps muted on the carpet. They enter the Salon Cleopatra. The President walking slowly, solicitously caring for his wounded Minster.

INT. THE SALON CLEOPATRE. ELYSEE PALACE. DAY

A small group of impeccably dressed Ministers and uniformed officers stand respectfully around an ornamental table. In the centre of the table is a walnut box. The President nods to the Aide, who takes out a heavy gold medal from the box. He carefully hands this to the President.

De Freyn stands rigidly to attention, his eyes on a massive work of art which covered a wall, while The President pins the medal to his chest. The President takes a step backwards.

PRESIDENT
It is fitting that a former Legionnaire
is now recognized by France's
highest Military Award, The Legion
d'Honneur.
(A beat)
This Award was established in 1802
by Napoleon Bonaparte, and today
there is no more fitting award for
extraordinary bravery and service to
France.

The President pauses amid subtle clapping, concern showing.

PRESIDENT (CONT'D)
And now my friend, we must allow
you to sit down and take some rest.
We have affairs of State to discuss,
but these will wait while you recover.

The Aide steps forward with an ornate chair, touching De Freyn's shoulder. The ripple of applause dies away as De Freyn sits, finally relaxing his rigid posture. The small crowd mills around him. The President stands back, smiling broadly, then glancing at his Patek Phillipe watch, quietly withdraws.

CUT TO:

INT. LAFITTE'S OFFICE. INTERPOL HQ. PARIS. DAY.

Jean Lafitte sits at his desk reading an article in a newspaper. He reads to the end, then spinning his chair slightly he gazes out of his window at the skeleton of the Notre Dame Cathedral several hundred meters away. After a beat he throws the paper away from him in distaste. It slides across his polished desk, coming to a stop in the centre.

The camera zooms in and we see a photograph of M.de Freyn, and the headline:

'FRANCE AWARDS ITS HIGHEST RECOGNITION TO THE NEW FOREIGN MINISTER'

FADE TO BLACK

INT. BELFAST INTERNATIONAL AIRPORT. ARRIVALS. DAY.

Georgie, Stiv and Bob emerge from Customs into the wider reception area. They stand in a small group looking around them.

Several meters away on the atrium, O'Leary looks down on the reception area, watching the crowd for any interest being shown in the new arrivals. On an opposite atrium, Benny also watches.

STIV
Over here guys, taxis.

GEORGIE
Not yet. Stay here a few minutes.

Bob snorts and wanders off towards the TAXI sign. Stiv looks questionably at Georgie but she shakes her to let him go, her eyes drifting upwards to the atrium.

High above them, O'Leary glances at Benny, who nods. O'Leary waves slightly to Georgie and she and Stiv head towards the Taxi rank, pulling wheelie luggage.

CUT TO:

EXT. BELFAST INTERNATIONAL AIRPORT. CARPARK. DAY.

Georgie walks past the taxis to the short-stay carpark, changing direction as she spots Benny's Transit. Stiv follows close with Bob trailing behind.

AERIAL

Benny's Transit exits the Airport, merging with traffic.

CUT TO:

INT. LARNE. YEWTREE FARM KITCHEN. MORNING

O'Leary, Benny, Georgie and Stiv sit around the table with mugs of tea. The table is covered with breakfast debris.

> MICHAEL O'LEARY
> Well, you are back and I'm glad
> to see you. But its not just returning
> from the wars is it...? There has to be
> a complete homecoming in body,
> mind, heart and soul.
> (A beat)
> At least your bodies are here, the
> rest will arrive in time.

Georgie searches her Father's face with concern.

383

                    GEORGIE
          Did you speak to Liam and Robbo's
          family...

                  MICHAEL O'LEARY
          I did, to be sure darling.
                    (A beat)
          I've had better days, but at least
          they won't have any money worries
          into the future.

Georgie reaches to hold her Father's hand, his head drops briefly,
then rises again, his mood becoming brisk.

              MICHAEL O'LEARY (CONT'D)
                    (To Stiv)
          Bob...?

                      STIV
          He's around somewhere, probably
          in his room, should I...?

                  MICHAEL O'LEARY
          No, leave him.

O'Leary looks towards Benny, but his return glance is opaque.
Georgie watches both of them, suddenly alert. Stiv sips his tea,
oblivious to the sudden rise in tension.

                                                    CUT TO:

EXT. LARNE, FARMHOUSE YARD. DAY.

Benny has the bonnet up and is fiddling with the Transit's engine.
Georgie is in the driver's seat dressed in an oily boilersuit.

                     BENNY
             (Muffled, head down in the
             engine)
          Try it now Podge

The Transit splutters into life, while Benny cocks an ear.

> BENNY (CONT'D)
> Hmm, she's not well this old girl.
> Getting old I guess, like me.

O'Leary joins them as they all gaze into the engine's innards.
Benny and Georgie exchange glances, then...

> GEORGIE
> Let's go in the barn shall we, out of
> the wind.

CONTINUOUS

INT. LARNE FARM. BARN. DAY

The interior of the barn is cluttered with bales on palettes,
machinery and tools. A bench runs along one wall with a huge
vice. A rack has several saddles, and riding tack hangs on
wooden hooks hammered into old oak beams.

Benny and Georgie sit on random bales while O'Leary paces
back and forth. They watch him. Eventually O'Leary seems to
remember they are there, he sits, rummaging in a pocket. he
brings out a red 12 Gauge cartridge. He turns it over in his hand,
shakes it to his ear listening to the rattle of the lead shot. He holds
it up, catching both their eyes...

> MICHAEL O'LEARY
> You see this? It is this. Its not
> something else is it? We know what
> it is.

Benny and Georgie are silent, waiting, knowing.

> MICHAEL O'LEARY (CONT'D)
> Our situation is the same, we know
> what it is. We all know it.

O'Leary puts the red cartridge back in his pocket. Both hands flat to his thighs.

> MICHAEL O'LEARY (CONT'D)
> Liam and Robbo are not coming
> home, that has to mean something.
> Stiv is now here and I want him in our
> family. Only him though, not...

O'Leary glances at Georgie, who blushes briefly, then shakes her head.

> GEORGIE
> (Emotional)
> We can't just kill Bob Dad. Stiv won't
> live with that. They grew up together.

O'Leary gets up, walks over and sits next to Georgie, takes her hand, appraising her sadly, his eyes full of dread.

> MICHAEL O'LEARY
> So, he goes back to Cumbria? Back
> to being Bob Kramer. Back to...

> GEORGIE
> OK Dad, I know. I do know.

Benny watches these two people, whom he loves more than life, both wrestling with the inevitable.

> GEORGIE (CONT'D)
> I'll talk to Stiv. Fuck knows what I
> will say.

She suddenly looks up her Father, her beautiful blue eyes filled with tears.

> GEORGIE (CONT'D)
> What if Stiv won't accept this
> situation Dad... What if he
> decides to...?

O'Leary puts his arm around his daughter as she sobs, hugging her to him. His hooded eyes locking on Benny.

FADE OUT

EXT. LARNE. FELL COUNTRY. NORTHERN IRELAND. DAY

Georgie and Stiv walk on open fell. Both are dressed in anoraks and wear heavy fell boots. They crest a rise and look out on a wooded lake.

> GEORGIE
> The last time I was along here there
> was daffodils along the lakeside.
> I guess the seeds had floated on
> the water and then grew up there. I
> never saw daffodils so beautiful.
> > (A beat, eyes out over the
> > water)
> I remember that day, there was a
> boat floating out there. Right in the
> middle. Nobody on it, I watched it
> for ages thinking maybe someone
> was sleeping just out of sight, but
> never saw anybody.

Stiv takes her hand and they both look out over the lake cocooned in a moment of stillness. She turns to him.

> GEORGIE (CONT'D)
> I love you Stephen.

Stiv's heart surges. They kiss, his arms holding her tight, feeling the strength in her, pulling back, sensing her tears before he sees them. He touches her wet cheek with his thumb.

> STIV
> What is it Podge? Is it Liam and
> Robbo?

                    GEORGIE
          Yes, it's that, but there's other stuff
          Stephen, stuff that I can hardly
          bring myself to utter. I'm reeling with
          magnitude of it all.
                    (A beat, earnest eyes
                    seeking his)
          I couldn't bear to lose you, I don't
          want to wake another day, but that
          you are with me, just there, so I can
          reach out and touch you.

Stiv gazes at this beautiful creature rapt with emotion, tears
streaming down her face.

                    STIV
          I want that too Podge. I love you
          more than my life. I've been on my
          own ever since my old man died,
          and my Mother re-married. I never
          needed much over the years. In
          many ways Bob was my family. He
          was always there, we did stuff, you
          know.
                    (A beat)
          I know Bob is going through some
          issues right now. He's in a mess, but
          he won't always be this way. He'll
          come through OK.

Georgie's eyes drop away, her head sagging. Stiv doesn't notice
her reaction.

                    STIV (CONT'D)
          Going round to Iris's place, Bob's
          Mother, was like going home. She
          treated me like her own, well mostly
          she did.

Stiv laughs to himself, Georgie's eyes locked back on his.

                    STIV (CONT'D)
        I fancied her rotten as I got a bit
        older. She filled all my fantasies and
        I'm sure she knew it. She used to
        tease me in a sexy sort of way, but
        there was nothing in it really. Not like
        this with you and me. I never knew I
        could feel like this Podge.

Georgie's arms go around her man, pulling him to her. Her eyes
over his shoulder filled with pain and uncertainty. She holds him
for several beats, then he pulls back and looks at her with worry in
his eyes.

                    STIV (CONT'D)
        What is it Podge, there's
        something...?

Georgie disentangles herself, walking off several steps, then turns,
suddenly bright.

                    GEORGIE
        Come on, let's go down to the
        shoreline, then let's get back home
        for some tea and toast.
                (A beat)
        Its getting cold, come on.
                (Taking his hand)

AERIAL

Camera rising high above a small lake in desolate fell landscape.
Two-minute figures making their way to the shore.

                                                        CUT TO:

INT. LARNE. FARMHOUSE KITCHEN. AFTERNOON.

Georgie is cooking. The table is covered with vegetables, meat,
chopping board, knives and pans. The light is fading, and the

kitchen is brightly lit and warm. In the fireplace a huge log is burning.

Bob enters, his face falling as he sees Georgie, he immediately turns to leave.

> GEORGIE
> You don't need to leave Bob. I'm
> civilized. I won't bite you know.

Bob pauses in the doorway, his mouth twisting in hatred, pondering. With an effort he comes further into the room.

> BOB
> I was just going to get a drink...

Georgie is chopping, she pauses momentarily, indicating the fridge and kettle.

> GEORGIE
> Help yourself to be sure. It won't
> bother me.

Bob looked at her, judging the distance. He goes to the fridge, taking out milk, then to the kettle, noisily filling it at the sink. He makes himself coffee with his back to her.

Georgie keeps busy but watches him surreptitiously. He goes to the door carrying his cup.

> GEORGIE (CONT'D)
> Oh, it's OK Bob thanks. I won't have
> a drink right now. But its good of you
> to ask.

Bob stops in the doorway, then slowly turns, his eyes malevolent and hostile.

> BOB
> How do you want it? In your fucking
> face you bitch. You are welcome

to this one right now, I can make
another one later.

Bob takes a step towards her. Georgie stands back slightly
from the table, alert, the carving knife in her right hand, point
quivering.

> GEORGIE
> The last time you threatened me
> Bobby, you ended up on your ass.
> This time you might not be getting
> up again.

Bob fights his rage down with an effort. Georgie watches him
without a trace of fear. After a beat and in control again, Bob
raises his cup to her in a mock toast, his eyes appraising her
balefully. He leaves the kitchen.

In the hallway eight feet away, out of both of their sight, O'Leary
stands stock still, every nuance of the exchange replaying in his
brain. After a beat he enters the kitchen, Georgie, busy with her
tasks, looks up at him and smiled.

> MICHAEL O'LEARY
> Irish stew tonight then is it Podge?

CUT TO:

INT. IRIS'S HOUSE. ULVERSTON. KITCHEN. NIGHT

Iris answers a knock at the door. It is Mike Kramer, concern
showing on his face. She stands to one side as he enters. She
gestures to the kitchen. They both sit.

Iris pushes a letter on the kitchen top towards Mike. He glances at
the Letterhead: 'Foreign and Commonwealth Office'. He looks up
at her, she turns away to make coffees. He reads, then looks up at
her again.

> MIKE KRAMER
> Bastards!

He reads again, then pushes the letter away from him.

> MIKE KRAMER (CONT'D)
> Well, that's it then. We don't even
> get a funeral.

Iris sits, pushes a mug towards him and drinks from her own -
dejected and low.

> IRIS
> My Bobby. I can't bear to think of
> him on some slab in the desert.
> Those two lovely boys.

She slides the letter so she can read again, her finger tracing the
written words.

> IRIS (CONT'D)
> "I am advised by the British Consul
> for Algeria that your request for
> authorization to remove Robert
> Kramer's body from Algeria is
> refused..."
> (A beat)
> They make him and Stiv seem like an
> objects, rather than our lovely boys.

Mike looked at her, gauging whether to comment on the fact
that her son and Stiv were multiple killers of other men. He
decided it wouldn't be a useful intervention right now. Instead, he
reached for her hand.

CUT TO:

**INT. LARNE. BENNY'S VAN DRIVING A COUNTRY ROAD. LATE
AFTERNOON**

Benny is driving expertly along a country road. Beside him
O'Leary sits, tense, his feet pressing into the floor at corners. Benny

notices with amusement but does not change his aggressive driving.

>   MICHAEL O'LEARY
>   Are we late?

Benny glances at his watch a millisecond longer than he should and overcooks a corner.

>   MICHAEL O'LEARY (CONT'D)
>   (Right foot stabbing the floor)
>
>   Shit Ben!
>   (Deep breath)
>   I am convinced that the last thing
>   that passes through my mind will be
>   my fucking ass when we pointlessly
>   die in a hedgerow somewhere in
>   the deep countryside.

Benny corrects the van's slide and continues, slowing down and smiling to himself.

>   MICHAEL O'LEARY (CONT'D)
>   In fact, I think you should drive
>   around with Bobby, then it would
>   solve two of my problems at the
>   same time, when you finally kill
>   yourself, and him.

They crest a rise and below is a village built around a small pretty bay. A cluster of buildings stand around the water's edge overlooking a small marina. Benny pulls into a lay-by and rummages behind his seat, producing a flask of tea and doorstep sandwiches. He hands one to O'Leary, taking one himself, looking at it critically.

>   BENNY
>   I love that girl to bits, but her
>   sandwiches are like fucking
>   tombstones.

> (Taking a bite)
> Taste like them as well. I pity poor
> Stiv if he has to eat these for the rest
> of his life.

O'Leary doesn't comment, gazes down towards the bay. Benny glances at him as they eat.

> BENNY (CONT'D)
> Sorry Michael.

O'Leary eats in silence for a few moments, easy in Benny's company.

> MICHAEL O'LEARY
> That's why I wanted to get away
> from the farm Ben. We need to talk
> about them two boys.

> BENNY
> I know.
> (A beat)
> Bob is losing it day by day, he's
> going to blow anytime soon, you
> know that don't you?

> MICHAEL O'LEARY
> (Nodding)
> I'm worried that he will blow in
> Podge's direction. They hate each
> other with a passion, and you know
> what a rattlesnake tongue she has
> on her. And she won't back down
> from him either.
> (A beat)
> Stephen is in the middle of them two
> spitting at each other.

Benny finishes his sandwich, takes a swig of tea, glances in the mirror, tenses.

                              BENNY
                    Hold up, cops.

A police car comes up behind them, slowing. The officer looking
across the empty passenger seat at Benny as he passed.
Benny raised his cup in salute, and the officer raised a finger,
accelerating away. They watch as the vehicle winds downhill
away from them and towards the town, brake lights flashing at
bends.

                         BENNY (CONT'D)
                    Bobby keeps threatening to go back
                    home. Its going to come to a head
                    any day. We have to get Stiv on
                    board with this, or both them have
                    to go down.

O'Leary nods, stretching, wiping his hands on his thighs.

                       MICHAEL O'LEARY
                    Its not an option to take both down
                    Ben, we both know that. Podge has
                    a big stake in this now doesn't she,
                    and Liam and Robbo's legacy has
                    to mean something, he put himself
                    on the line for them. We need Stiv.

                    Fuck it, come on Ben, let's get back.

AERIAL

Camera rising high above the landscape as the Transit pulls out
from the lay-by, side lights coming on. In the bay, streetlights glow,
reflecting in the water.

                                                    CUT TO:

INT. FARMHOUSE. LARNE. BOB'S ROOM. DAY.

Bob is alone in his room. He is restless. From his window he can see out over the farmyard and further to open fields. A TV shows a silent news article, he ignores it, pacing. A tap on the door.

                            BOB
              Hang on.

Opens the door, it is Georgie.

                          GEORGIE
              Can I talk to you?

                            BOB
                    (Hostile, glancing down the
                    corridor)
              About what? Relationship advice
              maybe?

                          GEORGIE
                    (Earnestly)
              Bob, we need to talk, OK? Can we
              at least try. We can't carry on like
              this.

Bob reluctantly stands to one side and Georgie enters the room
Stands awkwardly, hands thrust deep into levis.

                            BOB
              You threatened me with fucking
              carving knife yesterday...

                          GEORGIE
              Yes, I did, just after you threatened
              to throw boiling tea in my face.
                    (A beat)
              Look this is not getting us anywhere,
              and no, before you bring Stiv up, I
              don't need relationship advice.

Bob regards her with intense dislike.

                    BOB
                (Slowly)
            Maybe you do...more than you
            know...

Georgie appraises him, not wanting to pick up the inevitable
response, then succumbing against her better judgment.

                  GEORGIE
            OK, come on then, let's get this
            out of the way, then we can talk
            about what I really came for. What
            relationship advice do I need
            from you?

Bob smiles triumphantly, clearly enjoying the moment.

                    BOB
            You think that you and Stiv are a
            big deal now huh? Big love affair,
            and your old man dusting off his
            wedding suit.
                (A beat)
            Well, there might be a few things
            you might need to know to help you
            with your big decision.

Georgie is alert, in spite of her better judgment. Bob pursues his
perceived advantage.

                  BOB (CONT'D)
            How do you know that Stiv hasn't
            been playing with someone else?
            Has feelings for her, for years in
            fact...

Georgie is breathless, realizing that her decision to try to build
bridges with Bob was not going well. Angry with herself for
allowing Bob to penetrate her vulnerability.

BOB (CONT'D)
I happen to know that Stiv has loved
someone else long before he even
heard of you. And if she was here,
you wouldn't get a look in. Its only
because he's stuck here, and can't
see her. He's just amusing himself
with you.

Georgie gazes hopelessly at Bob, violently shaking her head.

GEORGIE
You're talking crap Bob.
(Losing patience)
I'm going to go. This was a bad
idea, coming here. I thought that
somehow you and me could call a
truce. But forget it. You are a fuckwit.
A worthless piece of shite. I've had
enough of this.

Georgie makes for the door, but Bob blocks her, leaning in the
doorway.

BOB
You think I'm making it up, don't
you? But I'm not because the person
I'm talking about is close to me.
(A beat)

About as close as you can get really.

Georgie is mute, her breath coming fast, eyes filling with tears, not
wanting Bob to see that he had shaken her.

GEORGIE
Let me go Bob. I've heard enough
of your rubbish. I'm going through
that door and you won't stop me.

                    BOB
          Not until you know who it is, you Irish
          bitch. Then you can ask him yourself.
          Have a heart to heart...

Georgie's hands come out of her pockets, fists clenching. Bob
grins savagely.

                 BOB (CONT'D)
          It's my Mother, that's how I know. My
          fucking Mother. Ask him about Iris,
          he's had...

Georgie launches herself at Bob, fists flailing, a barrage of
punches and kicks that drive him back against the door, but he
isn't going to let her sucker punch him again. This time he will fight
her, like he would another man.

He squares his feet and delivers a roundhouse swinging punch
that connected with the side of Georgie's head sickeningly. She is
poleaxed, dropping in her tracks, her head lolling sideways. Bob
grunts with the effort, wringing his hand, glancing at his knuckles.

                 BOB (CONT'D)
          Chew on that you Irish bitch. That's
          for the sucker punch you managed
          to get on me last time.

Bob Looks down at Georgie. There is something about the way
she is lying that catches his attention.

                 BOB (CONT'D)
          Come on now, get the fuck up. It
          wasn't that fucking hard.

Bob, still breathing hard, moves around Georgie, looking down at
her. Her head is a sharp angle, and her foot is twitching violently
for several beats, leaving incongruous scuffs on the floorboards,
eventually becoming still.

> BOB (CONT'D)
> (Slower, becoming
> concerned)
> Georgie, get up now, you are really
> pissing me off big-time.

Bob eventually drops down on his knees next to her. Pushing at her with a knuckle. She settles flatter onto the floor, her head at a grotesque angle. Bob, now panicking, tried to pick her up, but her head hangs sideways, her neck is clearly broken. He tries her pulse, it flutters, then nothing.

Bob scrabbles violently back and away from Georgie's body. His back flattening against the wall, horror etches across his face. Georgie's ethereal beauty is now grotesque, her face distorted against the floor. Bob is in hell.

                                                                    CUT TO:

INT. FARMHOUSE OUTBUILDING. LARNE. DAY

Stiv is laughing at something that O'Leary has said and Benny has responded to. The three men are working on a car engine that lies on a workbench like a primeval beast, its guts open and innards on display.

O'Leary and Benny both look at Stiv as he laughs, both their faces creasing into grins, all three men easy in each other's company. O'Leary's cell phone trills, he glances at the screen, then walks away from the other two.

> MICHAEL O'LEARY
> Enrique, my friend.

> ENRIQUE DADA
> Michael, I hope you are well. We
> may have some business. It is not
> imminent, but just checking your
> availability over the coming weeks.

MICHAEL O'LEARY
All good Enrique. Diary empty
right now.

ENRIQUE DADA
I'll come back to you.

The cell phone clicks. O'Leary exchanges a questioning glance
with Benny, shrugs.

CUT TO:

INT. FARMHOUSE. LARNE. BOB'S ROOM. DAY.

Bob gradually pulls himself together, all the time gazing at
Georgie's inert body. Somehow, she has sunk further down to the
floor than before, and he is now certain that she is dead, and he
has killed her. A livid bruise spreading across the side of her face,
blood pooling from her nostrils.

He fights down his heart rate and tries to think what to do next.

He knows that O'Leary will kill him immediately, and Stiv would
not defend him. Waves of panic sweep over him, tears running
freely down his face. All he can focus on is Iris's face, his Mother.
Somehow, he has to get back to Iris, she will put her arms around
him and know what to do next.

Bob goes to the window, no one is in sight. He opens his door
slowly, listening. The house is quiet, there is no one downstairs in
the kitchen. He softly closes the door, rummaging and throwing
possessions into a sports bag, finding and checking his new
passport.

Carrying his bag, Bob locks his room door, quickly trotting down
the stairs, through the kitchen, then checking the yard, exits the
farmhouse. Keeping away from the outbuildings, he drops over a
wall and heads through trees, disappearing into greenery.

INT. FARMHOUSE KITCHEN. LARNE. EVENING

Benny and Stiv wave goodbye to O'Leary as he drives out of the farmyard in the Range Rover. They enter the kitchen. The fire is lit and there is a smell of cooking.

                         STIV
                (Glancing around)
            Smells good Benny.

Benny sniffs the air appreciatively, grinning.

                         BENNY
            Irish stew I reckon. She's a good lass
            that one Stephen.

They make themselves tea, sprawling by the log fire. Soon Benny is snoring. Stiv stretches his legs and follows suit, the spitting logs lulling him gently into sleep.

                                                      CUT TO:

LATER

INT. FARMHOUSE KITCHEN. LARNE. NIGHT

Stiv and Benny are asleep by the fire. O'Leary pulls up outside, parks, and enters the kitchen, grinning to himself at the two sleeping companions by the fire. O'Leary checks the AGA, lifting the lid on a huge cast iron pot of Irish Stew. He glances at his watch with a vague frown.

                                                      CUT TO:

EXT. BUS STOP ON A COUNTRY ROAD NEAR LARNE. NIGHT.

Bob stands with his arm outstretched and an old, battered bus pulls to a stop by the bus-stop on the roadside. The door swings open and Bob climbs up the three steps, paying the driver in change. The bus is empty apart from an old lady dozing near the back.

The bus pulls away into the night, lights fading.

CUT TO:

INT. FARMHOUSE KITCHEN. LARNE. NIGHT

Stiv wakes, stretching. The fire has burnt down, and he leans forward throwing another log onto the embers. The sound wakes Benny and looks around the kitchen.

> BENNY
> Must have dozed off Stephen.

> STIV
> Me too. I'm bloody hungry now. I
> wonder where Georgie is.

> BENNY
> If she's put the dinner in the oven,
> she'll just expect us to help ourselves
> when we are ready. I wouldn't worry
> about that lady. She's a law to her
> own self to be sure.

> STIV
> She is that.

O'Leary enters the kitchen.

> MICHAEL O'LEARY
> Well lads, nice to see you two
> awake at last. Hungry?

O'Leary noisily bangs the huge pot of STEW onto the kitchen table and clatters spoons and bowls down.

MICHAEL O'LEARY (CONT'D)
Seen Podge?

STIV
Naw, not for an hour or two.
(A beat)
Haven't seen Bobby either come
to think of it. Mind you, he doesn't
seem to want to eat with us these
days.

O'Leary grunts, ladling three bowls of stew and carving a hunk
of bread. He sits down to eat. The other two follow suit. There is
silence other than the noise of spoons and eating.

CUT TO:

EXT. BELFAST CITY CENTRE. NIGHT.

The bus pulls up on a busy, orange lit, street, wet reflections
everywhere. It disgorges Bob, a dark figure in a heavy hooded
anorak, he hefts his sports bag, looks around for directions, then
heads for a sign showing AIRPORT.

FADE TO BLACK

NEWS ARTICLE: LA PARISIAN. MORNING EDITION

VOICE OVER, OR ROLLING TEXT

"France's latest and most colourful National HERO Jacques De
Freyn, who recently shot his way out of a Terrorist Ambush has
been appointed Minster for Europe and Foreign Affairs. Monsieur
De Freyn now occupies the 3rd most powerful post in French
politics."

"This accolade is a true recognition of De Freyn's contribution and
loyalty to his country. He is a former senior officer in the French
Foreign Legion and is now a holder of France's highest award,

The Legion d' Honneure. He demonstrated his bravery and total disregard for his own safety as he, while in handcuffs, shot dead two English Assassins, both men wanted by Interpol. De Freyn was himself shot in the exchange of fire, but he is now recovering, and many say he is the next natural successor for France's Presidency in the on-coming elections. When this paper asked his office for comment in this regard, we were told that this was speculation of left-leaning commentators"

CONTINUOUS

INT. LAFITTE'S OFFICE. INTERPOL HQ. PARIS. MORNING.

Lafitte read the morning's 'La Parisian' with distaste, quickly leafing through the paper for any other comments. Finding none, he pushed it aside as his cell phone rang.

TELEPHONE CONVERSATION

JEAN LAFITTE
Laffite.

CALLER
My apologies Sir, wrong number I think...

De Freyn glances at the 'Caller Unknown' legend on his screen. Closes down his handset and takes another handset from his pocket. He switches it on, looking expectantly at the screen. It trills.

JEAN LAFITTE
Lafitte.

ENRIQUE DADA
Hello Jean, are you able to speak?

JEAN LAFITTE
Yes, proceed Enrique.

ENRIQUE DADA
You read today's La Parisian I
take it?

Lafitte glances at the headline glaring up from his desktop.

JEAN LAFITTE
It is on my desk as we speak.

ENRIQUE DADA
Speculate with me for a moment my
friend.
(A beat)

Do you think De Freyn will stand
against the man who has just given
him France's highest award, and the
No3. Post in his cabinet?

Lafitte smiles bitterly, spinning his chair on its axis to gaze out of his
window.

JEAN LAFITTE
In a heartbeat Enrique. It will not
cost him a moment's thought.

There is silence on the Dada's side of the conversation as the
handset is muted. Lafitte waits, Dada comes back...

ENRIQUE DADA
We think so too Jean. Thank you, my
friend, we will speak further.

The phone clicks OFF. Lafitte switches down the handset, putting it
back in his pocket.

Lafitte gazes thoughtfully across several hundred meters of
cityscape to the vast reconstruction site that was the Cathedral
of Notre Dame. 30,000 tonnes of burned scaffolding and steel

tubing was being removed, men crawling like ants, silent through triple glazing.

FADE TO BLACK

INT. MANCHESTER AIRPORT. ARRIVALS. DAY.

AERIAL

Bob comes through Customs, hefting his sports bag, dropping Ray-Bans over his eyes. Following several other passengers, he crosses the concourse and exits the Airport, looking for the Rail Link north.

CUT TO:

EXT. PLACE DE HOTEL DE VILLE SQUARE. CENTRAL PARIS. DAY

AERIAL CIRCLING

People begin to gather in the elegant square in front of the Hotel De Ville to hear Republican and Socialist speakers in the nominations for the on-coming French primaries. A raised platform is set up near the bank of the Seine, a large screen playing live TV coverage from Al Jazeera and Sky.

CONTINUOUS

EXT. PLACE DE HOTEL DE VILLE SQUARE. PARIS. DAY

The crowd is calm but excited with many speculating that JACQUE DE FREYN will choose today to announce his Republican nomination standing against the man whom he had sworn loyalty to only scant days ago.

NEWS REPORT Commentary voice-over. Background screen showing candidates and various show-biz supporters milling around.

"We are expecting at least three candidates to speak today, but the name that is on everyone's lips is Jacques De Freyn, the new Minister for Europe and Foreign Affaires. M. De Freyn has assumed a 'Rock Star' persona in the weeks since he literally shot his way into the hearts of the French Public. In spite of his mounting popularity, many are concerned that De Freyn has not shown the expected loyalty to the incumbent President that should be due. The President has not only recently awarded De Freyn with France's highest Award but has inducted him into a post very close to the President himself.

Others look at De Frey's candidacy as a welcome change to the Republican centris perspective, bringing a more right-wing influence to stand against the growing Socialist political menace.

Whatever happens, today may be the day that de Freyn announces his candidacy. Something is happening now, we go to live coverage"

CUT TO:

INT. LAFITTE'S OFFICE. INTERPOL HQ. PARIS. DAY

Lafitte switches on his TV, sitting back, crosses his legs, arranging trouser creases.

CUT TO:

EXT. PLACE DE HOTEL DE VILLE SQUARE. THE STAGE. DAY

The crowds are now dense near to the stage, the rest of the SQUARE filling, blue lines of Police around the outer edges. Clusters of cameras in a barricaded off area, a technician taping microphones together, testing sound levels. Sporadic cheers as several celebrities appear on stage, waving, everyone smiling, atmosphere electric.

A Hollywood actress and star of NETFLIX's DAREDEVIL takes position at the cluster of microphones...she taps the microphones, the sound amplified massively.

408

                    ACTRESS
            (Arms outstretched, waiting)
          Everyone, please... Thank you.
The crowd gradually subsides, intermittent flashes from cameras
stark white, faces expectant.

ACTRESS (CONT'D)

                    (Smiling around)
                Thank you, and thank to all the
                people watching this from their
                homes. We have an exciting line-up
                for you today with nomination
                hopefuls from three political camps.

The crowd respond with surging levels of excitement and
enthusiasm as if they were waiting to hear their favourite bands.

                    ACTRESS (CONT'D)
            I know, I know...exciting!
                    (Smiling broadly around,
                    waving)

She looked off stage, exchanging words with someone off
camera, then turning back to the crowd...

                    ACTRESS (CONT'D)
                    (Shouting enthusiastically)

            Yes, he is here, Jacques de Freyn is
            here...

The crowd roared. Cameras swung to the edge of the stage, then
swept back to the speaker. The camera zooms back as Jacques
de Freyn walks on stage from the left. He is animated and waving,
he walks quickly to the cluster of microphones and embraces
the Actress as if he had known her for years. They both turn to the
crowd with broad smiles, waving. More roars from the crowd.

                    ACTRESS (CONT'D)
                    (Arms outstretched)

Please everyone, Jacques is here,
he's not going anywhere, are you
Jacques?

The Actress takes De Freyn's hand and raises it high, they stand
together wide legged, triumphant. She drops his hand and backs
away out of camera. De Freyn faces the crowd on his own, waits
for the roar to die away. Finally, after several beats...

                    M. DE FREYN
           Thank you, my dear friends...
                    (Waits)

The crowd subsides, De Freyn waits, savouring the moment. After
several beats there is silence.

                    M. DE FREYN (CONT'D)
           Today I announce my candidacy to
           run for for the Presidential elections
           of France.

The crowd roars, De Freyn holds up his hands for quiet.

                    M. DE FREYN (CONT'D)
           It is a Candidacy like several others,
           victory is not assured. And I pledge
           today that if my Candidacy is not
           successful, it will not diminish my
           total support for the person who
           wins.
                    (Hand to his breast)
           Because I stand here today in this
           battlefield, just as I have stood in
           many other battlefields with a gun in
           my hand, for France.

The crowd roared, De Freyn faced around, nodding.

                    M. DE FREYN (CONT'D)
           France is my mistress and my love.
           Saint Augustine, a saint of my

church, wrote that "A people was a
multitude defined by the common
objectives of their love". So, my
friends, today, I stand with you,
we have the same love, the same
objectives.

The crowd is silent, rapt. De Freyn pauses, his head down. Slowly
he raises his head, the camera zooms in, streaks of tears visible
down his cheeks. He allows the silence to extend. His face fills the
huge TV screen on the side of the stage.

> M. DE FREYN (CONT'D)
> (A break in his voice)
> Not long ago, close friends and
> colleagues died in hails of bullets in
> the Algerian desert. They were my
> people - French heroes. And it was
> my honour and my duty to put my
> own life on the line for them, to shed
> my own blood in the sand for them,
> and for France, and...
> (A beat)
> ...for you, and your families, and the
> families they will have.

Another roar from the crowd. De Freyn wipes his hand across his
face, smearing the tears. He waits, his face upwards, cameras
flash...

> M. DE FREYN (CONT'D)
> Some people say, because I was
> rewarded for these actions, that
> I should stand aside today, and
> consider myself lucky for the things
> that I have. That I should let others
> carry forward the banner of France.

The crown ripples, some people calling out. De Freyn waits.

> M. DE FREYN (CONT'D)
> To those people I say this. Slaying
> the enemies of France and taking a
> bullet, was yesterday's task. Now a
> new day has dawned, and I have
> new tasks.
> (A beat)
> Now it is time to stand against the
> challenges of today. Now it is time
> to press forward with speed and
> urgency...

The crowd roars, applauds. Falls silent. Cameras zooming, De Freyn's face again filling the TV screens.

> M. DE FREYN (CONT'D)
> Together, we have much to do,
> much to achieve in this winter of
> great peril, much to restore, much to
> heal...

Throwing his arm outwards towards the Cathedral Notre Dame.

> M. DE FREYN (CONT'D)
> (Nodding)
> ...and much to repair and rebuild.
> (A beat)
> Overcoming these challenges and
> restoring the soul and the future of
> France will take much more than
> words, more than good intentions,
> it will take great courage, ingenuity,
> unity, and above all, great and
> enduring love for our beautiful
> country...

There is a gradually rising roar from the crowd, people press forward, De Freyn shouts his final word, arms outstretched in a crucifix...a Messiah.

M. DE FREYN (CONT'D)
France!

There is pandemonium.

The police press against the sides of the heaving crowd. Camera flashes becoming almost continuous. The Actress runs from the side of the stage into camera, throwing her arms around De Freyn. He staggers back, holding her tightly like a lover. Even other candidates at the back of stage waiting to speak, rise to their feet, clapping in admiration, caught in the moment. The huge TV screen filled with De Freyn's face; eyes closed in ecstasy.

Paper bombs explode, tinsel cascades. The Actress leads De Freyn forward. They emerge amid fluttering sparkles of light, holding hands tightly, from behind the microphones, coming to stand at the front of the stage, arms outstretched, the Actress finally backing away from De Freyn, leaving him to stand alone in the centre of the stage, all cameras focused in tight.

AERIAL

Camera rises up, circling, showing vast crowds, rising further showing central Paris.

CONTINUOUS

INT. LAFITTE'S OFFICE. INTERPOL HQ. PARIS. DAY.

Lafitte finds himself on his feet, clenched fists outstretched towards his TV screen, he drops back into his seat, breathless, his eyes blurring, fixed to the closing scenes of De Freyn's speech.

CUT TO:

INT. RANGE ROVER, COUNTRY ROAD NEAR LARNE. DAY

O'Leary is driving. His phone rings on the dashboard, automatically muting his radio.

                    MICHAEL O'LEARY
            O'Leary.

                    ENRIQUE DADA
            Michael, we need to talk. I'll be
            heading to Belfast. Ill ring you.

The phone clicks OFF. The radio returns to Irish Country Music.
O'Leary reaches down to switch the radio off.

                                        FADE TO:

INT. FARMHOUSE KITCHEN. LARNE. MORNING

Benny is sat with tea and toast at the long table. Stiv comes in
from outside, pulling off an anorak.

                    STIV
            Ben, I don't know where Georgie is.
            I've just been down to the stables,
            she's not there. Horses haven't been
            fed. It's not like her.

Benny continues chewing, unperturbed.

                    BENNY
            I wouldn't worry about that lady.
            She does what she does, when she
            wants to do it.
                    (A beat, quizzically, winking)
            You didn't see her last night then?

                    STIV
                    (Annoyed)
            Fuck off Ben. This is her and
            Michael's home. We don't...

                    BENNY
            I'm joking with you son. I know you
            don't. Did you check her room?

414

                    STIV
          I knocked, no answer. I didn't go in,
          I thought she would be down here,
          then I checked outside, stables,
          barn, nothing.

The sound of a vehicle outside. Stiv walks to the window.

                    STIV (CONT'D)
          Its Michael. He will know.

O'Leary enters the kitchen.

                    MICHAEL O'LEARY
          Morning both, Its cold out there.
          Some tea and toast for me.

O'Leary takes a step towards the table, stops, looking quizzically
at Benny and Stiv.

                    MICHAEL O'LEARY (CONT'D)
          What...?

                    STIV
          Have you seen Georgie?

                    MICHAEL O'LEARY
          Not this morning I haven't. She'll be
          with the horses maybe...

O'Leary picks up the tension on Stiv's face, and stops, then...

                    MICHAEL O'LEARY (CONT'D)
                    (To Stiv)
          She isn't? Barn? Maybe out in
          the car?

Stiv shakes his head. The three men are silent for a beat, the
atmosphere chilling by the moment. O'Leary pales beneath his
tan, looks sharply at Stiv

MICHAEL O'LEARY (CONT'D)
Where's Bob?

BENNY
No sign of him since day before
yesterday, but that's nothing new.
He takes food back upstairs rather
than eat with us.

O'Leary leaves the room. Stiv and Benny now unsettled and tense.
Two minutes later O'Leary returns, his face registering concern.

MICHAEL O'LEARY
Her bed hasn't been slept in.

O'Leary faces Stiv, tense, Stiv colours.

STIV
No Michael, she didn't stay with me.
We wouldn't, I mean she wouldn't, I
mean...

O'Leary is distracted, he goes up the stairs, Stiv and Benny follow.
O'Leary pounds on Bob's door, no answer. Stiv passes him,
trying the door, it is locked. Stiv violently shakes the door handle,
pounding the door.

STIV (CONT'D)
Bob, open the fucking door...NOW!

O'Leary is now alarmed, he thrusts Stiv to one side, stands back
and kicks the heavy door. In two kicks the door smashes back
against the wall. O'Leary stands mute in the doorway. Stiv and
Benny are behind him with no view on the interior of the room.

O'Leary drops to his knees in mute shock. Stiv and Benny look over
his head at Georgie's broken body.

Stiv darts forward, dropping to his knees beside her, his hand
reaching for her shoulder. As he touches her, he freezes.

416

                    STIV (CONT'D)
              She's cold, she's fucking cold.

All three men know instantly that Georgie is dead. O'Leary
doesn't move from the doorway, still on his knees. Benny clutches
the door frame, his eyes wide in shock. Stiv leans down to see her
face.

                    STIV (CONT'D)
              Look at her face, she's been...

O'Leary is still, his eyes clouding with grief and shock. His voice
broken.

                    MICHAEL O'LEARY
                 (Small voice, wondering)
              I could tell straight away you know.
              Soon as I saw her. My baby, My
              Podge.

Benny walks very slowly to the bed, sitting down, showing his
age, never taking his eyes away from Georgie. Stiv tries to move
her body, but she is stiff. He bends down to her face again, tears
running freely down his face, a hoarse broken sound of anguish
wrenching from his throat.

                    MICHAEL O'LEARY (CONT'D)
                 (Very quietly)
              Leave her Stiv, please.

O'Leary gets slowly to his feet, leans down and gently picks up
Georgie's body. He places her tenderly on the bed, smoothing
back her hair. The livid bruising down her face and neck now
clearly visible. One of her arms sticks rigidly upwards, with an
effort, O'Leary forces it down to her side. O'Leary touches the
bruise, tracing his fingers down her neck.

                    MICHAEL O'LEARY (CONT'D)
                 (Faintly, voice breaking)

He broke my baby's neck. He hit her
so hard, he broke her neck.

Stiv remains on his knees in the middle of the floor. His entire world destroyed, his brain barely processing what O'Leary said, then slowly he looked up.

> STIV
> You think Bob did this? Killed Podge?
> Bob? He wouldn't...

Benny gets up, looks around the room. Checks in the wardrobe. Sits down again.

> BENNY
> (Flatly)
>
> His stuff is gone. He did this. He's
> killed our little Podge, and now he's
> fucking gone.

Stiv stares at Benny, shaking his head in despair. He gets up, moving around the room, checking for himself. The wardrobe and cupboards empty. Bob's passport gone. Benny watches him silently.

Stiv drifts to a stop by the bottom of the bed, his hand on Georgie's foot. O'Leary is gazing down tenderly at his daughter, his hand stroking her hair, his heart breaking. Without taking his gaze away from her face he gestures vaguely at Stiv and Benny, waving them away.

Benny stands, moving over to Stiv, he pulls his shoulder gently.

> BENNY (CONT'D)
> Come on Stephen, leave him alone
> with his little girl, give him some
> private time with Georgie.

Benny leads Stiv out of the room, guiding him down the stairs and into a chair at the kitchen table. He disappears momentarily,

418

returning with a half-empty bottle of Irish Whiskey and two glasses. He pours two slugs, pushing a glass towards Stiv. Stiv drinks and coughs, his streaming eyes to the top of the stairs, he drinks again.

Benny sits opposite him, his glass already empty. He pours again. His eyes straying to the tabletop - a plate with a slice of half-eaten toast, the shape of a bite in the cold crust, somehow reflecting how life can change in an instant. Benny turns away, not wanting to see it.

FADE TO BLACK

EXT. ULVERSTON RAILWAY STATION. DAY.

The two-coach diesel train rattles into Ulverston station and doors swing back, crashing against rubber restraints. Passengers exit, hurrying towards the street exit. Bob hefts his sport bag, looks both ways, pulls up his hoodie, steps into familiar streets.

AERIAL

Camera zooms upwards from close shot of Bob, circling, zooming up higher showing the Rail Station, then the wider town.

INT. FARMHOUSE KITCHEN. LARNE. MORNING

Benny and Stiv are in the kitchen. Stiv asleep with his head down on his arms on the table top. Benny slumped in a chair, staring into the embers of the fire.

Stiv wakes looking ravaged. He looks around, sees Benny, stretches.

STIV
Where's O'Leary Ben?

419

Benny doesn't reply but gestures vaguely at the stairs without looking around. Stiv looks to the top of the stairs, then his head sinks down onto his arms again in despair.

                    (A beat)

Stiv gets up from the table, making for the stairs. Benny turns to look at him.

                         BENNY
              Don't...

Stiv, stops in his tracks, nods, goes to sit back down at the table, then changes his mind. Slumps into an armchair next to Benny.

                    BENNY (CONT'D)
              He'll come down in time.

Stiv and Benny sit together by the fire, both staring into the embers.

INT. FARMHOUSE. BOB'S BEDROOM. LARNE. MORNING.

O'Leary sits on the side of the bed next to Georgie's body, his gaze locked onto her ravaged face. O'Leary's muscular frame is sunken and exhausted.

A sound behind him. Benny enters the room. He is carrying a plastic washing bowl with hot water, soap, sponges, towels and hairbrush. Benny places these on the bedside table. Benny stands there for several beats, then placing his hand momentarily on O'Leary's shoulder, exits the room.

After an eternity, O'Leary rouses himself and begins to gently remove the clothes from Georgie's body. When she is naked, he rolls her gently, placing towels beneath her, and begins to wash her with loving care. O'Leary is beyond tears, lost in the task, he murmurs to her as he works, as if she could hear him.

                                        DISSOLVE TO:

EXT. IRIS'S HOUSE. ULVERSTON. DAY.

Bob walks down the street, his face obscured by the hood, towards the house he shared with Iris. He turns in towards his old front door, the hood still obscuring his face. He looks up and down the street, it is deserted.

He raises his hand to knock, then changes his mind. He enters the house, closing the door behind him, then standing with his back to the door. Iris is in the kitchen.

> IRIS (O.S.)
> Is that you Mike?

Bob, by the front door, doesn't reply, and suddenly Iris stands in front of him.

> IRIS
> Who the fuck...?

Bob brushes his hood back from his face, savouring the moment. Iris steps backwards, retreating into the kitchen until she backs up against the units, then sinks down to her haunches in total shock. Her eyes bulging, gasping for breath.

> IRIS (CONT'D)
> Bob, it can't be... Bob...

Bob steps forward, reaching for her. She recoils, her hands to her face stifling a scream.

> BOB
> It's me Mum, I'm OK. I'm not a
> fucking ghost. Its me, Bobby.

Iris allows him to take her hands, raising her up, stepping close to her, and hugging her tightly, feeling her body shuddering.

                    BOB (CONT'D)
          I'm really OK Mum, we had to
          pretend we were dead. Stiv is alive
          as well.

Iris pulls back to stare at him in wonderment, pale with shock,
her hands going to each side of his face, feeling him, her hands
running through his hair.

                    BOB (CONT'D)
          I'm really here Mum, it's OK.

Iris finally cries. Huge wrenching sobs that shake her small delicate
frame. Her hair plastered to her cheeks, she repeats his name
over and over. Bob can do nothing except hold her as tightly as
he can until she subsides.

LATER

Bob and Iris are sitting on the kitchen floor face to face. Bob is
dabbing at Iris's face with a towel. She is white-faced with shock;
Bob is watching her with concern.

                    BOB (CONT'D)
          Mum, can we get up now. Let's
          have some tea eh...

Bob raises her and they sit. Iris gets up to make tea but can't do
it and just stands there staring at Bob, hands shaking. Bob sits her
down and takes over the task, making tea while she watches him.
He puts two mugs down between then.

                    BOB (CONT'D)
          Are you OK Mum? Shall I get Dad
          over here?

Iris violently shakes her head, clutches his hands.

                    IRIS
          No, please Bob, I'll be OK, it's just
          a big shock. Probably the biggest
          shock I've ever had.
                    (A beat)
          You can't just ring Mike, He'll have
          a bloody heart attack. Let's just sit
          here for a bit. I need to get used to
          this.

They drink tea, staring at each other with tear-stained faces.

                                        FADE TO BLACK

INT. FARMHOUSE. BOB'S BEDROOM. LARNE. EVENING.

O'Leary works in the light of several candles. He has washed and
dressed Georgie in her favourite clothes. Her hair is his last task,
brushing it carefully into a cascade across the pillow. Finally, he
stands and looks down at her with a soft smile.

                    MICHAEL O'LEARY
          You look beautiful my dearest love,
          beautiful.

                                        CONTINUOUS

INT. FARMHOUSE. KITCHEN. LARNE. EVENING.

Benny and Stiv are sitting in armchairs by the fire in semi-darkness.
Neither have eaten or moved for more than 24 hours. O'Leary
appears at the top of the stairs, looking down at then. He
descends and comes to stand beside Benny's chair.

                    MICHAEL O'LEARY
          Ben, Stephen, can you sit with
          Georgie, she cannot be left alone.

O'Leary leaves the kitchen, quietly closing the door behind him. Stiv turns, looks at the door, then back to Benny.

                    STIV
          Where is he going Ben?

                    BENNY
          Oh, I guessing he'll have some work
          to do son. Leave him be, let him get
          on with it.

Stiv looks at Benny, questioning.

                    BENNY (CONT'D)
          Come on son, we will go and sit
          with Podge, it's a dangerous time
          between her passing and burial.

Stiv follows Benny upstairs, compliant, not understanding.

                                        CUT TO:

EXT. GARDEN OF FARMHOUSE. BENEATH APPLE TREE. NIGHT.

In the light of a lantern, O'Leary digs a grave beneath the apple tree. He has removed his jacket and works in shirt sleeves, humming softly to himself. From time to time, he pauses and looks towards the bedroom where Georgie is laid. It is softly lit by candlelight.

INT. IRIS'S HOUSE. BOB'S BEDROOM. ULVERSTON. NIGHT.

Bob is sprawled across his bed fully clothed, deeply asleep, his sports bag on the floor next to him, gaping open. Iris leans in the doorway gazing at him in wonderment. Her eyes stray to the sports bag, a passport tucked in the side pocket. Glancing at Bob, she kneels and pulls the passport out, leafing through it. She sits back on her haunches, the camera looks over her shoulder at the page with Bob's photograph, and name 'ROBERT KRISTENSEN'.

She scans the passport, seeing the recent Morocco and Gran Canaria stamps. She rummages the rest of his sports bag quickly finding large amounts of cash in US Dollars and Euros.

LATER

Iris sits at the kitchen table with tea. She is using an iPad. She searches yet again 'Assassinations' and 'Morocco'. Shaking her head in disbelief as the Headlines appear. "British Mercenaries shot Dead in the Massacre of French Trade Delegation on Moroccan/Algerian Border'. Later she reads 'France Celebrates her new National Hero, Jacques De Freyn'.

Iris's eyes raise to the ceiling, where Bob lies sleeping, in front of her on the screen, photographs of Bob and Stiv.

CUT TO:

EXT. FARMHOUSE LARNE. ORCHARD. NIGHT.

Benny and Stiv stand next to a deep open grave. A large heap of fresh soil next to it, shovel sticking up at an angle. Several lanterns are lit, illuminating lower branches of a dense apple tree.

O'Leary walks slowly into the light; he is carrying Georgie's body wrapped in white sheets. He places her body gently on the ground next to the grave, then climbs laboriously down into the hole. Stiv starts forward to help him but is restrained by Benny. Benny catches Stiv's eye, shaking his head.

O'Leary reaches up, cradles her and gently lowers Georgie into the grave. He arranges her carefully, drawing the sheets to cover her completely. The two other men watch as he gently covers her with a layer of soft soil, working with his hands.

Stiv and Benny are distraught, O'Leary is calm and statesmanlike in his demeanour. Finally O'Leary climbs up and out and begins to fill in the grave using the shovel. He works continuously until the soil is mounded up in an oval shape. Benny and Stiv stand to one side silently. Finally, O'Leary stops, looking down at Georgie's grave.

                    MICHAEL O'LEARY
          'For us who see another day! Bless
          us all this night I pray. To the next
          day's Sun, we all will bow, and say
          goodbye - but just for now.'

For the first time, O'Leary acknowledges the existence of Stiv and Benny, meeting their eyes.

                    MICHAEL O'LEARY (CONT'D)
          She will be safe here now boys, my
          lovely Podge.

The three men, united in their grief and savagery, stand together. The magnitude of their loss evident in their stance. Somewhere off to the East near Larne, the distant sound of a ship's horn wailing is carried on the wind.

                                        FADE TO BLACK

INT. IRIS'S HOUSE. KITCHEN. ULVERSTON. DAY

Iris and Mike are sitting at the kitchen table, both are emotional, holding hands. Mike is in shock. Iris's iPad screen shows the Algerian headlines. Mike's eyes go upwards to the ceiling.

                    MIKE KRAMER
          I want to see him.

                    IRIS
          No, let him sleep Mike. He's
          exhausted. He's slept now for 12hrs,
          straight, never moved.

Mike subsides, shaking his head.

                    MIKE KRAMER
            I'm not taking this in Iris. So, he just
            turned up, out of the fucking blue.

                         IRIS
            Just like that.

                    MIKE KRAMER
            And he's now Robert Kristensen - on
            his passport?

                         IRIS
            Yes. According to the stamps,
            travelled from Morocco via Gran
            Canaria to UK, through Northern
            Ireland.

Iris pulls the iPad screen around.

                    IRIS (CONT'D)
            The Moroccan exit stamp is two
            days after the Algerian Massacre,
            where him and Stiv were supposed
            to have been shot by that
            Frenchman.

                    MIKE KRAMER
            Obviously, a setup.

                         IRIS
            Obviously.

Mike looks incredulously at Iris.

                    MIKE KRAMER
            Who the fuck could set that up? This
            is big stuff, involving Governments,
            how could our son be involved with
            people like this? How does he even
            know people like this?

From the doorway...

                    BOB
        You don't know the half of it Dad...

Iris and Mike spin towards the doorway in shock. Bob smiles
whimsically at them.

                                    DISSOLVE TO:

INT. FARMHOUSE OUTBUILDING. LARNE. DAY

Stiv watches while Benny tinkers with an engine on a workbench.

                    STIV
        It's been days now Ben. How long
        do we leave him?

Benny looks up, resting oily hands on the rocker cover of the
engine.

                    BENNY
        Pass me that Lump Hammer
        Stephen. This needs a bit of
        persuasion, I think.

Stiv looks around, then passes over an oil covered lump hammer.
Benny taps and tinkers. Stiv watches.

                    BENNY (CONT'D)
        He never lost a daughter before
        you know son. Its new ground he's
        treading.

Benny glances keenly at Stiv.

                    BENNY (CONT'D)
        You lost someone as well. You and
        her were just getting started.

                    STIV
                 (Bitterly)
         Losing people is what happens to
         me Benny. My Dad, then my Mum,
         now Georgie.

Benny taps away at the engine for a beat.

                    BENNY
                  (Slowly)
         You lost Bobby as well.

Stiv gets up, walks to the door, gazing out over the fields, his back
to Benny.

                    STIV
         Bob is a dead man walking Ben.

Benny looks at the set of Stiv's back, his hands thrust deep into
pockets, wide legged, resolute. He bends back to the engine.

LATER:

INT. FARMHOUSE KITCHEN. LARNE. EVENING

Stiv and Benny enter the unlit kitchen noisily. O'Leary sits by the
fireplace wrapped in a blanket, looking into the flames. He
doesn't acknowledge their entry. Benny puts lights on and makes
tea for all of them, taking a mug and placing it by O'Leary's side.

                    BENNY
         Will you be eating something
         Michael?

O'Leary doesn't reply. Benny busies himself with making toast,
carving hunks of roughly cut bread. Suddenly he spins, slamming
down a plate of butter in the middle of the table, he turns to face
O'Leary, uncharacteristically angry.

                                                        429

BENNY (CONT'D)
Well fuck you too Michael. We
all lost her you know, all of us.
She belonged to all three of us in
different ways. She was only partly
yours. And we lost Liam and Robbo.
(A beat)
So, that's it, is it. Now we give up. All
of us, fucked.

Benny throws the carving knife with great force across the
kitchen, it sticks into the back of the front door with a thud,
quivering. It is a demonstration of Benny's potential for violence
that he mostly hides behind a veneer of gentle humour. Benny
and Stiv look at it. Benny slumps down at the table disconsolately,
Stiv goes to get the carving knife, carefully levering it so he
doesn't snap the blade.

By the fire, O'Leary, looking older than his years, turns slightly,
acknowledging Benny's anger.

MICHAEL O'LEARY
Oh Ben, my true friend. You are
greatly loved you know.

O'Leary laboriously gets up and walks stiff legged to the table
and drops into a chair, cradles his mug.

MICHAEL O'LEARY (CONT'D)
I think I must have slept a bit earlier.
It's the waking you know, the rising
up, emerging into reality from a
confusion of dreams, thinking that
everything's all right, and that she's
still here, my girl.
(A beat)
But she's gone. Georgie has gone.

Benny and Stiv are silent, watching O'Leary. Both of them vaguely
glad that he is least talking.

                    MICHAEL O'LEARY (CONT'D)
          I understand death you know my
          lovely boys. It has been my business,
          and it's been integral with Ireland,
          and being Irish, for generations.
                    (A beat)
          Without death, life would not be
          bearable, I know that. I know it. But
          a world without my Georgie in it is
          no world at all, to be sure.

O'Leary raises his eyes to Stiv, who sits mute. The two men
lock eyes for several beats. Then O'Leary nods slowly to the
younger man.

                    MICHAEL O'LEARY (CONT'D)
          "Let the word go forth from this time
          and place, to friend and foe alike,
          that the torch has been passed to a
          new generation"
                    (A beat)
          A great Irishman said that, John F.
          Kennedy.

O'Leary smiles gently at Stiv, his hands flat to the tabletop.

                    MICHAEL O'LEARY (CONT'D)
          This business is yours now Stiv. It's you
          that will carry it forward, I knew it
          when I first saw you. Georgie knew it
          as well.
                    (A beat)
          Gideon said he chose his generals
          from the ones who didn't lay down
          on their bellies to drink at the
          waterhole. He wanted men who
          were watchful, you were always that
          Stephen.
                    (A beat)

> Take whatever you need Son.
> You know what you must do now,
> don't you?

Stiv looks from O'Leary to Benny, then back at O'Leary's level eyes. He nods.

FADE OUT

INT. LE CINQ RESTAURANT. PARIS. DAY

Lafitte exits a taxi outside the Four Season's Hotel in the City Centre. He nods to the doorman and enters the reception area, immediately turning right, stepping onto soft carpeting, into a broad space of high ceilings, gilt, shades of taupe, biscuit and 'fuck you'. The Le Cinq Restaurant is designed for people for whom guilt is unfamiliar and who don't expect menus to display prices.

Lafitte pauses, glances around the half-filled room, raises a finger and is approached by an earnest waiter, confers, and is led to a table in a semi-private alcove. Lafitte sits where the chair is proffered, then gets up and sits in another seat facing the main room, his back to the wall. After a beat an iced Perrier with lime is placed before him. Lafitte sips and waits.

From the side of the room, Enrique Dada watches the room for a few minutes, then moves smoothly between tables, sliding into a seat facing Lafitte. They exchange nods.

> JEAN LAFITTE
> I am told the flaky brioche is
> compelling Enrique, with salted
> butter, Irish of course.

Enrique Dada appraises his immaculate colleague.

432

ENRIQUE DADA
I hope the things we will discuss
today will not take away your
appetite my dear friend.

JEAN LAFITTE
The last time I was here I was
less than impressed anyway. The
stickiness of the scallop mush made
my lips purse like a cat's arse that
has brushed against nettles.

Dada allows himself a vague smile as the waiter appeared. They
order a light lunch of eye-wateringly expensive tit-bits and wine
from a list that includes bottles at $15,000. Neither man inquire
about prices.

JEAN LAFITTE (CONT'D)
So, Enrique, you bear news?

ENRIQUE DADA
Indeed. My principals have some
concerns regarding our mutual
friend, and his meteoric rise into
'Messiah-dom'.
(A beat)
Which of course, both you and I
have played a part. The 'Law of
Unintended Consequences' Jean...

Lafitte acknowledges the comment with an arched brow, his
vaguely amused gaze sweeping several 'older man - younger
women' tables in the room behind Dada.

ENRIQUE DADA (CONT'D)
His rise into super-stardom has been
quicker than many people could
have visualized, there is much in the
way of unfinished business with the
current incumbent before we could
countenance any change.

(A beat)
Perhaps we could slow things down
and remove a little heat from this
situation.

Lafitte holds his companion's gaze for a beat, considering, then
he tastes his wine with a grimace, placing his glass carefully
down, dabbing his lips and signalling the waiter. The waiter arrives
and Lafitte points disdainfully downwards at his plate.

JEAN LAFITTE
(Lip curling)
What is this green stuff?

The waiter frowns leans over to look, then straightens, his face
clearing.

WAITER
It is frozen parsley powder Sir. It's
very nice.

Lafitte leans back, his gaze sweeping the grandeur of the room.

JEAN LAFITTE
No, it isn't. It tastes of grass clippings.
It's one of the worst things I have
ever eaten, and this food reminds
me of a crime scene.

Enrique Dada smiles widely at the exchange, leaning back,
pushing his own plate away. The waiter apologizes profusely,
Lafitte waves him away irritably, then turns back to Dada.

JEAN LAFITTE (CONT'D)
Things have indeed moved on
a-pace since we last met Enrique.
I assume that you may be passing
through Belfast on your return
journey.

Enrique Dada dabs his lips and rises fluidly to his feet, his hand outstretched. Lafitte takes it, rising slightly, and the two men lock eyes.

                    ENRIQUE DADA
          Thanks, you for the lunch Jean.
               (Glancing at his watch)
          My flight to Belfast is in two hours.

Dada leaves the restaurant. Lafitte raises his finger for the Bill. The waiter spots the signal immediately from across the room and moves smoothly towards Lafitte through the tables, flicking through his notepad with a sad expression.

                                        CUT TO:

INT. IRIS'S HOUSE. KITCHEN. ULVERSTON. EVENING.

Iris, Mike and Bob are in the front room. All are sitting upright around the coffee table, which is covered by cartons of Chinese take-away.

                         IRIS
          We ordered too much as usual. We'll
          never eat all this.

Mike Kramer is thoughtful. He has come down from his state of shock but is still very alert and tense.

                    MIKE KRAMER
          So, Bob, after you left us at the
          Sinkhole, what...

                         BOB
          Dad look. I'd rather that we didn't
          go over all that stuff. It's better for all
          sorts of reasons that you and Mum
          don't know details and stuff. They
          call it 'Plausible Deniability'...
               (A beat)

It's so that when you really do
deny that you know something,
the person questioning you, then
believes you, its plausible because
you really truthfully don't know.

Iris and Mike gape at Bob, feeling like he become the parent, and
they the children.

                    IRIS
          How do you know stuff like that
          Bobby? You are from Ulverston.

Bob looks between his parents, wondering if he had done the
right thing in coming home. There is a knock at the door, they all
freeze, exchanging glances.

                MIKE KRAMER
                  (To Iris)
          Are you expecting anybody?

Iris has paled.

                    BOB
          Mum, it's OK. Nobody knows I'm
          here. It's probably just the neighbour
          wanting something for tonight's
          meal. Go on, it's OK, answer it.

Iris goes to the front door, opens it a little way. It is Dave Geddings.

                DAVE GEDDINGS
          Hi Iris, sorry to bother you. I'm looking
          for Mike, his car is out front, so I
          guessed...

                    IRIS
          Dave, it's not really convenient
          right now...

Dave's face falls, immediately backing away.

DAVE GEDDINGS
Oh hell, sorry Iris, I didn't mean to
intrude. I just...

Mike appears over Iris's shoulder, pulling the door wider.

MIKE KRAMER
(To Iris)
Let him in Iris, he knows everything
we know anyway.
(To Dave)
Come in mate, you'll need to sit
down for this...

Dave enters the hallway, looking curious. Mike scans the street
both ways before closing the door.

MIKE KRAMER (CONT'D)
Come in mate, there's someone
here that you'll be surprised to see.
(A beat)
You may need to sit down for this,
I did.

CUT TO:

**EXT. BELFAST INTERNATIONAL AIRPORT. OYSTER BAR IN CENTRAL
SHOPPING AREA. DAY.**

O'Leary and Stiv, smartly dressed, are sitting at the Oyster Bar with
drinks. O'Leary watches the Arrivals Screen above their heads.
The area is crowded with luggage and travellers, a dozen sit
around the circular bar eating and talking.

MICHAEL O'LEARY
Here he is.

Enrique Dada appears in the crowd, picking his way towards
them carrying a leather hold-all over his shoulder. He is dressed
smart/casual. Dada greets O'Leary cautiously, looking guardedly
at Stiv. O'Leary rises to his feet.

MICHAEL O'LEARY (CONT'D)
Enrique, this is Stephen, his friends
call him Stiv. How was your trip?

Dada shakes hands with Stiv while looking expectantly at O'Leary.

MICHAEL O'LEARY (CONT'D)
Stephen, Stiv, is one of us Enrique. He
knows what we know - everything.
(A beat)
The French Connection...

Dada's face cleared slightly. He takes his seat, looking around the
other occupants of the bar. He turned back to O'Leary.

ENRIQUE DADA
Michael, I have always dealt with
you. We go back a long...

MICHAEL O'LEARY
It's different now Enrique, things
have changed since we last met.
As Mr. Spock once said "It is illogical
to assume that all conditions will
remain constant"

Dada glances at Stiv measuring him shrewdly, then turns back to
O'Leary.

ENRIQUE DADA
In Star Trek Episode 24, 1968, Spock
also said "Insufficient facts always
invite danger"
(A beat, checking watch)
What the fuck is going on Michael?

Dada looks at O'Leary, his weariness and the dark circles
beneath his eyes, his pallor, his demeanour.

ENRIQUE DADA (CONT'D)
Are you unwell my friend?

                    STIV
            You could say that Mr Dada.
            Michael lost some people who were
            very close to him.

Dada digests this information, looking between the two men,
then to O'Leary.

                ENRIQUE DADA
            I understand, maybe. You lost your
            two men...?

                MICHAEL O'LEARY
                    (Wearily)
            More than that Enrique, very much
            more than that.

O'Leary looks away across the crowds, then his eyes come back
to rest on Dada. Dada waits, but O'Leary does not elaborate.

                ENRIQUE DADA
            I take it then that you are still in
            business, but now, because of the
            changes, you are stepping back,
            and bringing this young man
            forward into our arrangements.

                MICHAEL O'LEARY
            He's already in them Enrique,
            Scotland and Algeria.

Enrique Dada appraises Stiv with respect, nods.

                ENRIQUE DADA
            Only one of you? I had thought
            there were two?

                MICHAEL O'LEARY
            No, only the one Enrique. Only
            the one.

Enrique is silent for several beats, then consulting his watch.

                    ENRIQUE DADA
              OK, can we do this in stages please?
              I am sure that Stephen is up to the
              job, But I want to feel confident
              when speaking to my Principals in
              the next few days.
                    (Glancing at Stiv)
              No offence Stephen.

                    STIV
              None taken.

Dada rummages in his bag, taking out a brown A4 envelope and
sliding it across the bar towards O'Leary.

                    ENRIQUE DADA
              Target, contract and background
              information gentlemen. Timescale is
              to be advised.

Dada held his hand on the envelope as O'Leary reached for it.
The two men locked eyes for a beat. In the moment, Stiv reaches
forward, placing his hand on the envelope also. Enrique looks
at him.

                    STIV
              Mr. Dada, Enrique, men have died
              by my hand, and in your service.
              There is nothing new here, nothing
              new. This is a continuation of what
              has gone before, and Michael's
              hand will still be the guidance and
              the control.
                    (A beat)
              I am learning this trade. I concede
              that, but I am some way along this
              route now. I am not a raw recruit, or
              a rookie as you might say.

Both Enrique and Michael are looking at Stiv now, both rapt.

> STIV (CONT'D)
> Michael and me both have lost
> someone very close to us recently.
> That person's loss has stripped away
> everything that was unnecessary to
> both of us. I can only speak for me,
> but what I have left now, is this.

Stiv leaned in towards Dada, his eyes searching his, fierce and unyielding.

> STIV (CONT'D)
> I am traveling light right now. If I
> don't work for/with you...

Stiv turned his face to O'Leary's.

> STIV (CONT'D)
> ...or him, then I'll work for someone
> else.
> (Back to Enrique)
> And it may be against you. It's your
> choice.

Enrique's eyes drop, he takes a deep breath, then releases it, betraying nothing. O'Leary leans back, drops his hand from the envelope.

> ENRIQUE DADA
> I want to work with me Stephen, and
> with Michael. Thank you for your
> service thus far. It is exceptional work
> and greatly appreciated.

Dada held Stiv's eyes for a beat, then suddenly brisk, he drops his hand away from the brown envelope. Stiv pulls the envelope towards him.

Dada glances at his watch.

ENRIQUE DADA (CONT'D)
I am gone gentlemen. I will be in
touch, enjoy your reading.

Dada nods to the two men and disappears into the milling crowd. O'Leary takes a long shuddering breath, his eyes moist, and places his hand on top of Stiv's.

The camera pulls back, and the two men are lost in the crowd.

FADE TO BLACK

INT. FARMHOUSE O'LEARY'S BEDROOM. 0245AM

O'Leary's bed is in the midst of a fortress of bookshelves around the walls. A faint glow comes from the window. O'Leary, fully clothed, lies awake staring at the ceiling in the darkness. The old farmhouse is quiet and still.

A faint sound from somewhere causes O'Leary's hand to drift sideways, resting on the Glock17 handgun on the bedside table. He raises his head, listening, the sound does not repeat, but now he is fully alert, eyes looking towards the door, then the window.
(A beat)

Silently O'Leary sits upright, his bare feet flat to the floor, the Glock making a faint snick as a shell is chambered. O'Leary pads to the door, listens, nothing. He goes to the window, standing to one side, he peers out into the night towards the Orchard.

At first, he can see nothing in the darkness, but his hair prickles at the back his neck. He senses a movement below in the direction of Georgie's grave. A match suddenly flares below, silhouetting a male figure down on one knee. A candle splutters into flame, the dark figure straightens, then settles down on haunches.

O'Leary, with a shock, recognises Stiv, a black silhouette against the candlelight, unaware he is being watched. O'Leary places the Glock on the sill, his breath catching in his throat, a scarred knuckle against his teeth, both men staring at the pinpoint of orange light, each man separate in their own worlds, but united in their pain.

INT. FARMHOUSE. STIV'S BEDROOM. MORNING.

Stiv packs a hold-all. A rifle, handgun and Passport lay on the bed. O'Leary comes to the door, standing watching. Stiv glances at him and continues folding and packing.

> MICHAEL O'LEARY
> Leave the guns Stephen.

Stiv nods, not turning round, straightens.

> MICHAEL O'LEARY (CONT'D)
> Wherever it is you are going, call
> me if you need guns. Taking them
> through an airport will get you shot.

Stiv turns to face O'Leary, initially a resolute expression, then softening.

> STIV
> Look after her Michael don't let her
> be alone.

> MICHAEL O'LEARY
> Cumbria...?

> STIV
> Yes. I'll be back.

> MICHAEL O'LEARY
> (Nodding slowly)
> This is your home now Stephen, you'll
> come back here when you are
> done?

The two men come together and embrace. O'Leary feeling the strength is his shoulders, then O'Leary is gone, Stiv zipping his travel bag, face into the wind, journey started.

                                                                    CUT TO:

INT. DIVE CENTER OFFICE. WALNEY. DAY

Dave and Mike are in the cluttered office, facing each other knuckles down on the desk. There is tension between the two men.

                    DAVE GEDDINGS
          You seem to be coping with this
          better than I am Mike. You have to
          face it, your son is a multi-murderer,
          an assassin. He has killed several
          people now, we even saw him shoot
          Daniel Laidlow at the Sinkhole, no
          hesitation. How can you just forget
          that?

                    MIKE KRAMER
          He's my son Dave, my fucking son.
          Don't you get that.

              (A beat)

          Well, you wouldn't you, never
          having any...

Dave turns away from the desk, his back to Mike, looking out of the window.

                    DAVE GEDDINGS
              (Quietly, with menace)
          Fuck you Mike!

Dave drops into a chair, spinning it away from Mike.

>   DAVE GEDDINGS (CONT'D)
>   Look at us! Bloody hell.

Mike is still glaring at Dave, eyes glittering.

>   DAVE GEDDINGS (CONT'D)
>   Oh, come on for fuck's sake Mike.
>   You know what I'm saying. He's
>   going to bring us all down; he should
>   never have come back here. It was
>   better that he was...

>   MIKE KRAMER
>   Dead?

Dave looks away, gulping, his head down.

MIKE KRAMER (CONT'D)

>   That's what you were going to say
>   mate, wasn't it. Dead!

Dave spins his chair to face his partner, quietly...

>   DAVE GEDDINGS
>   So, how do you envisage this story is
>   going to end Mike. You and Iris and
>   your lovely son all watching TV quiz
>   shows together. Him going out to
>   shoot a few rabbits...
>   (A beat, bitterly)
>   Instead of people.

Mike slumps into his own chair, subsiding, lost for a reply. They both
fall silent, the atmosphere changing from anger to despair. Then...

>   DAVE GEDDINGS (CONT'D)
>   Where is he now? Home, with Iris?

Mike nods.

DAVE GEDDINGS (CONT'D)
(Shaking his head)
He has to go away mate,
somewhere safe, but away from
here. He can't just stay in Iris's house.
(A beat)
How do you know there isn't
someone coming after him?
Someone like him, maybe even
another pro? He's killed people,
important people. There's always a
payback. They don't just leave it...

Mike stares at Dave, his face paling.

CUT TO:

EXT. HERTZ RENT-A-CAR. MANCHESTER AIRPORT. DAY

AERIAL, Close, then Zooming up.

Stiv exits the prefabricated shed which serves as the Hertz office
dangling keys and spins on his heel, surveying the car-park, finally
spotting a non-descript car and blip-ping the keypad. Light's
pulse, he throws his hold-all into the back, glances around, drops
into the driving seat, then drives off the carpark, camera zooming
up as he filters into traffic.

LATER

EXT. SCRAP DEALER'S YARD. INDUSTRIAL ESTATE. DAY

WIDE

Raining, muddy yard. Wrecked cars all around stacked up high.
Stiv is in conversation with a rough-looking man in his 50s as they

stand outside rusty shipping container that serves an office. The man passes a package to Stiv. They shake hands. Stiv drives away.

CUT TO:

EXT. IRIS'S HOUSE. DAY.

Bob, wearing a hoodie, exits Iris's house with a heavily laden rucksack and dumps it in the tailgate of his old car. Iris stands disconsolately on the doorstep. Bob embraces her briefly, bending slightly to look into her eyes.

> BOB
> It's for the best Mum, we both
> know it.
> (A beat)
> Look, what about you and Dad?
> You should be back together you
> know. Neither of you are any good
> without the other.

Iris nods mutely trying to keep tears at bay. Bob glances up and down the street.

> BOB (CONT'D)
> Go on back inside Mum. I'll be in
> touch eh.

He drops into the driver's seat and pulls away quickly, waving and gesturing at Iris to go inside, then speeding up along the street. Iris stands there for several beats looking after him, disconsolate, then goes back in the house, shutting the door.

Aerial: Camera zooms upwards.

EXT. M6 NORTHBOUND, JUNCTION 36. DAY

Stiv indicates left and takes the Kendal ramp, filtering onto the Barrow-in-Furness road, A590, then accelerating away.

INT. DIVE CENTER. WALNEY. OFFICE. DAY

Mike and Dave are working separately in the office. Dave sits at his computer while Mike tinkers with a diving valve, his back to Dave.

> DAVE GEDDINGS
> So where has he...

> MIKE KRAMER
> Leave it Dave! He's gone and that's
> it. Its what you wanted isn't it?
> (A beat)
> And don't bring up the issue of those
> fucking Sinkhole guns again please
> mate, its over, enough already.
> (A beat, quieter)
> Over...

Dave shakes his head and goes back to what he is doing. Mike sits there for a beat, then throws the brass valve system noisily onto the bench and exits the office, slamming the door behind him.

CUT TO:

EXT. A590 GREENODD, NEAR ULVERSTON. LATE AFTERNOON

Stiv pulls into a lay-by on the busy A590 three miles outside Ulverston, rummages in the boot, recovers a package and gets back into the driver's seat.

CONTINUOUS

INT. STIV'S RENTAL CAR. A590. GREENODD. LATE AFTERNOON

Stiv checks the driver's mirror, nothing to concern him. He unwraps the package revealing a Glock17 handgun and two full clips showing the rims of bright brass cartridges. He checks the gun expertly, then chambers a shell and places the weapon beneath his right thigh on the car seat.

He checks the mirror and pulls into traffic, heading the last few miles to Ulverston.

CONTINUOUS

EXT. INT. STIV'S RENTAL CAR. A590. LATE AFTERNOON

Stiv drives towards Ulverston in heavy traffic. Two miles outside the town he sees the track leading to the Sinkhole coming up on his left. He watches as it gets closer, then on an impulse, he suddenly indicates and takes the turnoff, immediately free of the heavy continuous traffic behind him. He slows, bumping onto the familiar unpaved track.

He stares around him, hardly believing he is here again. He continues into brush, the sound of traffic quickly becoming muted. As he approaches the Sinkhole, he pulls off the track, leaving the rental car behind some trees, and continues on foot. The area is still, deserted and quiet.

CONTINUOUS

EXT. SINKHOLE. LATE AFTERNOON

As Stiv approaches the Sinkhole he is aware that the light is fading. The black water mirror still, as he remembered it. He glances to where the Bulgarians were shot, their bodies laid by the huge rock, then over to where Daniel Laidlow met his end, simultaneously marvelling and appalled at the momentous events that had happened in this place.

He walks to the edge of the water where the crates had been hauled up. His reflection in the black water high-def perfect with misty pale green scatters of floating pollen. No trace of previous activity was left now, new grass growing where once it was muddy and bloodstained.

Fascinated by this place, he wanders around the Sinkhole to where he and Bob had hidden, watching the Bulgarian Divers hauling up guns from the black depths. Something catches his eye, he bends, parting the grass. It is a brass shell, 22 calibre. He examines it, turning it over in his fingers, his whole attention consumed.

He looks up, suddenly aware that something in the woods has changed, his scalp prickling, heart rate rising, he stares around. He looks towards the track, nothing, he spins slowly.

The feeling persists, he spins a full circle, nothing, he begins to relax, then suddenly Bob is standing on the other side of the Sinkhole 30M away.

The shock jolts both men.

They stare silently at each other across the circle of black water. Stiv is shocked by Bob's appearance, he seems older. Bob is holding a scoped rifle in his right hand, barrel down.

For several beats the two men are totally still, facing each other across the dark abyss of the Sinkhole, the rest of their peripheral world fading to grey in the intensity and starkness of their mutual connection.

STIV:

Begins to move with infinite slowness 90 degrees to his left, stepping carefully, placing his feet precisely. His right hand slipping behind him to the butt of the Glock pushed into his waistband next to his spine.

BOB:

Is shocked to see Stiv, feelings of love flooding through him for an instant, then followed immediately by the image of Georgie falling to the bedroom floor, her head twisted grotesquely sideways. He watches fascinated as Stiv turns sideways to him as he moves, the target of his silhouette reducing. Bob moves slowly

450

to his right, the two men slowly and deliberately circling each other, watchful, the black water between them, still, bottomless.

Bob thumbs the safety catch off his rifle, watching as Stiv's right hand comes into view, holding a Glock, barrel downwards.

                    BOB
         I never meant to do it you know Stiv.
         She didn't give me a choice...

The silence draws out, both men sill moving with infinite slowness.

                    STIV
         There's always a choice Bobby,
         except for now. There isn't a
         choice now.
                  (A beat)
         I wish it was different, but it isn't.

Both men continued to circle the Sinkhole, stepping carefully sideways, watching each other like hawks.

                    BOB
         It there any way we...

                    STIV
         No.

Stiv stops, a second later Bob also stops. Both men immobile, then...

SLO-MO SEQUENCE

STIV:

Stiv fires twice one handed, both misses, dust impacts, ricochets screaming. He shifts his hold to cup his right hand with his left, wide-legged, sighting along the barrel to Bob's upper torso.

BOB:

Bob feels the airwaves of two shots passing close to him as he brings up the rifle from his hip, firing one-handed at the same time, knowing that he missed. The rifle continues upwards into his shoulder with infinite slowness, he tries to aim without using the telescopic sight, knowing that its 4* magnification will disadvantage him with such a close target. His works the bolt, brass shell spinning away, clinking.

STIV:

The Glock rises to his eye-line, centering on Bob's torso. He double taps, knowing immediately that his shots had connected. Bob's silhouette is thrown violently backwards, landing flat, legs spread. Stiv sights the gun on him, holding his aim, seeing the soles of Bob's feet incongruously upright, twitching. He waits, chest heaving...
                    (A beat)

Stiv advances around the Sinkhole, holding the Glock on Bob's form. As he approaches, Bob's rifle, partially obscured in the grass, blossoms white. An immediate hammer blow to Stiv's upper thigh. He goes down onto one knee with the impact. Stiv fires again, double tapping, both shots missing, kicking up dust on both sides of Bob, screaming ricochets.

END SLO-MO SEQUENCE

                         BOB
              Enough. You've killed me mate. I'm
              fucked.

Stiv gets up painfully. Blood spurting down his thigh. He limps to Bob, holding the Glock on him with both hands. Bob lets go of the rifle, holding both palms upwards. Stiv kicks the rifle away with his good leg, sinking down onto the grass next to Bob.

                      BOB (CONT'D)
              I think you hit me twice, good
              shooting old mate.

STIV

You got me as well, not bad for a
rifle with a scope on it.

Bob is deathly pale, he grins wolfishly, eyes impossibly bright,
holding up a hand.

BOB

Give me hand up here mate, I can't
see shit from down here.

Stiv, handgun in his right, reaches for Bob's hand with his left hand,
pulling him into a sitting position.

BOB (CONT'D)

Can you get me over to that rock, I
need to lean against something?

STIV

Bob, I might...

BOB

No, its ok, it doesn't hurt Stiv. I felt the
thump, but it doesn't hurt at all yet.
Pull me...

Stiv pulls Bob over to the rock, Bob helping himself as much as he
can. As he settled him, Bob glances down at Stiv's thigh pouring
blood.

BOB (CONT'D)
(Concern on his face)
You need to be a belt around that
Stiv. Here let me...

Bob tries to take his own belt off, but fails, giving up.

BOB (CONT'D)
Don't think I can...

                            STIV
                  It's OK, I'll sort it.

Stiv makes his gun safe, puts it down beside him, takes off his own
belt, tightening it around his thigh. Bob watches, bemused. Stiv's
blood flow eases. Bob looks down at his chest, feeling around
with both hands.

                         STIV (CONT'D)
                      Here, let me...

Stiv checks Bob's chest area, parting his jacket, seeing one
central hole pumping blood punched through his clothing.
Another hole high in the right shoulder, less blood. Stiv pulls him
away from the rock, looking at his back. He gently lays him back
against the rock. Bob searches his eyes.

                            BOB
                  Big exit huh? Fucked?

Stiv nods, tears in his eyes.

                         BOB (CONT'D)
                  Thought so. Will you stay here
                  with me?

Stiv nods again and moves around so they are both leaning
against the rock side by side. They are both silent for a beat,
then...

                         BOB (CONT'D)
                  It's not so bad you know. I was
                  dreading this, but I guess it's OK. I
                  thought I'd be scared you know, of
                  the pain, and being alone.

Both men are gradually coming down off their high, calmer,
facing the Sinkhole.

454

> BOB (CONT'D)
> I'm so sorry about Georgie Stiv. It
> was losing you that hurt me the
> most. I've always had you next
> to me my whole life. We were
> partners. You always had my back.
> Always just a phone call away. She,
> Georgie, took that away from me,
> everything changed.

Stiv allows the tears to flow down his face as Bob speaks, loving the familiar sound of his friend's voice, being in Cumbria, two lifelong friends, back together again, almost as if their Cumbria life had been continuous, and nothing else had happened.

> BOB (CONT'D)
> (Voice faltering)
> I didn't want just anyone else to
> do this you know, I'm glad it's you.
> I didn't want some fucking SWAT to
> shoot me, some guy who I never
> met. Who would get a bloody
> medal, or a commendation or
> something, then drive home to have
> supper with his family in his fucking
> Vauxhall Astra?
> (A beat)
>
> There's something right this, about
> you and me being here, doing this.

Bob goes silent for several beats and Stiv thought he had died. Then, in a smaller voice...

> BOB (CONT'D)
> If it had been the other way around
> you know, I would have sat with you.

Bob doesn't speak again, and Stiv stares hard, through the failing light, at the still water of the Sinkhole. He sits there a long time in the deepening darkness, not wanting to look sideways at Bob.

In the last light of the day, Stiv painfully gets to his feet and using Bob's rifle for support, stands looking down at his lifelong friend. He reaches down, ruffling Bob's hair gently, then hobbles to his car. He starts the car and turns it, the headlights swinging across the black water of the Sinkhole, then bumps away along the track.

CUT TO:

EXT. TEAM BASE. HAKIRA'S HOUSE. REMOTE DESERT. MOROCCO - ALGERIA BORDER. NIGHT.

Hakira and Zami are sitting outside their house by an open fire. Hakira is cooking flatbread. The desert sky has deepened to streaks of deep orange and purple and the heat of the day has dropped as night creeps in.

Hakira suddenly stops, looks up, alert. Zami watches her, startled. Hakira's eyes go skywards, tracking along the black horizon, seeming to sniff the air. She holds the pose for several beats, her hijab swept back from her face. Finally, she turns slightly and for an instant in the firelight, Zami sees streaks of tears down her cheeks, then her hijab is pulled across her face again, she bends back to her cooking.

CUT TO:

EXT. A590 TOWARDS GREENODD. CUMBRIA. NIGHT.

AERIAL

Stiv's car filters onto the A590 towards Greenodd, speeding up and merging in the traffic flow, getting lost. Camera zooming impossibly upwards showing white and red car lights in a continuous stream.

FADE TO BLACK

EPILOGUE

EXT. PLACE DE HOTEL DE VILLE SQUARE. CENTRAL PARIS. DAY

AERIAL and WIDE

Jacques De Freyn stands with several others at the edge of a raised stage while technicians prepare microphones. Vast crowds surge towards the stage, jostling, press and TV straining for images and sound bites, security personnel alert, watchful.

De Freyn approaches the microphones, smiling around, the crowd roars, cameras focus, he raises his arms wide, rock star grin, right hand punching the air with a triumphant fist.

The camera zooms impossibly back above the crowd, finally showing Stiv crouched over a sniper's rifle. He is focusing on De Freyn's centre chest.

VIEW THROUGH SCOPE

Crosshairs moving, then centering on De Freyn's chest. Camera tracks along gun barrel, a finger clicks off the safety catch. Camera continues tracking along a metallic gun stock, finally showing Stiv's face. He smiles, head dipping, his eye moving to the scope.

Silent view from above/behind Stiv's hunched back, pulsing crowd below. De Freyn out in the distance, brightly lit, arms outstretched in a crucifix pose.

LONG FADE TO BLACK

TITLES and CREDITS

SYNOPSIS

Part 1. Scenes 1 - 121.

Two young HUNTERS stumble unwittingly onto some guns being recovered from a SINKHOLE in the Cumbria countryside. One of them is discovered by the perpetrators. To save his friend's life, one of the HUNTERS kills two criminals. Following the thwarted crime, A SENIOR CRIMINAL converges on their small town, closing in on the two HUNTERS's personal lives. Local and international law officers collaborate to solve the murders, which are rooted in another crime that happened 16 years previously. The POLICE investigations do not go well.

Two PRO DIVERS, one them, FATHER of one of HUNTERS, see an opportunity to intervene, steal the, as yet un-recovered GUNS for themselves, and capitalize on the situation.

The SENIOR CRIMINAL takes up a relationship with the HUNTER'S MOTHER, and both hunters are brutalized by him. They both become focused on taking revenge on him, in the process, discovering hidden personal skills and talents for assassination.

The international police investigation gains momentum with collaboration with a SENIOR FRENCH INTERPOL OFFICER, but they are still on the wrong track. The PRO DIVERS collaborate with the SENIOR CRIMINAL to jointly recover the GUNS from the SINKHOLE, but this is predicted by the HUNTERS, who lay in wait at the SINKHOLE. The local police also finally connect facts and converge on the SINKHOLE.

The HUNTERS, who have finally become ASSASSINS, but haven't yet processed this fact, kill the SENIOR CRIMINAL at the SINKHOLE. The PRO DIVERS, and the local POLICE OFFICER who remains hidden in undergrowth, witness the ASSASSINATION.

The PRO DIVERS, one of whom is a HUNTER'S FATHER, help the HUNTERS escape, while still planning their own take-over of the HIDDEN GUNS. The PRO DIVERS clear up the new crime scene, while the two HUNTERS board a

FERRY TO FRANCE. The LOCAL POLICE OFFICER contacts his French colleague to intercept the escapees.

The HUNTERS are met by the SENIOR INTERPOL OFFICER as they arrive in France. He is also working as a CRIMINAL AGENT to provide PROFESSIONAL ASSASSINS for WORLD-WIDE HIRE. He makes the two HUNTERS an offer they can't refuse.

Part 2. Scenes 122 - 264

Inspector Jean Lafitte of INTERPOL meets with his superior M. Jacques de Freyn, a senior Minister in the French Government. An agreement is made to use the two 'CLEAN SKINS' to assassinate 2 spies who have infiltrated the French political machine.

Stiv and Bob travel to Scotland and successfully assassinate their first pro target. Back in Cumbria, a senior Irish Criminal ((O'Leary) arrives in Ulverston to continue the recovery on Sinkhole guns. He suspects Stiv and Bob's involvement in the killing of the Bulgarians and begins to follow them.

Cumbria Police close in on Stiv and Bob. Pressure is brought to bear from French Govt. To kill the Clean Skins, and a SWAT Team is activated to arrest them. An unknown shooter foils the Swat's arrest, and with O'Leary's help, they escape to Ireland. The Head of the SWAT (Anders) takes the blame for Stiv and Bob's escape and is sacked.

Stiv and Bob are inducted in charismatic Michael O'Leary's criminal family on the remote farm near Larne, NI. Stiv is attracted to O'Leary's beautiful daughter, Georgie. The two men begin to prepare for a contract HIT of the second French Diplomat Target. Because of their supreme firearms skills, they quickly become indispensable members of the HIT Team. Anders joins the HIT Team, crossing the line from legal to criminal.

O'Leary is drawn to Stiv, but remains deeply suspicious of Bob, even though he rates Bob's marksmanship. Stiv's attraction to Georgie begins to blossom, much to Bob's disgust. De Freyn meets with Lafitte and Enrique Dada, a CIA contractor, and tells them of his plan to enter the highest level of French politics by killing two of the assassins himself in the fray of shooting exchanges at the planned HIT site in Algeria.

The HIT team led by O'Leary arrive in Morocco and travel to the Algerian border to set up the HIT. The rising tension explodes into violence, and O'Leary almost kills Bob. The

HIT takes place successfully, but two of O'Leary's men are killed. De Freyn becomes a national French hero and is decorated. He uses this as a political springboard.

The HIT team leave Morocco in disarray with Anders also dead.

Part 3. Scenes 265 - 344

Stiv and Bob escape via Gran Canaria, where Georgie has
flown to meet them. Stiv and Georgie fall in love, leaving
Bob brooding his developing hatred for Georgie.

Stiv, Bob and Georgie arrive back in Larne, where
Stiv and Georgie's romance intensifies. Bob become
increasingly isolated, and tensions begin to boil over.

De Freyn's star continues to rise as he assumes Messiah like status
in France. He declares his intention to contest the Presidential
elections, as international alarm bells begin to ring. Enrique Dada
meets with Lafitte and O'Leary to discuss De Freyn's assassination.

Tensions rise in the Larne farmhouse with Bob's increasing
alienation. O'Leary is also still brooding about the loss of
his two men during the HIT. Against this backdrop, Stiv
and Georgie's love affair deepens. NEWS Media reports
that the two men shot in the Algerian HIT firefight are
Stiv and Bob, Iris and Mike Kramer, back in Cumbria are
devastated. The hunt for the two assassins is discontinued.

An explosive confrontation between Bob and Georgie
leaves Georgie dead. Bob escapes back to Cumbria, much
to his parents' shock. O'Leary and Stiv are devastated.
O'Leary, shocked to his core begins to withdraw into himself,
pushing his protege, Stiv, into the forefront of his assassination
business. A contract is agreed with Stiv to kill De Freyn.

But before that Stiv vows to hunt down his former friend and
comes back to Cumbria to kill him in revenge for Georgie.

Stiv meets Bob in a momentous showdown at the Sinkhole. The
two friends engage a savage western-style duel, with both
taking hits. Bob's hit is fatal, and in his dying moments, the two
young men rediscover their lifelong love and friendship.

Stiv returns to his new home in Ireland as part of
O'Leary's family, but now older, wiser and alone.
The planned HIT on De Freyn begins...

Sid Stephenson is a former Education/Aid Pro, re-inventing as an Author and Screenwriter

Aaron Diebelius is a BAFTA Scholarship recipient, London Film School graduate and British Film Institute funded Screenwriter.

'SCROVEL', a unique writing genre existing in the Story's crossover between a NOVEL and a SCREENPLAY. There are two main elements to a Novel, (1) Introspective perspectives of characters, and (2) Externalised actions descriptions.

A Screenplay is made up of Formatted externalised actions and dialogue.
SCROVEL is a 'Formatted Novel'.

It would be great if someone read this and decided to make it into a movie... Ring us!

Printed in Great Britain
by Amazon

84682734R00274